W9-AQL-938

TROUBLEMAKER

TROUBLEMAKER

Let's Do What It Takes to Make America Great Again

CHRISTINE O'DONNELL

ST. MARTIN'S PRESS

NEW YORK

For my mom and dad

www.stmartins.com

ISBN 978-0-312-64305-8

First Edition: August 2011

10   9   8   7   6   5   4   3   2   1

ACKNOWLEDGMENTS

First and foremost I want to thank my parents for their unconditional love and support and for allowing me to share our story; and my sisters and brother, cousins and aunts, who were extremely supportive throughout my whole life, but especially during the campaign and with this book. Thank you, also, to my nieces and nephews for your love and support. I particularly want to thank Jennie, who was there just about every step of the way in my life, my campaign, and now with this book. Thank you for keeping a campaign journal and reminding me of the many things I'd sooner forget, but were important to the story. Also, thanks to Matt, without whom none of this would have happened.

I'm grateful to have such a fun, supportive team at St. Martin's for navigating this rookie through the process: Matthew Shear, Elizabeth Beier, Michelle Richter, Mariann Donato, and Dana Trocker. Thank you to John Murphy and Joe Rinaldi for spreading the word. I'm also grateful to Eric C. Meyer, Laura Clark, Christina MacDonald, and Eva Diaz for working so hard to get this done right and on time; to David Rotstein and Omar Chapa for the design; and to Laura Wilson for the audio edition.

Thank you to Dan Strone for believing in me and for always having chocolate in your office. Thank you to Dan Paisner for jumping in at the last minute and helping me smooth out a very bumpy manuscript, and thanks to your wife for taking out the trash while you were busy helping me. Thank you to Deb and Bryan McCarthy for your insight; Jen French, for your friendship and pages of invaluable notes; and Chuck and June Piola for reminding us to not get caught in the weeds. Thank you to Annemarie MacWhinnie for teaching me how to enjoy life regardless of circumstances; you are an inspiration to all who know you.

I also want to thank everyone who played a role in my previous campaigns and all the work leading up to them. Whether it was donating a dollar or stuffing an envelope, you made this happen. Thank you to every 2006 campaign supporter, every 2008 supporter and volunteer, and especially to the 2010 primary supporters who jumped on board early—you risked a lot to defy the powers that be in order to get behind me. There are so many I want to personally name, but there is not enough room. You know who you are, and thank you! Now go make some trouble of your own!

CONTENTS

*So let us not grow weary in doing
what is right, for we will reap a
harvest if we do not give up.*

—Galatians 6:9

INTRODUCTION

My Book

*Democracy is two wolves and a lamb
deciding what to have for dinner.
Liberty is a well-armed lamb.*

—Benjamin Franklin

Don't Tread on Us

This book is not about me.

Or, I should say, it's not *just* about me. It's not a memoir, although I plan to share bits and pieces of my life story, which I hope will place my views and my political journey in context. After all, you can't know where someone's going, or why they're even headed in that direction, until you know where they've *been*, right?

It's not a campaign journal, although there'll be insights and anecdotes from the 2010 midterm elections, specifically about my own race for U.S. Senate in the great First State of Delaware. As is the case with many upstart candidates, it was my third try for the office, but this time out I won a state primary, upsetting our current congressman and former governor, while capturing the attention of some of our most prominent political leaders, and took my place on the national political stage. Of course, I would have much preferred that place to be a U.S. Senate seat, still there's no denying that my candidacy made an impact. In fact, a recent study published by the Pew Project for Excellence in Journalism reported that my campaign received more coverage than that of any other 2010 political figure, which I guess means we must have hit at least a couple of positive notes along the way.

(At the very least, those notes were surely *loud*!)

My goal here is to inspire others to join me in the resurgence of American values that is reshaping our political landscape: to take part in a growing middle-class movement and to help them realize that meaningful political involvement is within reach—and we all have a responsibility to get started on the reaching.

In case you're wondering, the title is from a tag given to me by *Time* magazine, in a 2010 roundup called "The Party Crashers: Behind the New Republican Revival." The article focused on four conservative candidates making serious headway in four key races around the country: Marco Rubio—"the upstart"—who's now the junior United States senator from Florida; Rand Paul—"the populist"—who's now the junior United States senator from Kentucky; Meg Whitman—"the billionaire"—the former CEO of eBay who'd won the Republican nomination for governor of California before losing the general election to Jerry Brown; and yours truly—"the troublemaker"—a designation I take as a compliment, for the way it signaled that I wasn't afraid to speak my heart on the campaign trail.

Okay, so now you know why this book is called what it's called, and what this book is *not*. So what is it, then? Well, it's all of the above. Categorize it however you want—a political memoir *slash* campaign diary *slash* position paper *slash* rallying cry, with an emphasis on the *slash*. I'll be dipping into all these different genres, writing about my family, my call to political action, and the "trouble" I've made along the way. In the end (hopefully!), there'll be a hard-to-pigeonhole book that might stand as a telling barometer of the values I hold dear, a snapshot of what it was like in the campaign trenches, and a template for others looking to push some of the same buttons (albeit in their own communities, in their own ways).

You might wonder: Why write a book at all? And why now? Well, first and foremost, I'm writing this book because I now have a platform. That's one of the silver linings of all the fanfare that surrounded my race. After participating in a high-profile election, you have an opportunity to reach out to people in a new way. Win or lose, folks seem to want to hear what you have to say—so here I am, saying it, as long as I have your attention. Not because I'm so full of myself to think I've lived a book-worthy life, nor do I think that the nuts and bolts of my background are of interest to anyone outside my family, my close circle of friends, or my most ardent supporters. But because there are lessons to be gleaned—and shared!—by looking over one's shoulder and revisiting the paths that have led to the present place.

Second, I'm hoping to gain some perspective on my own experiences, while at the same time gathering my thoughts and strengthening my resolve for what lies ahead. If there's one thing I've learned from my first tries at elected office, it's that fighting this good fight can be wearying, even demoralizing, so one of the impulses behind this book is the chance to set the record straight on a number of issues that surfaced during the campaign, and in doing so to set them aside. And as long as I'm on it, here's another thing I've learned: The establishment elite will not always welcome you with open arms. In Delaware, as elsewhere, the "establishment" isn't defined by party or ideology. It's endemic, and it cuts across labels and affiliations. It's the same all over.

The "establishment" is a mind-set. Not every incumbent or "established" politician is part of the establishment. Not every successful person is "establishment." The phrase, as a pejorative, applies to "establishment-minded" people, those in power and those who *want* to be in power, those who share an eagerness to compromise their supposed principles and a willingness to step on people in order to get ahead. You can even find such people in the Tea Party movement, sad to say.

Establishment-minded people plague *all* levels of government, all arenas; those who've made it *and* those who are still trying to make it. Think back to where we were just after our last presidential election. Remember the despair, the frustration? Maybe you even experienced a palpable fear for the future of our country. The news out of Washington was troubling to someone like me—to someone like you, perhaps. I still shudder when I recall some of the very first initiatives crossed off the to-do list of our newly elected leaders—the *hardly established* establishment, if you will. Forcing us to pay for abortions overseas? *Check.* Ending the D.C. Opportunity Scholarship program, the one sliver of hope for low-income families in our nation's capital? *Check.* Drafting a so-called stimulus bill that would spend almost a trillion dollars on a Keynesian fantasy, while millions of working Americans lost their jobs and watched their savings disappear? *Check.*

It didn't end there, did it? Next came ObamaCare, and the bailouts—one industry after another. With our forces in Iraq and Afghanistan, there was confusion everywhere, with a persistent chatter about withdrawal dates that seemed to belie our actions on the ground. Plans for closing Gitmo, trying terrorists in Manhattan, and our looming Supreme Court vacancies . . . Do you remember it? I know I do.

In the face of all this uncertainty, the message sent to those of us who didn't like what we saw was to curl up in a fetal position and stay there for the next eight years, thank you very much.

Oh, how things have changed! During those dark, dark days, when common-sense, patriotic Americans were looking for even the faintest silver lining behind the blackest clouds, they stumbled across something else: The Constitution. You see, a funny thing happened on the way to our assigned seats on the sidelines. Those of us who had toiled for years in the values movement found ourselves surrounded by like-minded Americans who had rediscovered the most fundamental value of all.

Liberty.

Try as they might, the establishment elites will never have the last word on liberty. There's something in our national DNA that gets our backs up and leaves us shouting at our would-be masters: "You're not the boss of us!" It's been this way for centuries. Thomas Jefferson said essentially the same thing, perhaps a bit more eloquently: "The issue today is the same as it has been throughout all history, whether man shall be allowed to govern himself or be ruled by a small elite."

Make no mistake, there are more of *us* than there are of *them*. And the thing of it is, the ruling elite don't get us. They call us wacky. *They* call us wingnuts. *We* call us "We the People." We the People don't always agree. We don't always share the same strategy memos, endorse the same candidates, or speak off the same talking points. But what we share is a love for liberty and a willingness to fight for it. We're loud, we're rowdy, we're passionate.

And yet underneath the ruckus there's an echo that takes me back to those great C. S. Lewis Narnia books I used to read as a kid, where a little girl asks about Aslan the lion, the fearsome beast who comes to represent God in Lewis's universe. She asks whether he is safe. Her friend answers, "Safe? . . . Who said anything about safe? 'Course he isn't safe. But he's good."

That's the way I feel about what's happening in America today with this grassroots groundswell, this revolution of reason, this love affair with liberty. It isn't tame . . . but boy oh boy, it sure is good!

Will the ruling elite come after us when they feel threatened? Yes. Will they smear our backgrounds and distort our records? No doubt. Will they lie about us, harass our families, and try their darndest to intimidate us? Better believe it. There's nothing safe or sure about what we're trying to do. But is it worth it? Well, let me ask you, is freedom worth it? Is America worth it? Are those unalienable rights worth a little alienation from the Beltway in crowd?

Yes, yes, yes, a thousand times yes!

Some have accused us of being just an aging crowd of former Reagan supporters and home-schoolers. They've tried to marginalize us and put us in a box. They don't get it, either. We're not trying to take back our country. We *are* our country. We've always been in charge. That's liberty. You don't have to assert your authority when everyone's on good behavior. It's when the wheels fall off that the grown-ups have to step in and step up.

And I'd say we've been awfully patient so far. We've let the incremental assault on our freedoms, on our values, on free enterprise, on property rights, and on our economic stability go on way too long. We've watched the tentacles of Big Government reach into every part of our lives. We've held our tongues as Washington bureaucrats and politicians told us what kind of lightbulbs we can use, what kind of toilets we can flush, what kind of cars we can drive, what kind of food we can buy or sell. They want to tell small businesses what kind of jobs to create or what kind of commercials they can run. They even want unelected panels of administrators to decide who gets lifesaving medical care and who is just too old or too expensive to be worth saving. They'll buy your teenage daughter an abortion, but they won't let her buy a sugary soda at a school vending machine. In Delaware—to note another powerful example—a teenager can't even use a tanning bed without a parent's permission! But that same teenager *can* get an abortion without parental consent. How could a tanning bed be more dangerous than risky surgery?

Consider: Every American child born today already owes over $200,000—his or her piece of the national debt and unfunded future liabilities. Folks, what kind of parent sticks the bill for today's spending to kids who'll have to pay for it tomorrow? Did your mom and dad do that to you? Think about your parents, or your grandparents, and the sacrifices they made so that you could have a chance at the American Dream. Think what that dream has become.

I'm one of six kids. There were a lot of meatballs to make

and mouths to feed. My parents struggled to make ends meet. It was never easy. As I grew older and set out on my own, it was still a struggle. I never had a cushy job or a company car. It took me over a decade to pay off my student loans. I never had to agonize over where to dock my yacht to reduce my taxes—and I'm betting most of you never had to either.

Today the richest, most recession-proof segment of society is the one made up of government workers. They average twice the salary and benefits of those in the private business sector; their jobs, for the most part, are secure. In Washington, D.C., over the past couple years, the recession has hardly been felt at all. After all, it's a "company town."

Meanwhile, those of us on the outside looking in are told that we're not taxed enough. We're told that the dry cleaner down the street as a small business owner is somehow rich, and that he may need to pay more taxes. This neighbor of ours has first to pay his rent and utilities, and the salaries and benefits for his four employees, before he feeds, clothes, and shelters his own family with the moderate amount of money he takes in through his dry cleaning. We're told we're heartless and somehow unpatriotic if we let on that we're sick and tired of government budgets increasing every year, while our salaries are frozen or cut.

This is not the America we've known.

My generation grew up in a time of peace and prosperity, big dreams and bold risks. As the Berlin Wall came down on our TV screens, we saw the hunger for freedom from the heavy boot of government. As one lone student stared down a Chinese tank in Tiananmen Square, we saw the audacity of liberty. As the backlog grew in the requests for political asylum, we saw the shining City on the Hill beckoning all to imitate and create the refuge that only freedom can build. The Golden Arches went up in Moscow. Family businesses became national chains like Walmart and Home Depot.

My generation saw American economic genius and glory on full display. We saw what freedom can do, what it *must* do. We saw what happens when people have control over their money, their property, their ideas . . . their *risk*, their *reward*. . . . And now we've sat and watched the great American engine of prosperity seize up and stall out. We watch as if we are powerless against it. Our job creators are in lockdown; our economy has choked like it hasn't since the Great Depression. My generation—*our* generation—didn't really feel the full impact of the Carter inflation when we were riding our bikes on safe hometown streets. This is uncharted territory for us and for so many Americans younger than us. And so it's easy for some of us to believe the politicians telling us we simply need to spend more on unemployment benefits. Or to pass thousand-page laws that even the lawmakers admit they haven't read.

When I talked to Delaware voters, I heard frustration, loud and clear—not only over the direction our country appears to be headed, but also because of the anti-American sentiment that taints every outlet of the ruling class. In diners and truck stops, in town halls and church halls, I heard a vibrant conversation about American values. The good people I found on the campaign trail rejected the narrative that had been imposed on them from the D.C. cocktail crowd. They wanted leaders to defend our values, our culture, our way of life, instead of offering weak-willed apologies that tear us down.

Like many, I believe that the American values enshrined in our Constitution and in our Declaration of Independence are not mere relics from the past, but the landing lights on a clear path to a strong and secure future. I believe that these core values were worth fighting for then, and that they're worth fighting for today.

There are more of us than there are of them.

The same principles that made our country great will keep our country great. If we err, let it be on the side of liberty. If we stumble, let us pick ourselves up and press on. If we benefit, let it be from working hard and saving smart. Let us meet our obligations to God and neighbor by way of our own hearts and checkbooks rather than some cold government bureaucracy. Let us entrust our nation to public servants who serve the public rather than themselves, and who place the next generation above the next election. Let America make peace in our world and on our borders through strength, friendship, commerce, and good common sense.

These are the values and principles that built—and can still *rebuild*—a great nation. But it wasn't easy then and it won't be easy now. We will be resisted and we must resist as well, but we must set about it. And so I ask you readers to join me in taking the same pledge as our first generation of dissenters. They saw only Lexington and Concord. They didn't see the dynasty of dissent they were founding. They couldn't see Gettysburg, Normandy, or Fallujah.

What was required of them though, is still required of us and will no doubt be required of our children and grandchildren. They took a pledge together, and that pledge closes out the Declaration of Independence. The same pledge will preserve this, the last, best hope for our planet. Let us pledge now, as they did then, to one another and to posterity. For the sake of life, liberty, and the pursuit of happiness, let us pledge our very "lives, our fortunes, and our sacred honor."

May God ever bless America.

Don't tread on us. You're not the boss of us.

And so, no, this book is not just about me. It's about you. It's about us: We the people!

PART ONE

My Life

If you don't like the road you're walking,
start paving another one.

—Dolly Parton

"I hung around people who were doing these things . . ."

I'll cut right to it: My lowest moment of the 2010 Delaware U.S. Senate campaign, was when I was caught in a swirl of negative press over a decade-old comment I'd made on the late-night ABC-TV talk show Politically Incorrect, *hosted by comedian Bill Maher.*

It wasn't much of a comment, if you must know. Frankly, it wasn't much of anything, but from the moment it started recirculating in the media it put our still-small campaign team on the defensive. Big time. We went from autopilot to damage control in a flash—over a nothing comment on a nonissue, made when I was hardly a factor on the political scene.

In an effort to be candid and relatable to the audience, I had opened up about a time back in high school when I went out on a blind date with a guy who believed in the occult. That's all it was, really.

When Bill Maher pressed me on "dabbling," the word I used to describe the extent of my passing interest in such matters, I said, "I hung around people who were doing these things."

As a side note, let the record show that "dabbling" means that a subject is "lightly explored," with a "superficial interest." You wouldn't hire a lawyer who'd dabbled in law school. You wouldn't see a doctor who'd dabbled in medicine. With this definition in mind, the word was exactly right. Dabbled. Lightly explored. That about said it. I never embraced this young man's religion. This was at a time in my life when I was open and curious and searching for meaning and spiritual guidance. And then I moved on.

When the show first aired in October 1999, nobody seemed to notice or care—boom, end of story. Back then, I was an aspiring political and social advocate, traveling the country on behalf of my own grassroots ministry, hoping to get young people to think a little more conservatively (and, I maintained, more responsibly). Politically Incorrect was a frequent and favorite stomping ground for me, because it offered such a wonderfully direct pipeline to America's young people—who, after all, accounted for much of Bill Maher's late-night audience. And Bill and his producers must have liked my cheerful, hopeful, no-nonsense style, because they kept asking me back. Or maybe they were getting good feedback from the audience, and that's why I was getting booked. Either way, I ended up appearing on that show twenty-two times. (According to the show's producer, that put me right up there with Ann Coulter and Arianna Huffington as one of the most frequent guests on the show.) And each time out it felt to me like I was making more and more of a connection with the teenagers and young adults I was trying to reach.

This, I thought, was a great, good thing.

Now, more than a decade later, it was nearly my undoing. Bill Maher dug out that old clip to show on his new late-night show, HBO's Real Time with Bill Maher, *and before I even had time to wonder what he might be up to the thing had gone viral. Suddenly, it was the talk of the campaign— and not in a good way. In putting it back out there, I didn't think Bill Maher was stirring up trouble so much as he was baiting me to appear on his new show to debate the issues of the day. At first, that's how I looked at it, giving him the benefit of the doubt.*

A lot had happened in the intervening decade. I was now making some noise all of my own, having just defeated our current congressman and former governor Mike Castle in the Republican primary, stunning the party establishment and in the process winning the support of the Tea Party Express; political commentators like Rush Limbaugh, Mark Levin, and Sean Hannity; and even the de facto *standard bearer of the Tea Party movement, Sarah Palin. In the language of late-night talk show producers, I'd become "a good get." Since I was no longer doing many national interviews, in order to focus on the needs and concerns of my fellow Delawareans and to address the issues of the campaign, I figured the* Real Time *producers were just doing their jobs in going after me.*

Did I regret making those remarks, now that they were coming back to bite me? I'm tempted to say yes, but it wouldn't be true. It was a different time in my life when my purpose was different, long before I could ever imagine that I'd one day run for the United States Senate. What I said referred back to an even earlier time in my life, when I was just a kid and my front-and-center worries had more to do with boys and grades than taking on the liberal establishment.

Absolutely, a whole lot had changed since my time on the Bill Maher show, and even more since the time twenty years earlier that I had spoken about. I got that. I understood full well that these nothing revelations meant one thing from the lips of a relatively unknown grassroots advocate, but coming from a candidate for the United States Senate, they meant something else entirely. I got that, too. And yet to hear the firestorm of controversy that was now coming my way, you'd think I'd started turning my political opponents into toads. Bill also showed a clip where I said I read the Bhagavad Gita, *but no one accused me of being a Hare Krishna. And anyway, aren't the liberals who slammed me for this the very same ones touting tolerance?*

All this fuss and bother over a blind date when I was a teenager, for goodness' sake! It was all very innocent, and very weird, and nothing more. This guy shared some of his views with me, and that was pretty much that. I saw him a few times after that, and I did a bit of reading on paganism, because it was a time in my life when I was searching for my own footing, but I never signed on to this guy's beliefs.

I was curious, that's all.

CHAPTER ONE

Where I Come From

The O'Donnell family quilt is a colorful patchwork of classes and cultures, *and* political affiliations, but the common thread that knit us all together is a tireless work ethic, a fierce determination to stand for something (and for each other), and an enormous sense of pride, place, and love.

We have our disagreements, just like any other American family, but we work past them and set them aside because we love each other. We come together from all these different, sometimes opposing views and opinions, and we find our way to common ground, to a place of shared purpose and meaning.

I think every American family is its own little melting pot. In ours, there was a whole lot of Italian and Irish, with a healthy dose of American blue blood thrown into the mix.

Initially, I wasn't really sure about including any stories from my childhood, because they don't *only* involve me. My parents and siblings were put through so much scrutiny and hardship when I ran for office and declared myself a public person. The moment I became a candidate, my life became an open book—and my life is so intertwined with their lives that my family was thrown right out there with me. Then I realized that my goal in writing this book is to inspire real people to engage in the political process. And real people have real lives and real problems.

When we share the hard truths of our lives they often stand as an inspiration to others. We've all had our share of rough patches, and I believe we lift each other up when we talk about them; we can learn from each other's mistakes, and find strength in the struggle.

My family is close. We all have our own special relationships with our parents and with one another and this extends to the next generation as well; my siblings have great spouses and well-adjusted children. By all outward appearances, we're one big happy family. And this is true from our own perspectives as well. That's not to say we didn't have our problems. We did. Along with the great times, we had some tough times as a family. To the outside world it might have looked like we were the Waltons—living in the suburbs instead of the mountains. And in a lot of ways, that was true. But in addition to the financial struggles that you could imagine would arise in raising six children—yes, there were six of us—my dad drank heavily during my childhood. He doesn't drink like that anymore. And I'm proud of the way we've powered past it all. Our difficulties don't define us. It's how we deal with them that shape who we are. Frankly, I'm a little wary of politicians with "perfect" pasts, and I've come to regard the imperfections that have found my family over the years as badges of honor, not marks of shame.

My parents are the true heroes of my story—and were it

not for their strength, their faith, and their boundless courage my journey could have gone another way. My mother's refusal to let her family fall apart on the back of my father's alcoholism was, and remains, an inspiration. My father's willingness to let himself be lifted by the love of his family to a place where he could do the hard work necessary to make himself whole . . . well, it's been a kind of revelation.

Ah, but I don't mean to get ahead of the story—my story, *our* story . . .

My parents grew up in the same Philadelphia neighborhood, so they knew each other as kids. My mom, Carole Chillano, is Italian; her parents were first-generation Italian-Americans. My dad, Dan O'Donnell, is Irish-American, with family roots in this country that quite possibly reach all the way back to our Founding Fathers. My parents lived on opposite ends of what they've always called the Corpus Christi part of town. You won't find that name on a map of the city, but in those days, to hear my parents tell it, Philadelphia neighborhoods were known by the churches in each community. My mom lived on the Italian side of the neighborhood and my dad lived on the Irish side, with a playground in between, on Clearfield Street. They started dating as teenagers, and they've been together ever since. (They even *married* as teenagers, so they got a good running start!) And they still keep in touch with their neighborhood friends from the playground.

My paternal grandmother, Kathleen Carroll, had a real zest for living. She was witty, charming, and full of spunk. I remember visiting in the hospital when she was dying and she said, "Go get my purse, let's go dancing!"—and she was serious!

Kathleen Carroll came from a long line of Carrolls—for a time, one of the most prominent families in Philadelphia. We were always told that one of Grandmom's great-great-great uncles was Charles Carroll, a United States Senator from Maryland, the longest-living and last-surviving signer of our Declaration of Independence. We were never able to confirm a direct relation, but I mention the connection here because I know my nay-saying critics are fact checking this book. I'm hoping to use their scrutiny to my advantage—either to corroborate our long-presumed link to Charles Carroll of Carrollton or to set it to rest.

Just in case, we'll have it covered!

At a young age, my grandmother found herself "in the family way" after taking up with my grandfather, Francis O'Donnell. The circumstances surrounding their relationship and the pregnancy caused a great scandal and in the end she was estranged from her family—and cut off from what would have been a sizeable inheritance.

I can't imagine what my grandmother suffered, for the choices she made as a young woman, but in the years to come her courage and great conviction came back into play, because it turned out my grandfather was an alcoholic, the same disease that would later haunt my father—only in Grandpop O'Donnell's case, sad to say, the battle didn't exactly go his way. The marriage didn't last, and my grandmother eventually found someone special—a wonderful stable man named John, who worked hard in a gas station and was utterly devoted to my grandmother. We called him Grandpop John, because in time he became more of a grandfather to us than Francis. In fact, later on, my grandmother's dying wish was to make sure my father would look after John once she was gone—and, as always, my father was true to his word. Grandpop John ended up moving in with my parents the last couple years of his life, and here again the takeaway for me was the importance of family.

There's one cherished memory that grew out of my grandmother's estrangement. My grandmother's siblings, for the most part, were fearful about keeping in touch with their sister because they did not want to go against their father's wishes. However, a couple of my father's aunts and uncles did on occasion secretly defy him to maintain a connection with my grandmom.

On one such occasion, my grandmom was having a family barbecue and her sister, my Great Aunt Urse, snuck around to take part. Not in the habit of showing up empty-handed to a gathering, she brought a plate of deviled eggs arranged on a blue Limoges plate. To Aunt Urse, the plate was an everyday plate, but to the rest of us, it was clearly a fine piece of china. Grandmom O'Donnell recognized it right away from her mother's china collection. At the end of the party, Aunt Urse left in haste, forgetting the plate. Grandmom thought about returning it—but the temptation to have something that belonged to her mother was just too great, so she kept it. A few days later, the plate took a place of honor up on my grandmother's wall. It was the only keepsake she had from her mother, so it meant a great deal to her. She proudly showed it to everyone who came by for a visit.

She would point to it up on the wall, and say cheekily, "That's my inheritance." Except, of course, when good ol' Aunt Urse came over. For her visits, the plate was temporarily removed.

Well, the story of my grandmother's prized blue plate did not end there, because after she and most of her siblings had passed, the provenance of the plate was thrown into question. At one point, one of my father's relatives reached out to him to see if he planned to challenge the estate. My father didn't want any of their money, he said. All he wanted was his Aunt Ursula's blue plate.

And so it was settled—and now the blue plate hangs proudly on my parents' living room wall.

I never really knew my paternal grandfather, Francis. He was out of the picture by the time I was born. He was a difficult character. He drank . . . a lot. I share the broad details of his life with a heavy heart. He was my grandfather, after all, and it's difficult to cast a member of your own family in such a vulnerable light, but this was who he was. We do not lift or improve ourselves by ignoring the mistakes or missteps of others; rather, we must consider the bad paths they've taken or the turns they might have missed and weigh them against the roads that spread out before us. We don't do ourselves or our loved ones any favors by avoiding the truths of our lives, however ugly or heartbreaking those truths happen to be.

I only met my grandfather once. I was in fifth grade, and he was living down in Clearwater, Florida. My father hadn't been in touch with him for years, but out of the blue his father sent him a check for $1,000, as a kind of make-amends gesture. My dad recognized that check as the lonely, desperate cry that it was, so with his $1,000 he packed us six kids and my cousin Evelyn into a run-down passenger van we'd borrowed for the occasion, and we drove down to Florida for a family reunion he said was long overdue. Even as a kid, I saw this as a great lesson in forgiveness and turning the other cheek. I was old enough to understand the depths of my grandfather's mistreatment of his family, but here was my father, taking what for us was a lot of money and spending it on the man who'd showered so much abuse on him for so many years.

It was a beautiful moment of redemption, and a wonderful opportunity for us kids to see our father rise above his raw emotions to do the right thing, and set the right example. Even in retelling it, it still moves me.

Grandpop O'Donnell was thrilled to have us visit, and we kids were able to tune out all of the anger and anguish that had been built up over the years. To us, he was just a fun grandfather, and my father was happy to see us all getting along so well. In fact, things were going so well, from our little kid perspectives, that the night before we were due to leave we pleaded with our parents to take my grandfather back with us. He seemed so lonely down there in Clearwater, his days so dark and dismal; we all thought he could use a change of scenery. My parents, a bit reluctantly, agreed.

It was quite a frantic scene, as we got ready to leave early the next morning. It was barely daylight, and my mother had her hands full getting her six kids and her niece all packed and washed and into the car. I believe now that my grandfather had probably been up all night drinking, so in addition to worrying about us kids my mother had to wonder what he might do next, but somehow we got past the chaos and were ready to leave. The last thing my mother had us do, just before leaving, was to shuttle us each into the bathroom, so we wouldn't have to stop on the way. One-by-one, we took our turn and then headed out to the van.

I was the last—and by the time I stepped out of the bathroom everybody had gone. I thought they were all waiting for me in the van, so I raced outside, but the van was gone, too! It was a real *Home Alone*-type moment, back when Macaulay Culkin was just a baby!

Amazingly, surprisingly, I didn't panic.

They'd driven a couple miles before anyone figured out I was back in the apartment. Remember, this was before cell phones, so they couldn't call to tell me they were on their way. Before heading out, my mother, as usual, did a quick head count, and in the rush of the morning had simply forgotten that we also had my cousin Evelyn in tow, so when she got to six she left it at that, and now all they could do was race back to my grandfather's and hope against hope I hadn't gotten into any trouble.

My poor mother was absolutely mortified that she could leave me behind like that. To this day, she gets embarrassed when we tell this story, but I didn't see it as anything to be embarrassed about. I still don't. There was a lot going on that morning, that's all. There were a lot of kids to track, and my cousin Evelyn, and my ornery grandfather, and all of our stuff. It's a wonder they got out of there at all, with *most* of their kids—I count this to my mother's great credit.

Meanwhile, first thing I did, after assessing the situation, was plan my new life in Florida. I didn't know how long I'd be there on my own. So I searched my grandfather's kitchen cabinets, and saw a couple cans of tomato soup, so I figured I was covered in the food department. Then I went out back, and started exploring. It occurred to me I might need to find some way to make a living, so I gathered a bunch of *sticky-gooks* from the trees behind my grandfather's building. I don't know what these things are actually called, but I used to collect them with a friend of mine at Strawbridge Lake, near our house in New Jersey. We always knew them as *stickygooks*— brown pods, with a hard outer shell, filled with seeds and green sticky stuff. If you dry them out, you can shake them like maracas, so my idea was to decorate them and sell them, and if I couldn't find a market for them I told myself I'd at least have a nice collection going.

I was wearing a sundress, and I lifted the hem so the dress made a small basket in front of me, and gathered as many *stickygooks* as I could carry, and when my family pulled back up, I was out by the curb in front of my grandfather's building, trying to sell my wares to folks as they passed by.

I must have made quite a picture.

We've told that story into the ground in my family, and it always gets a good laugh at Sunday dinners, but we've never told it *outside* the safe harbor of our own family . . . until now. I share it here for the way it stands as a precious family memory, but also for the gracenote it offers to this one extended visit with my grandfather. There were all kinds of lessons in it. Self-reliance wasn't meant to be one of them, but there it is alongside the all-important lessons of forgiveness, tolerance, empathy, and all that good stuff.

We didn't always get it right, in our family, but we made the effort.

I fared a bit better in the grandfather department with my grandpop Chillano, my mother's father. Actually, he was pretty great with us kids. My grandmom Chillano was a jewel all around. She was beautiful on the inside and the outside. She had ocean blue eyes and dark blond hair. Although she came from limited means, she was always dressed to the nines and had an amazing fashion sense. We were extremely close to them throughout my childhood, and both my grandmother and grandfather had as much of a role in shaping me and my worldview as anyone.

My grandpop was a hardworking man with a fascinating background. He was one of those cantakerous old men that you couldn't help but love. He was born in New Castle, Delaware, but moved to the rural outskirts of Philadelphia by the time he was an adolescent. Throughout his life he had several different careers, which meant he had an endless supply of stories to tell his grandchildren. He was a foreman for the railroad. He was an MP in the army during World War II. He was a cook. He worked as a taster in a local brewery—Ortlieb's, a one-time Philadelphia institution. He'd tell the story of how he once alerted his boss to a bad batch of beer that was nearly sent out into the marketplace. Apparently, my grandpop could taste that the yeast was about to turn, but he couldn't get anyone else to agree with him on this. They ran a bunch of tests, since discarding an entire batch would have cost the company a lot of money, but everything kept coming back fine. Finally, my grandfather's boss turned to him and said, "Pete, if you tell me it's a bad batch, it's a bad batch." Sure enough, within a week to ten days, the beer had soured and Grandpop was proven right. But this was almost beside the point. What mattered to my grandfather was that his boss believed in him, even when all the tests and all the other tasters didn't agree. He'd built up enough credibility and goodwill to be taken at his word, and this to him was a tremendous accomplishment.

And he always had a story or two he'd share to instill that same work ethic in us. The most memorable was a kind of parable about hard work and determination, centered on a bag of peanuts. He told it to us so often that years later it made its way into my campaign speeches. He used to sit us down and in his gruff voice he'd say, "Listen, no one is going to hand you a bag of peanuts. If you want a bag of peanuts, you have to earn it." Then he'd go on. "Instead of banging your head against the wall in frustration, you could work hard and earn enough money to buy two peanuts at the end of each day. Then, eat one peanut and put the other in a bag. The next day," he'd continue, "do the same thing." As he spoke, he'd raise his hand to his mouth as if he was eating a peanut. "Eat one," then gesturing as if to toss a peanut into a bag, "put one in a bag. And before you know it, you've earned yourself a bag of peanuts!"

It was a simple bit of homespun wisdom, but he handed it down to us kids as if it held all the secrets of the universe.

To this day if anyone in my family says, "Eat one peanut . . ." whoever's in ear-shot will respond, "Put one in a bag . . ."— complete with hand gestures!

Lessons about hard work didn't only come from Grandpop, but from Grandmom, too. She grew up during the Depression, one of nine children, and as soon as she and her siblings were old enough they had to go out and work. At the end of the day, they gave what they earned to their father, my great-grandfather. My Grandmom was nine years old when she got her first job, working in a dress factory earning a penny for every tag she sewed on a garment. It was painstaking work, but she never complained because she loved it. Eventually she worked her way to floor supervisor. She was happy to contribute to her family's finances. She used to tell me that no matter how difficult things were, she was always able to move about with her head held high. She considered herself very much a lady, throughout her life, never more so than when she had so little.

"Class is about character, not money," she used to say. "Doing the right thing and treating others with respect is not something you can buy."

To my grandmother, this was what it meant to be a lady, which was (and *is!*) all about character.

During the worst of the Depression, she told me, there was barely enough money. Sometimes a meal for all eleven of them would be stewed tomatoes picked from their garden and poured over stale Italian bread. That was how families did it back then, making a little go a long, long way.

Over time, Grandmom Chillano came to think she was richer for having suffered through that period in her life with her sprawling family. She might have minded sewing all those penny labels at the time, but she never let on that she minded it in retrospect, because it helped to define her, and build her character, and put food on the table.

Grandmom's last days were difficult. When I got word that

she didn't have much time, I was living down in D.C., trying to make my way as an activist. My grandmother was in the final stages of Alzheimer's, a slowly devastating disease that can drag down whole families in its wake. Some folks, when they get a grim prognosis like that, they simply check out. They say, "Oh, that's awful. Call me when it's over." But that's not how we O'Donnells roll. We hear a piece of news like that and we rally. We say, "Oh my gosh. Only three more weeks? That's not nearly enough time." And we drop everything to be at our loved one's side, for whatever time we have left.

That's how it happened with Grandmom. We all rallied together. At the time, my father and grandfather hadn't been getting along, but even they put aside their differences. We did it because we wanted to make Grandmom as comfortable as possible, to make her death as peaceful and beautiful as possible. It became so much more than that, because the experience knitted us more deeply together as a family, in a profoundly beautiful way.

That colorful quilt I wrote about earlier? We wrapped ourselves beneath it and held each other close.

There's a profound encyclical on suffering from Pope John Paul II, in which he talks about how suffering can unleash love. That's how it was for us at my grandmother's passing. Her death brought us together and reminded us what it meant to love each other—fully, truly, unconditionally.

In many ways, my grandmother's death played a formative role in my life. On paper, and in every outward respect, I was already a young woman; I was deep into my twenties, making my own way in the world; and yet when you're swallowed back up by family, surrounded by aunts and uncles, you fall into some of your old roles, your old ways of being with each other. I think in times of extreme stress or hardship, this is especially so. We all had our roles within our family dynamic. My brother and sisters and I were all "kids" in the eyes of the "adults," and it fell to *them* to make all the really, really important decisions.

But that all changed through this experience. At one point my grandfather turned to me and said, "I don't know what I'll do without Grandmom. I don't know how I'll manage."

It wasn't just the *thought* of losing her that was weighing on him. It was the *process* of actually losing her. Caring for her was hard, really hard, and it was taking its toll. He didn't say as much but it was clear, so I said, "Grandpop, how about I spend the night and take care of Grandmom for you?"

As soon as I put it out there, it was clear that my aunts and my mother didn't want to put that kind of burden on "us kids." "No, no, no," one of them said. "You don't have to do that." The others concurred. They were trying to protect us from the pain of caring for a loved one and facing the loss of that loved one in such a full-on way. And, since I was one of the youngest and was used to yielding on stuff like this, I backed down from what would have been a good, helpful turn.

I came back the next morning to find that Grandmom had had a rough night. As a result, Grandpop was more on edge than ever. I could have kicked myself for not helping out.

The way things were working back then was that all of us would gather at my grandparents' apartment each morning, and stay until very late at night. Spending all that time together gave me the chance to see this grumpier side of my grandfather that didn't quite fit with what I knew growing up. So the very next day, when he was even more out of sorts than the day before, I made the very same offer, and this time I didn't back down from it.

Once again, one of my aunts said, "No, honey. You don't have to do that."

I loved them all for loving me so much that they wanted to take on this burden themselves, but this was something I wanted to do, something I *needed* to do.

It was a milestone moment for me, to push this course of action, and to have it be so. Just like that. And for my mother and her sisters, too, it was a great relief. They were so grateful that I'd put myself out in this way—but it really didn't feel like I was putting myself out at all. It was my pleasure, my duty.

And it turned out to have a very calming, very reassuring effect on my grandfather. We stayed up talking, remembering, for a good long while. We talked about my grandmother's gnocchi. She was famous in our family for her gnocchi—tiny Italian potato dumplings she'd slather with gravy, which was what "real" Italians called their tomato sauce, which she made with "real" tomatoes grown from their own garden. There was always a friendly tug-and-pull between my grandparents and us grandkids over which one was the better cook, and any talk of my Grandmom's gnocchi was almost always met by a challenge from my Grandpop's meatballs. And so it was on this night as well, even though my grandmother was no longer able to defend her kitchen honors.

"You always liked my meatballs better," Grandpop said, as he finally drifted off to sleep.

I sat there for a long moment, watching him sleep, his gray-black hair parted to the side. His healthy olive skin made him look younger than he really was, and I remember thinking that he was still strong and handsome—at least in his granddaughter's eyes.

The next morning, after getting a good night's rest, he was much more like himself, much more like I remembered, so we "kids" (and I use that term loosely, because we were all in our twenties and thirties!) put together a schedule for taking turns on the overnight shift and spending as much time as possible with Grandmom during her last days on Earth.

As I set this down on paper I realize it might seem like such a tiny thing, but to me it was a pivotal moment. It was somewhat of a coming of age.

It was taking responsibility, which can be a beautiful burden. That's how it made me feel, taking this on. Like it was a challenge I wanted to meet for my grandmother. For my grandfather. For my mother. For my aunts. For me. And it *was* a challenge. I remember sitting with a woman from hospice who came by one afternoon to tell us what to expect in caring for a patient with Alzheimer's. She told me that the hardest part for a caregiver was to think like the patient. "You have to try to enter what's going on in her mind," she explained. "If your grandmother thinks something is happening, or if she thinks she's someplace long ago, don't try to convince her that she's not, because she'll just get scared."

That very night, I had a chance to put this counsel to the test. It was my turn on nightwatch. I was lying on the floor next to her bed so that I could be close. Suddenly, the sound of the bed rattling made me open my eyes. There was Grandmom, standing on the mattress, chatting calmly and specifically about going to work. In her head, she was a teenager, getting ready to go to the dress factory and start sewing tags. My first instinct was to reach for her and pull her down from the bed. I thought she'd fall and get hurt. But each time I reached for her she became more and more agitated. Then it came to me what the hospice worker had said about going along with my grandmother's "reality." Grandmom thought she was talking to one of her sisters. So I talked to her as if I was right there with her, like I was one of the girls.

"Betty," I explained, reaching for her arm, "the bus isn't coming right away. Maybe we should sit down and wait."

She responded, "No, no, no. I'm going to be late for work."

She didn't settle down, and again I was afraid she'd fall. So I tried a different approach. When we were younger, my grandmother would sing to us as we were falling asleep. So I started singing to her.

Without even thinking about it I started singing one of the hymns I remembered from going to church with her when I was a child. I recall feeling like I needed to pray, and this was what came out.

> *Holy, Holy, Holy*
> *Lord God Almighty . . .*
> *God in three persons*
> *Blessed Trinity.*

I should mention here that I can't really carry a tune, but that didn't stop me—and Grandmom didn't seem to mind. I sat there in the dark room and quietly sang. The glow of the streetlamp outside her window cast a soft, blue light across her face. After a verse or two her mood began to change. The words, the melody . . . it seemed to reach her. Whatever had been upsetting her melted away, and she calmed down. I held her arm and guided her as she lay back down, then sat on the bed beside her. She rested her head on the pillow and I stroked her hair the way she had stroked mine so many times when I was a little girl.

"Good night, Grandmom," I whispered.

This was how we took turns saying good-bye to Grandmom, and taking care of Grandpop, and reconnecting with each other—reestablishing the relationships that would sustain us for the rest of our lives.

Later I overheard my aunt Karen telling my sisters, the next overnight team, "And Chris learned that if you sing her a church hymn, she really responds to it." To me, her words signaled a sea change in our family dynamic. It felt to me like there had been a shift. I had taken my place at the adult table.

The whole experience of losing my grandmother in such a long, painful way was really very beautiful. It was so full of love, and growth. It strengthened us as a family. It was transitional, transforming. I went into the experience in some ways as a child and came out as an adult. Changed. In fundamental ways.

"You're going to hate this, Christine, but hear me out. . . ."

Okay, so that's the setup to the crisis that came on the back of Bill Maher showing that old interview, and once it found me I couldn't think how to respond. Not at first, anyway. The general election was a little more than a month away, and we still didn't have any television commercials running throughout the state. Meanwhile, the Coons campaign, the Democratic Senatorial Campaign Committee, and other groups had launched a whole series of misleading and distorted ads, quite a few of them attacking me, my family, my background, or my beliefs. They were also running false ads about Coons's record, claiming he had brought New Castle County to solvency when in reality our county had gone broke on his watch—a sad fact that our local newspaper wouldn't report until over a month after the election, by the way.

Like it or not, like me or not, this nothing comment about a guy I'd known back in high school had set in motion what was starting to feel like a modern-day witch hunt—with me cast as . . . well, as the witch. It would have been silly, if it wasn't so darn serious, if there wasn't so much at stake.

For a while, I managed to defuse a lot of the talk. I even tried to joke about it. When a reporter asked me about the Politically Incorrect clip, I said, "If I was a witch, I would have turned Karl Rove into a supporter by now"—referring, of course, to the architect of George W. Bush's presidential campaigns and his former chief of staff, now one of the Grand Old Men of the Grand Old Party whose only acknowledgement of my campaign was to lead attacks against us.

It was a good line, but it didn't get a whole lot of play, because by now there was a great deal riding on this one Senate race, and not just for me personally. In fact, there was so much at stake in this midterm election that the Democrats were sending out the heavy artillery to stem the tide of support that had been coming my way since I'd announced my candidacy earlier that year. The Democratic Senatorial Campaign Committee was running ads against me, while national unions came out with a barrage of hateful direct mail campaigns. My fellow Delawarean, Vice President Joe Biden—who'd opposed me in the race for this same Senate seat back in 2008—was traveling through our home state, beating the drums for Chris Coons, and even President Obama was coming to Delaware to campaign against me.

It felt a little bit like being David lining up to do battle with Goliath . . . again. Even without the bubbling controversy of that ancient Politically Incorrect footage, we were facing an uphill climb without any support from my own party. I didn't think we could compete, so I huddled with my key advisors—my campaign manager, Matt Moran; my sister Jennie; and Cleta Mitchell, our campaign general consultant—to go over our options. The consensus was that we would reach out to a production company called Screaming Dime, since we were familiar with their work and liked their vision and approach to our message. Trouble was, Screaming Dime couldn't make it to Delaware for at least another week, because they were booked on a commercial shoot out in Los Angeles—ironically, for a series of ads endorsing various Democratic candidates.

Matt felt strongly that we needed to get our response ads on the air as soon as possible. A week was too long to wait, he said, and I agreed, so we looked instead to a media strategist named Fred Davis, who came highly recommended by John Cornyn, the U.S. Republican senator from Texas who was also the head of the National Republican Senatorial Committee (NRSC). The endorsement was a big deal because the NRSC had seemed to be twiddling its thumbs about helping us, so we thought we'd do well to follow their lead on this and go with one of their established vendors, hoping this might move the needle in our direction.

Still, I had an uneasy feeling about hiring Fred to help craft our response. Oh, he knew his business, make no mistake. He was very, very good at his job. And he'd run a number of effective campaigns for a number of candidates I admired—all of them men, I should point out. It troubled me that he didn't have much of a track record with female candidates, and as any political consultant will tell you, the marketing of a female candidate is a whole other ballgame. It also troubled me that he charged a lot more money than other media consultants, and I didn't think that sent the right message to our supporters.

Our support came in five, ten, or twenty dollars at a time, and it came with powerful, personal notes filled with stories of hardship and sacrifice. We felt duty-bound to spend every dollar wisely, purposefully, thinking we had a duty to sacrifice as well. In my mind, that duty reached to our vendors. If a hardworking farmer sent us ten dollars, I wanted to use it to pay for printing a hundred postcards. These aren't knocks against Fred, mind you. He's entitled to set his own terms, and he's done enough good, influential work to justify them. Good for him. Yet I worried that it wasn't so good for us, and I came away thinking we might not be a good fit. What troubled me most of all was that Fred wanted creative control, which meant he would run the entire ad campaign. This was a giant red flag. I was not comfortable with it. I mean, I was the one getting ripped in the press. I was the one being called a witch by Letterman and Leno. Also, the campaign was very much a team effort, so it was not just my neck on the line, my reputation, my career. The entire campaign and the entire Delaware Tea Party movement was hanging right out there with me.

To hand over the keys to a guy I hardly knew, at a price tag I could hardly justify . . . well, it didn't sit right.

I weighed the pros and cons of hiring Fred Davis and concluded I didn't have much choice. Don't misunderstand me, it was my decision to make, bottom line, but I felt like I was being pulled in this one direction. My advisors wanted me to go one way, while I wanted to go another, so I tried to look at the decision qualitatively. Fred was the choice of the National Republican Senatorial Committee, and we hoped going with their guy would be a gesture of good faith. He did good work; he was available immediately, and perhaps most important was that a big part of the pitch was that his production company almost always brought his clients a double-digit bump in the polls. And we needed a double-digit bump. So what did I do? I ignored my gut, listened to my advisors, crossed my fingers, and hoped like crazy this guy would put us ahead. The moment I did, I regretted it. I started thinking of Ronald Reagan, one of my all-time political heroes, a guy who didn't always listen to his closest counsel. You see, all great leaders know when to ignore those advisors and follow their own instincts instead. It's a delicate balance, and President Reagan managed it quite heroically with his landmark speech at the Berlin Wall. Historians recall that key members of Reagan's staff urged him not to utter the words that would become one of the most memorable phrases of his presidency: "Mr. Gorbachev, tear down this wall!"

Reportedly, that one line was cut from and restored to the president's speech a number of times. For the most part, the advisors were doing the cutting, while the president was doing the restoring. Even the State Department warned of global consequences if President Reagan dared to make such a provocative comment in such an important setting. However, according to firsthand accounts, the president took one last look at his prepared remarks as he stood at the podium . . . and he went on his own way. Without telling anyone what he was about to do, he read the speech the way his heart told him to. It wasn't an act of rebellion or defiance so much as one of doing the right thing. He knew how important those six words could be, delivered in just the right way, at just the right moment. And indeed they were: They changed the course of history, and Reagan's monumental speech now marks the beginning of the end of communism.

Now, I'm not suggesting here that the decision before me carried anything like the weight and importance of President Reagan's decision at the Berlin Wall. Not at all. I'm simply saying that in this instance I didn't measure up.

And then—get this!—right after we signed an exclusive, ironclad contract to work with Fred Davis, we learned that the quick turnaround he'd promised wasn't about to happen any time soon. Turned out we couldn't set up our commercial shoot for another week or so, which meant we could have gone with our first-choice production company, Screaming Dime, all along.

We set a date on our calendar to shoot the commercial and waited to hear from Fred with a script. We waited and waited. Each time we reached out for an update, we were told to be patient, and to rest assured that Fred had it covered. (Believe me, I wasn't resting, and I certainly wasn't assured!) Finally, after a week of waiting, Jennie and I went to Philadelphia for the taping, before any of us from the campaign had signed off on a script or a concept. As we drove, the whole thing struck me as a fool's errand. Basically, we'd boxed ourselves into a corner and now had no choice but to sit back and watch Fred do his thing.

Big mistake, it turned out—and not because Fred Davis wasn't creative or talented or even well-intentioned, but because, in our case, his instincts were off. He came to see us that night, to go over a new idea he was all excited about.

He said, "You're going to hate this, Christine, but hear me out."

I thought, So much for sweet-talking the buyer. *Here I'd been prepared to be excited by Fred's new concept, and he all but told me it was all wrong—or, at least, that I would think it was all wrong, and that I should be smart enough to trust him to know better.*

And then he finally came out with it: "I want to start the ad with you saying, 'I'm not a witch.'"

CHAPTER TWO

Five to a Room: Growing Up O'Donnell

It was 1969—the summer of Woodstock, the first man on the moon, the debut of *Sesame Street*... and in that August I was born in Philadelphia, but we didn't stay there long. We moved to the suburbs that very same day, to a modest house in Moorestown, New Jersey—a pretty little town with good schools, safe streets, and wide open spaces for us kids to roam.

I was the fifth of six children, and our big family was bursting at the seams of our Clearfield Street row home, so we needed a bigger house. We needed a bigger yard. Plus, my parents were nearly choking on just three Catholic school tuitions—for my brother Dan, who was nine, and my sisters Jennie and Carole, seven and six. (The next in line, Elizabeth, was a year and a half older than me, so she wasn't in school just yet. Eileen, the youngest, wouldn't turn up for another three years.)

The *real* reason for the move, though, was to get us kids on the right track for college. Neither of my parents went, so it was important to them that their children go. They did a lot of research and concluded that the Moorestown Public School District was one of the best, with a college-prep curriculum.

Their strategy was to buy the least expensive house in the best school district, that's how important it was to them to give us the best possible education. Still, it was a struggle. Back as far as I can remember, we always had just enough to get by, but not nearly enough to get ahead.

Even at the modest end of the local housing market, the house was more than my parents could afford, so my father had to work three jobs to cover the mortgage payments. Over the years, he worked a whole host of jobs in a variety of fields. In my memory, he almost always had three separate gigs; he was forever coming and going; some nights, we wouldn't see him at all, but when he'd get back to the house too late for our bedtimes, he'd slip bags of bubblegum or pink popcorn by our beds, so we would find them first thing in the morning—just a little something to show that he was thinking of us. Despite his relentless work schedule, he made it a special point to carve out time for us, in what ways he could. He was one of the only dads in the neighborhood who'd go outside with his kids after dinner and teach them the games he remembered from his own childhood, like Kick the Can and Jailbreak.

My father was a bit of a ham—still is! —with a gregarious, outgoing personality, so he naturally gravitated toward performing. He was a deejay on a local radio station. He had a variety show on a small television station, which he sometimes trotted out to area theaters, including an occasional gig in Atlantic City. He was never able to make a whole lot of money at it, even though it's what he loved doing most.

Between gigs, he started a career as a car salesman—and he was pretty darn good at this. He said the key was to ask a lot of questions to find out what the consumer wants, and know your product well enough to give it to them. He was always taking "demo" cars home from the lot to try them out; we were known around the neighborhood for our eclectic collection of cars. We'd have a station wagon one week, a microbus the next week, and then an antique sedan. (We even had a hearse at one point, and a big blue school bus that had been converted into a camper.)

After a while my father realized that he could not pursue an acting career and support six kids, so he set aside his dreams of a career in show business to focus on the steady jobs that would support us—but not before one particular "star turn" that stands out in my memory, as Bozo the Clown on a local television station in Philadelphia. In each city, there'd be a local Bozo hired to introduce the cartoons from the national program. My father still worked his other jobs, but he was regularly appearing as Bozo.

One winter a giant snowstorm had pretty much brought everything to a standstill. The streets weren't plowed, so there wasn't much to do but romp around in the snow. This was a great treat for us kids, but it wasn't so great for Bozo, who had to somehow make it to the studio to film that week's show. And it wasn't enough to get the clown and crew to the studio—they had to get an entire studio audience down there too, because the show was filmed in front of a live audience.

Snowstorm or no snowstorm, Bozo couldn't do his thing on an empty soundstage; there'd be nobody to laugh at his jokes. That's where we came in. About an hour or so before the cameras were due to roll, my father called the house in a panic.

"No kids showed up," he said to my mom. "They're going to cancel the show if we can't fill the studio."

That's all that my mother needed to hear. She burst into action. She called our neighbor, Mrs. Rooney, who lived two houses down from us and also had a houseful of kids. They drove a Volkswagon mini-bus and we had our trusty station wagon. It was big enough to hold six kids under normal circumstances, but in a pinch could fit more than twice that number.

We lived in a kid-friendly neighborhood with close to a hundred kids living on our block (really!) and somehow my mom was able to cram a studio's worth of them into the two vehicles that could make it through the snow to the television studio. Remember, this was back before seatbelt laws, so they piled us right in, two on a lap, more on the floor. And then, in the back of the wagon you could squeeze in even more.

Boy, did my mom really save the day for Bozo that afternoon! In fact, it must have looked like a couple of clown cars from the circus, with all these kids spilling out in front of the studio, but I guess that was only fitting considering our mission. When my father stepped out on stage and said, "Hi, Kids," the studio erupted with applause—which I guess wasn't surprising, since the audience was made up mostly of neighborhood kids. What *was* surprising, though, was one voice that cried out above the din.

One boy took a look at my father on the set and shouted, "Hey, that's not Bozo! That's Mr. O'Donnell!"

We O'Donnells weren't a regular church-going family. We weren't even what you'd call "Christmas-and-Easter" Catholics.

We'd celebrate all of the holidays, but we'd rarely make it to Mass. Religion can be a tricky business in families. My mother didn't want to force it on us, because it had been forced on her.

In this way, I guess, we were like a lot of families in our neighborhood. The Rooneys were the one exception. They were our good, good friends. Their daughter Eileen was one of my closest friends, other than my sisters. We matched up in age. Whenever I was invited to Eileen's for a Saturday night sleep-over, I had to agree to go to church with them on Sunday morning. That was the deal—and I happily accepted it.

For several summers, my parents sent us to Vacation Bible School. The Moorestown Bible Church had opened up on Main Street, and they ran a summer program for area children; they even sent a bus around to pick us all up. For me, it was the place where I had my first *real* memory of truly experiencing or feeling an awareness of God in my life.

It was the summer I turned five. I was young, but I still carry a vivid picture of that summer Bible school because it had such a huge impact on me. I remember the feel of the cold metal chair against my swinging legs that couldn't reach the floor. I remember wearing my favorite yellow-and-white gingham sundress. I also remember being completely fascinated by what our teacher had to say. He talked about a loving God who was close to us and very much a part of our daily lives. And that day, I felt a very real, very powerful need for a savior. I didn't know the phrase at the time, but looking back, I knew the feeling.

In addition to Vacation Bible School, my mom sent us to catechism classes and made sure we received the appropriate sacraments. I can still picture my first Holy Communion. Leading up to the big day, they taught us about the Eucharist and reminded us how sacred it was, and how we couldn't dare touch it. This was a big, big deal, but I was the kind of kid who, when you told me I couldn't do something, that just made me want to do it all the more. It wasn't mischievousness as much as curiosity. One day I was wandering around the church when I stumbled upon the small side room where they kept everything for the communion ceremony. Right there in front of me was a golden plate piled high with communion wafers that practically glowed like a halo was around them. Right there with an easy reach, I thought about grabbing one. *No one will ever know.* But then I thought, *God will know, right?* It was one of those *just maybe* dilemmas that was enough to hold me back, because somewhere deep down, I did believe in God, even then, though I didn't understand Him just yet.

As long as I'm on religion, there's one Christmas story I'd like to share, for the way it shows some of our family traditions. In our household, the routine each year was to wait for Christmas Eve to pick out our tree. The tradition started because when my parents were first married they didn't have a lot of money and on Christmas Eve the trees were free at this one particular corner lot in Philadelphia, so they would wait out the holiday season until the last possible minute. To stretch their Christmas dollars even further, my mother would sometimes make homemade ornaments.

My parents kept up the practice even after they'd moved us to New Jersey because the last-minute deal was that the trees were half price. They didn't let on that the reason for this tradition was financial, rather, they set it up like an event leading to the big day. We looked forward to it every year. On Christmas Eve, we'd set up and decorate our new tree, and then we'd all pile into the station wagon for the drive to my grandparents' house, where we'd enjoy a hearty seven-fish feast in the Italian tradition.

In case you're wondering, the seven fishes are: smelts (tiny fish fried whole, sans head), bakala (overly salted cod), shrimp (fried, steamed, and spicy), octopus, scallops, calamari, and *cioppino* (clams, mussels, cod, calamari, scallops, and more shrimp, cooked in a tomato and garlic broth).

We still maintain this tradition, by the way. The day before Christmas Eve my mother buys the fish from the Italian Market, then spends that whole day (her birthday!) cleaning it. She then cooks up a storm on Christmas Eve, and after dinner we pose for our annual family photo. If any of us even suggest we'll miss the seven fish feast, we risk breaking my mother's heart. Even now, my little niece talks about which one of them will get to be the one hosting the tradition when they are the grown-ups.

When I was little, each year we'd take turns going with my dad to pick out a tree. Only one of us would get to go with him. We always got a potted tree, which we'd plant in the yard after the holidays, because we never had the heart to throw away a living thing that had played such a big part in the life of our family. The tree usually died by summer, but one tree in my parents' yard managed to survive and thrive over the years and now stands taller than the house. We're unclear on which one of us actually picked that one out, but we all point to it with great pride.

I was about six when it was my turn to go pick the tree with my father. He had to work that afternoon, so we got to the lot a little late. It was already getting dark and the air was crisp and cold. I could smell the pine needles and as I stepped out of the car, I could hear them crunch under my feet. The next sound I heard was a big machine being fired up to turn the remaining trees into mulch. Although there were still a few full trees that had gone unclaimed, I was drawn to a lonely looking tree off by itself in the corner; its needles had already started to brown and fall off. It was a real *Charlie Brown Christmas* moment, and I told my father that the other, healthier trees still had a last-ditch chance of finding a family to take them in, and that we owed it to this one tree to give it a home.

"Good choice," he said.

And it was—or so I thought, until we brought it home.

As they were every year, the entire family was back at the house waiting for us. Everyone came rushing to the front door to admire our new tree, except this year the welcome wasn't nearly as warm or enthusiastic as in years past. My sisters just didn't like "my" tree, and I didn't like that they didn't like it. Here I'd been so excited, bringing this sad little tree home to my family and my family didn't seem to want any part of it.

I was devastated.

We kids bickered over whether or not we had to keep this tree. On the one hand, nobody wanted to disappoint me, since it was my turn to choose that year and I'd clearly had my heart set on this one. On the other hand, everybody wanted a "real" Christmas tree. After a whole lot of discussion, we decided to go back to the lot to see if we could find a suitable replacement.

As we left, my dad asked my brother Dan to take my original tree to the curb to make room for the new one we'd be bringing home. It was the first time I could remember that an O'Donnell Christmas tree was sent to the curb for the garbage man instead of being sent off to die a natural death after being planted in the yard.

On this second trip to the lot, I picked the biggest, fullest tree I could find. And it was huge! In fact, we ended up having to chop off the top so it could fit in the living room, but before we even got the thing inside I had to get past another disappointment. The original tree was not at the curb when we'd returned home, and I could only imagine that it had already been collected by the garbage man and sent through his dreaded crusher.

I couldn't help but cry. (Hey, I was six! This was traumatic stuff!)

When we walked through the door with the new tree, everyone sighed with relief and hastily began setting it up. But I wasn't excited. My brother Dan pulled me into his room. I went halfheartedly, thinking he was about to give me one of his big brother pep talks to try to cheer me up. But he had something else in mind. He had a surprise for me, he said, and when he opened the door to his room I nearly dropped to the floor. He'd taken my sad little tree into his room and decorated it. While everyone else was out in the living room decorating our new tree, my brother and I were putting the finishing touches on this tree because this is where Santa would leave *my* presents.

To this day, it's one of my favorite Christmas memories.

•   •   •

The Moorestown house may have been a little out of reach for my parents, but it wasn't exactly a mansion—it was cozy and we loved it. We were packed in there pretty tight. My sisters and I all shared a bedroom, which was a great adventure. For many years, there were five of us in that one room, so you can just imagine the scene. There were two sets of bunk beds, which meant my little sister Eileen had to move around each night. We all loved it when she crawled in with one of us, because she was so cuddly.

For years and years, this was the sleeping arrangement. We'd stay up half the night, all five of us, whispering about boys or school or sometimes my father's drinking.

My sisters and I were extremely close. We'd share each other's clothes (usually without permission!) and help each other with homework. And of course, we'd tease each other, like all sisters do.

We actually had a blast. Whenever the *Wizard of Oz* or *Willy Wonka and the Chocolate Factory* came on TV, we'd stage the room like a movie theater and sell tickets to our parents. This was before VCRs or DVDs, so it was a can't-miss event!

As the oldest sister, Jennie was often asked to babysit. She had a whole philosophy about how to take care of us. She didn't want us to be tempted to misbehave, so she encouraged us to "get it out of our system" under her supervision. One time she told us we could each say *one* curse word. That was our allotment. Liz, who was also older than me, took some time before saying anything. She wanted to use her one curse word wisely, and after a while she came out with it. We laughed and laughed, because none of us were in the habit of speaking like this. We all knew these words, but we would never use them, not even in the privacy of our own bedroom.

(Not yet, at least!)

When it was my turn I couldn't bring myself to say anything. I was no goody two-shoes, believe me, but nothing would come out of my mouth. I guess I just needed a little more coaxing, but Eileen was little and eager. She saw my moment of hesitation and jumped right in.

"I'll take Chrissy's curse!" she hollered. "I'll take it!"

And then, before I could even object, the word came bursting out of her mouth: "Shit!"

For a moment, we all sat there in stunned silence, which was very quickly followed by fits of contagious laughter.

Jennie looked after us outside the house, too—and on one occasion she even saved my life. Every summer, we'd take day trips with the Rooney family to picnic and swim at the Bridgeport Rod & Gun Club lake. Once we got there, we'd all split up, older kids one way, younger kids another, and do our thing.

One time, when I was turning five years old, a group of older kids I'd never met wanted me to swim with them. I told them I wasn't allowed to go out past the rope, that I'd been told not to let the water get above the yellow stripe on my bathing suit. But these kids told me it was okay, that they got special permission—and, since I was five, I believed them.

I wasn't an especially strong swimmer, but I was pretty good for a little kid. But once we got out into deep water, they started pushing me under and holding me down. At first I thought they were just playing, but then I heard one of them say, "Hold her down, let's see if she stops breathing." Like it was a game. I kicked and splashed and tried to resist, but these kids were all bigger and stronger, and they kept pushing me down and the murky brown water seemed to swallow me under.

Around this time, Jennie noticed a commotion out in the deep part of the lake. She turned to one of the boys she was with on the shore, pointed to where I was struggling, and asked if he knew what was going on. The boy told her some of his friends had wanted to see what it was like to drown someone. Like this was no big deal.

Jennie turned to this kid and shouted, "You idiot!"

Then she swam out to the rescue. She didn't even know that it was me on the receiving end of all this stupidity. But when she got out to the middle of the lake and saw it was her little sister, she was enraged. She didn't think I was breathing, and for a long, sick moment she thought I was dead. Meanwhile, the idiot kids were *laughing*. She pushed her way past them and grabbed me in her arms and brought me in.

I was terrified, but mostly okay. Jennie, on the other hand, had to be restrained from going after those jerks. To this day, none of us O'Donnells or Rooneys remember what happened to them; quite possibly they just swam away and pretended to be innocent. But I'll never forget what happened to Jennie; she was rewarded for her heroism. For saving my life, my parents bought her the latest Partridge Family album. This was a huge deal.

We all caught the acting bug from my father. As kids, we spent a lot of time putting on skits and puppet shows and reviews. At family gatherings, we'd put on performances. My brother Danny would write plays, Jennie directed, and the little ones were the performers. There were Easter plays, Thanksgiving and Christmas plays, Fourth of July parades, and backyard talent shows. We'd organize all the neighborhood kids into a kind of competition. We'd break up into teams, and then perform our little routines for the grown-ups, and they'd have to vote with their applause to see who had the best skit. Other kids played competitive sports; we played competitive skits.

My mom got in on the act, too. She helped out by painting sets, or making popcorn, which we then stuffed into bags and sold to the other kids for a nickel apiece.

(By the way, today, you couldn't do this without a permit. Really. In Oregon, California, and way too many states, child-run lemonade stands have been shut down like criminal operations. Lemonade stands! A harmless, homespun activity that's just about as American as apple pie, and introduces kids to the virtues of entrepreneurship. The reason for the lockdown—the kids don't have a food or beverage license!)

Hand in hand with his thoughts on the theater, my father believed it was important for us to speak properly, to enunciate clearly, and to express ourselves fully. Jennie didn't want to speak with a New Jersey accent, so my dad had her try to speak with perfect diction while having a mouthful of marbles. It was an old television trick, he said. He'd have her read a sentence and keep correcting her until she got it right, and then she'd practice it over and over. She never asked for a glass of "*woodah*" or a cup of "*coofee*."

Family dinners were a great outlet for us to express ourselves. As busy as my father was with all his different jobs, he always tried to make it home for dinner. The rest of us had to do the same, no matter what, and our dinners could be boisterous, affectionate, and wonderful. Sometimes, we couldn't eat, because we'd all be laughing so hard; other times, we couldn't eat because there was so much yelling.

Usually, my father had us go around the table and share something we did or learned that day. My dad sat at the head, my mom at the other end. He'd say, "Sit up straight, elbows off the table, and don't say *um*." When it was my turn, he'd look at me and say, "Christine, tell us what you learned today." There always had to be some takeaway, some lesson we could share with our siblings. I remember looking forward to these dinners, and thinking about what I might share when my turn came around that night. Something would happen at school, or on the playground, and I'd catch myself thinking, *This is something I can tell everybody tonight at dinner.*

Sometimes, we'd even talk politics, which was often a bit of an adventure. We were all over the political spectrum in our house. My father has been a lifelong Republican; my mother, a Democrat. These days, we kids are split down the middle, and heated political discussions at Sunday dinner are often interrupted with "Pass the meatballs." This is where I learned that you can disagree on issues and still respect and admire those on the other side.

Anyway, as early as 1976, when I was only seven, I took an interest in the upcoming Presidential election. I came home from school one day and told everyone I'd written about the election in class.

The assignment was for a time capsule project. We each had to write an essay for the class journal, which we buried in a time capsule. My entry was about Gerald Ford. The journal was recently on display at our twentieth high school reunion, and I had a chance to read what I wrote. It was something like: "Jimmy Carter is not my president. Gerald Ford is. I love him. I want to marry him."

(Remember, I was only seven!)

I don't know what it was about Ford, but he was my candidate. Perhaps I'd seen a photo of him with his family and he seemed like a very nice man, so he had my vote. Trouble was, my vote wouldn't have gotten him very far. Even at seven I could see that, so as the election approached I hounded my mother to be my proxy and vote for Ford. This was no easy task. As an independent-thinking, Democratic-leaning woman in 1976, she was voting for Carter. Still, I kept after her. When she went out on Election Day to cast her vote, I waited patiently by the front door for her to return. As soon as she did, I raced over to her. I shouted, "Did you do it, Mom? Did you vote for President Ford?"

"No, Chrissy, I didn't," she said. "I'm so sorry. I voted for Jimmy Carter."

My heart sank. The very next day, hearing everybody in school talking about Jimmy Carter's victory, it felt to me like it was partly my fault. For the first time in my political life, I came away from an election night disappointed, thinking I hadn't campaigned hard enough.

My father always put the needs of others before his own and his generosity knew no limits. One day, a man we called Jeep needed some help. Jeep, an old man with special needs, had been a fixture in our neighborhood. He used to ride his bike up and down the streets all day long, his basket filled with groceries, newspapers, or whatever he'd retrieved on one of his errands. After we hadn't seen him for a couple days, my father went to check on him. It turned out Jeep's old bike had been damaged beyond repair, so the poor guy couldn't get around. His bike was his life and now it was gone. My dad was saddened by Jeep's misfortune and looked straightaway for some way to make things better for him. Well, it just so happened that I'd just gotten a new brown 3-speed for my birthday, so my father went straight to our garage and gave the bike to Jeep.

My father did this under the assumption that I'd be just as happy as he was to help out Jeep—but I wasn't, at least not at first. I went to the garage one day, hoping to ride around the neighborhood, and my brand-new bicycle was gone. When my father saw how upset I was, he realized he'd been impulsive and should have asked me first. He wanted to help a lonely old man in need. Even though we didn't have a whole lot, he hoped we would learn to share whatever it was we *did* have. And in this way it was an invaluable lesson. Of course, my father doesn't advocate going around and giving away other people's things without asking first. He didn't feel great about that part of it, but he'd gotten so caught up in the idea of doing what he could for this man that he didn't really stop to think how his kindness might have felt to me, but after I heard his explanation I wasn't so upset. In fact, I'd see Jeep riding his new bike up and down the street and take a special pride in knowing we'd brought a little bit of joy into his life.

My mother also had a strong selfless streak she hoped to pass on to us kids, and it was never more apparent than in the long hours she'd put into her work with the Parent Teacher Association (PTA). One thing you need to know about my mother: She's extremely responsible, fiercely loyal, and truly devoted to all her loved ones. She was always involved in the community, and I guess that's partly where I picked it up. She was president of the PTA, ran for town council, held down a job, managed our household, raised six kids, and found time to stay connected to her friends and family . . . so she was a walking inspiration to a young girl growing up with her own dreams of having and doing it all.

One year, our school desperately needed new playground equipment, but there was just no money in the budget. That was hardly an obstacle for someone like my mom, who was endlessly resourceful. She ended up leading the playground improvement project through the PTA, in an out-of-the-box sort of way. She rounded up volunteers and solicited donations of old tires from local tire stores, in order to build a uniquely creative kid-safe playground, at no cost. It was an incredible example of what you can do when you put your mind to a task, even against impossible odds. And the most remarkable piece was that she spearheaded this entire project in just one weekend.

There's a lesson about government bureaucracy here, too. The town had both the PTA and the Home and School Association, and both groups needed new playgrounds for different schools, so at first they tried to make it a joint effort. But our HSA was so bureaucratic that nothing was getting done. They had committee meetings to form committees. Budget committees, equipment committees, volunteer committees . . . it seemed like one giant wheel-spin. My mom finally threw up her hands and set out to do it on her own—and, as a result, "our" playground renovation was completed in one weekend, while the HSA was still holding committee meetings and hadn't even broken ground.

My mom's extra effort was held out as such a shining example of community activism, it even made the papers.

To show their appreciation, at their next meeting the PTA presented my mother with an unusual trophy—a round bundt cake with black icing, made to look like a tire. It had been shellacked so that it'd hang on the wall like a plaque. (Shellacked baked goods were a decorative fad at the time . . . for reasons I still can't quite figure out.)

My mom came home from her meeting that night and showed us all the trophy cake. She was so proud—and, of course, we were so proud of *her*. When we all went to bed, she left the cake trophy on the table, but the cake met a quick and regrettable end. That night, my father came home from work particularly late—and, particularly tired and hungry. He was so worn out from his long day, and so plainly famished, he took one look at the tempting cake on our table and dug right in. He didn't even notice it was coated with chemicals—in fact, the next morning, as his Irish eyes smiled, he told us that it tasted pretty good.

Of all our childhood stories, this one—*ahem!*—takes the cake!

"I think I've just made a terrible mistake. . . ."

Fred Davis was right; I hated his concept for our first campaign commercial. In fact, I hated it so much I immediately set it aside. A part of me thought he must have been joking on some level. I mean, it was such a ludicrous, preposterous approach. I flashed Jennie a look that meant, Is this guy serious?

Well, he surely was.

And here's the thing: Once he put it out there, the idea became like a runaway train. I'd come up with a couple concepts and ideas of my own that I wanted to discuss, and Jennie had input as well, but Fred could only half listen to us, that's how intent he was on following through on his own concept. I'd also brought along dozens of heartbreaking letters and testimonials from supporters, which I thought we might be able to weave into the narrative of our campaign, like the one from an older couple that had sunk all of their retirement savings into AIG, only to watch those monies disappear while AIG executives enjoyed their bailouts and bonuses and Benzes. I told Fred about a woman I'd met at a rally who approached me with tears in her eyes and a five-dollar bill in her hand, telling me with a sweet mixture of pride and embarrassment that it was all she could afford to contribute to my campaign but that she and her husband wanted to give something because they believed in what I was doing. I explained that I wanted my commercials to reflect the fact that families were hurting all across Delaware—indeed, all across this great country—and that a good deal of that hurt had to do with the selfish policies coming out of Washington, D.C., I wanted to put out the all-important message that we needed to elect a new generation of citizen politicians who would serve their constituents as a kind of sacred responsibility.

At the end of our meeting, Fred took the pile of campaign letters I wanted him to read and promised he would revisit his concept, and I went to bed that night thinking we had set things right. I've always tried to be a positive person, to put a hopeful spin on a situation even when it appears to be spinning out of control, and that was my mind-set here. It would all work out in the end, I told myself. It had to.

The next morning on our way to the Philadelphia studio, I could see the famous statue of William Penn, the state's founder, which stands proudly atop the Philadelphia City Hall. Until the mid-80s, no other building could be taller than William Penn's hat. Now, the city's skyline is a jagged horizontal of skyscrapers that reach into the clouds, and smaller structures that stand below William Penn. On this particular morning all the taller buildings were swallowed by a low-hanging fog, so what I saw was the skyline I remembered from my childhood, and I took it all in, thinking this was where my own story began. Somehow only the figure of

William Penn shone through the thick fog. It was a remarkable, stirring thing, seeing only a symbol of preservation and sacrifice, and from there I went about my morning, filled once again with great hope and good cheer.

It would all work out, I told myself again—this time, almost willing it to be so.

First I had to get through hair and makeup. They told me my face was too round and suggested I try a poker-straight hairstyle to make it appear thinner. Maybe they knew what they were doing in this one regard at least, because when Saturday Night Live *lampooned the ad the following week they cast Kristen Wiig to play me. If you've seen the show, you'll know that Kristen's a skinny girl with a thin face, so it's possible to conclude that my odd new cut did the trick. That, or maybe Kristen was the only* SNL *performer able to deliver the ridiculous lines with a straight face.*

I didn't recognize myself when I left the makeup chair to hunt Fred down to talk about the script, but by that point it didn't much matter. The runaway train had already left the station. This became clear the moment I was led onto the set and positioned on a stool, beneath the hot studio lights. There, glaring at me from the teleprompter, was Fred's script, in big, bold letters. And right there at the top was the same opening line: "I'm not a witch."

I winced. No, strike that. I believe what I actually did at just that moment was cringe. What I wanted to do was scream.

I thought once again of Ronald Reagan at the Berlin Wall, and his famous back-and-forth with his staff over those six simple words. And then I set that image alongside the ab-

surd back-and-forth that was playing out here in this Philadelphia studio. Four simple words, and try as I might I just couldn't get rid of them.

It's like I'd stepped on gum and now it was stuck on my shoe.

I still hadn't had a chance to talk to Fred, and by now I was fairly tethered to my stool, held down by my microphone wires, so I called off-set to him. I said, "Fred, I can't say these words. This isn't the message I want to put out there. I thought we've been over this."

He said, "You're right, Christine. We have. I want you to be comfortable. But let's just run through it a time or two the way it's written and see what we've got. If you don't like it, we won't use it."

He gave me his word—in front of a studio filled with people. His people, my people . . . many, many people.

Sure enough, after I said those words, I didn't like it, and I said as much. In fact, I said a little bit more besides. I told him I hated it. I told him it didn't get close to capturing what was going on in the campaign. It didn't reflect the magnanimous sacrifices being made by our supporters and team. It was missing the heart of what was going on. And, worst of all, it was beating the heck out of a really dead horse. We'd already put this issue to bed, I told him. There was no reason to bring it back up again ourselves and throw my candidacy back into the fire. It was time to move on and address the very real issues of the campaign.

Finally, he agreed. We made a last-minute call to our supporters. Bob Thornton, a businessman; Mike Brown, a Wilmington elected official; Melissa, a single mother; and *many others dropped everything, raced to the studio, and cut brand new campaign commercials. The content of these ads was drawn from the simple unscripted words of my supporters. It was powerful and humbling to hear how they spoke from their hearts.*

By the end of our session, we'd cut several new ads that I really loved, yet I still left the studio with an uneasy feeling, wishing like crazy I hadn't filmed that ridiculous "I'm not a witch!" ad. I couldn't shake it, that ad. The others we'd managed to put together were actually quite strong and persuasive, so I tried to get my head around the bump we'd enjoy in the polls once those ads started to air, but I couldn't stop thinking about that stupid witch spot. It's like it was following me around the whole rest of the day.

It was raining when we left the studio, and as I climbed into our campaign truck for the drive down the I-95 corridor back to our Wilmington headquarters, I found myself really looking forward to the next stop on my schedule: a meeting with several Delaware pastors. But even the support and calm I felt with these good people couldn't shake me from my doubts and worries, and as we concluded with a prayer I shared my feelings with the group.

"Guys," I said, "please pray for the campaign and for our commercials. I think I've just made a terrible mistake. . . ."

CHAPTER THREE

Moving On

For the most part, I had a pretty terrific childhood. All was (mostly) right in our little corner of the world. But as I hinted at earlier, there were some hard times and most of them stemmed in one way or another from my father's alcoholism.

I've struggled long and hard about whether or not to share what my family went through. In the end, I've decided to touch on these things and to shine what I hope will be a positive light on my father's struggles and triumphs. I do so knowing that somewhere out there a family is about to break up or a child is going through a similar anguish. Perhaps they feel like life is so messed up it's beyond repair. I keep coming back to the thought that by sharing my story, in some small way, they might be helped and my family's journey might offer real hope.

There is no sin so great that cannot be forgiven when there is true repentance—and, true repentance includes a commitment to setting things right, even when it hurts, even when there is an easier way out.

Elsewhere in these pages, I write about bravery in the

political arena, but I hope to call attention to the bravery and self-sacrifice that resides within the family—for that surely resided in our house, in my father most of all.

Growing up in an alcoholic home, you see a lot of hard things, and you learn hard lessons. I came to realize at a too-young age that life with my father was a mixed blessing. It was great and horrible, fun and scary, light and dark. There was a specific moment when I realized this, and I remember it vividly, and in that moment I saw him for what he was . . . a broken man who loved his family dearly and tried his darnedest to make things right. Looking back, I recognize this as a sort of rite of passage, when you leave your childhood behind and discover that your parents are human, full of great pride and great regret all at the same time.

It's a powerful realization.

As a result of an iron will and fierce determination to change, my father's much better now, thank God. He is the man he was always meant to be all along.

The "rite of passage moment" found me in a family counseling session. It is a freeing thing to be able to admit that you need help. In some cases, that assistance can come from a nurturing support network of friends and family, while in others it comes from trained professionals—but I don't believe it matters *where* you find help, only that you do.

When I was a teenager, my sister Jennie graduated college and moved out to California to make her own way in the world. There, she began to put my father's alcoholism into perspective—she finally had some distance from it—and, sadly, she began to recognize some of the same addictive behaviors in herself. One of the things I love about my sister is that she's not the sort of person to sit idly by while the world unravels around her, so here she took a proactive approach. She got some help for herself, and once she was deep into her own counseling sessions she asked if we would do some family sessions with her. It wasn't just about my dad. We realized that we had all been affected by this disease, and it either tears you apart or you can take the opportunity to grow stronger from it. And that's what my family chose to do.

Jennie came back and set it all up. It was tough coordinating everybody's schedules but it was important to us, so we made it work. It was even tougher getting all of us through a session, which turned out to be gut-wrenching, yet we managed this, too.

The idea was that we would take turns telling my father how we felt about his behavior. We were meant to be very specific, and I remember being unsure what to say, the first few times around. I mean, I didn't know what it was to have a *normal* father, so I didn't know what was expected of *my* father. I had nothing to compare him to, and didn't know how to put my anger or frustration into words.

Whenever one of us told him how we felt, whatever we pointed out to him, he listened. He was never defensive, never in denial; he always copped to it, whatever it was, even if he didn't remember. He'd say, "I'm sorry. If you say this is what I did, then I'm sure this is what I did." And he always apologized. Finally he said, "I never had anyone teach me how to be a father. I was trying to figure it out."

He was so honest with us, so open, so eager to repair any

damage he'd caused. I was struck during these sessions at his humble vulnerability.

Through these sessions, I developed a lot of respect for my father, along with a deeper love . . . I'd always loved my father, of course. But now I came to admire him as well, because I started to see his struggle for what it was—a struggle. He was so brave. My mother, too. To have to listen to all of us spill our guts, about how Dad's drinking made us feel, about how his illness made us feel . . . it must have been a nightmare. It was hard for them, no question. It was hard for us, too.

But it was necessary. It helped me to see our dad as a noble, courageous man, able to admit his own shortcomings in order to become a better father, a better man.

It wasn't easy, and at times it was rough. I think all families have their challenges to overcome. This was ours and we love each other more for having gone through it all together. I think we appreciate each other more, because we aren't just people who were born into the same family, we are a family who also chose to stick with each other, chose to work through difficult things, and came out better for it. As a result, I think my siblings, my parents, and I, in any situation, can sort of see through the bad to the good and cherish and focus on the good . . . and that's what we do. I think the important takeaway from all of this for me is that families can not only survive; but if they choose to, they can heal, and thrive, and find real joy . . . and there is a greater joy as a result of knowing the bad and appreciating the good that is left.

•   •   •

Toward the end of high school, I started taking acting classes at the Walnut Street Theater in Philadelphia, and when I was sixteen I apprenticed at the Surflight Summer Theatre in Beach Haven, New Jersey. This was a significant change of scenery for me, and I loved it. It was also the first time I moved about "on my own," in an independent way, and I relished the chance to grow outside of friends and family. I was starting to think that theater was the path I should follow.

When I got back to school that fall, I made a conscious effort to get a job. I needed the money, because a lot of my friends were starting to go out, and some of our older friends were driving. I wanted to be able to join them on occasion and at the same time bring home a little something to balance our family budget. I worked at The Gap as a sales associate and cashier. And I logged long, minimum-wage hours, learning the proper way to fold sweaters around a clipboard. After just a few weeks, I could have folded those sweaters with a blindfold—and they would have been perfect! Soon, I took a second job in the domestics department at John Wanamaker's department store, where I learned the proper way to fold towels.

Outside the house, away from my family, I was an adventurous spirit—bold, curious, outgoing. My ideas and ideals were not quite fully formed, so I was willing to try on a bunch of ways of looking at the world, and I suppose this is as good a spot as any to revisit the story that would come back to haunt me during the 2010 campaign—my now infamous high school blind date with a guy who believed in the occult.

We were an unlikely pair, but we got along well enough.

He asked about my faith, and I asked about his. We were just a couple of average teenagers: confused, finding our way in the world, searching for meaning.

The old adage about girls being attracted to dark, mysterious types held true for me here, so I ended up seeing this guy. As a teenager searching for my own beliefs, I made an effort to learn a little bit more about his. In the end, I never got to that place in my thinking where I could sign on to his views, but for a short time I had been intrigued enough to keep the conversation going.

Just to give you an idea of the funny picture we made, one of my sisters came home one night from a date of her own and noticed me with my one-time blind date sitting under a tree in the front yard. My sister's date was a much more conventional sort, all blond, blue-eyed, and buttoned-down. Mine was dressed in all black, and hardly conventional, as he sat with his legs crossed and his back straight. He looked more than a little out of place, in a Goth sort of way, especially since he was sitting across from me, dressed far more conservatively in my turtleneck and faux pearls.

My sister's date pointed to us as they walked to the porch and said, "What's up with *that*?"

"Oh," she replied. "That's just my little sister. She's going through a phase."

I graduated from Moorestown High School in 1987. For the next two years, I attended Burlington County College to save on tuition. The idea here was to get all of my core curriculum courses out of the way at a less expensive community school and then transfer to a four-year college.

I lived at home while I attended classes at BCC and worked as a waitress at a local Red Lobster, as well as a few other restaurants. The money was pretty good and the hours were flexible. I even got to learn a few new recipes every now and then.

After two years, I transferred to Fairleigh Dickinson University because they had a good financial aid package, so I moved away from home and into one of their dorms in Madison, New Jersey.

Madison is a picture-perfect college town in the northern part of the state. It turned out I only had enough credits to enroll as a second-semester sophomore, so that's what I did. I was a psychology major, to start, with a plan to also take a bunch of theater courses and to participate in campus productions. I landed a great job as a waitress at a local country club. It was a high-end place that held weddings and anniversaries, bar and bat mitzvah celebrations, and big-ticket fundraisers. I signed on with a couple friends as part-time servers, and we earned a hundred dollars per party, plus tip. That was great money at the time. (It still is!) The real perk, though, was the food. We were friends with the kitchen crew, and at the end of each night they'd send us home with nearly a week's worth of whatever the entrees had been, along with assorted appetizers and sides. We'd be feasting on filet mignon or lobster, and looking ahead to our next gig.

By this point, I was starting to think seriously about a major. The theater was still my passion, but it wouldn't be in my future. My coursework began to reflect this shift. One semester, I looked up and realized that all of the elective courses I'd been taking were in English and communications, and I realized that without really planning on it I was fulfilling the requirements for a major in English and a minor concentration in communications, so I figured if my interests were suddenly announcing themselves in this way, I'd do well to listen to them. I declared this as my major.

I was performing in campus productions and keeping up a busy social life. My primary extracurricular activity, though, was earning as much money as I could. Throughout my entire time in school, this was my front-and-center worry, even more so than what I was actually *learning* in school. Each semester, I'd meet with my financial aid advisor to see how much I needed to earn to re-up for the next semester. At least once or twice, I had to borrow my mother's credit card in order to register for classes, because they required you to pay a certain amount up front before the start of each term.

It was during this time that I had a life-changing conversation with my childhood friend Eileen Rooney. We'd remained close all through college, and one day we found ourselves talking about abortion. I'd always thought of myself as a liberal person—leaning to the left on the issues of the day—and I found myself in the middle of an intense back-and-forth with Eileen. I no longer recall what prompted the conversation, but here it was, on the table.

"Do you even know how an abortion is performed?" Eileen finally asked in frustration.

I had strong emotional soundbites and because I was with a friend during her initial phone conversation with an abortion provider, I felt like I had a deeper understanding. I even thought I had pressed the clinician for the truth.

"Isn't it already a baby?" I had asked.

"No, no, no," she reassured us. "It's too early for that. The baby hasn't formed yet."

My friend was already showing, and yet I took the woman at her word, which only goes to show that you can be made to believe whatever it is you want to believe in the first place.

And now here I was, going around and around on the issue with Eileen. I told her what the woman at the clinic had said. In truth, I didn't know the specifics.

"You can't listen to what either side says on this issue," Eileen said. "You have to read and see for yourself."

She wasn't proselytizing, she was just being pragmatic; she wanted me to know what she knew; she wanted me to know the truth.

I found some time between classes and went to the library. I pulled a pile of medical books from the stacks and sat down on the floor and started reading. It was appalling to me, the way they described the procedure. I sat there feeling stunned and a little betrayed by my own beliefs. The description alone was quite clear: it talked about "realigning the body parts" and "making sure that all foreign matter is removed." They used very specific language, to describe a very specific procedure.

It shattered my entire worldview, to the point where I came away thinking, *If I've been wrong about abortion, what else am I wrong about?*

I couldn't reconcile what I was reading with my own pro-choice position that was also held by so many women I respected—like Hillary Clinton, for one. She was very much in the news at the time, campaigning on behalf of her husband,

and I found a lot to admire about her, but now I saw that her deeply held position on this issue was profoundly different than my own emerging view.

And here's a strange thing: The closer I came to embracing a pro-life mind-set privately, the more adamant I was on the other side in my discussion with Eileen. It's like I was refusing to give up my views without a fight. I was in serious conflict. Eileen's ideas were in my head and taking root. Slowly over time, however, once the ideas and truths settled into my heart, mind, and soul, my perception shifted entirely.

The shift seemed to jump-start the activist in me, because I ended up sounding the campus drumbeat for the pro-life movement. Unfortunately, it wasn't much of a drumbeat. Frankly, in the beginning, it was just me. As a matter of fact, I was met with a lot of resistance. I thought all I had to do was show people what I read and they'd change just like that. I was wrong. I finally found a pro-life group on another campus, went to a couple of their meetings, and offered to start up a chapter at Fairleigh Dickinson. And this became my thing.

Within a couple months of my "epiphany" following that push from Eileen, I was setting up vendor tables in our student union, handing out flyers, and organizing meetings and rallies. I wrote to several national organizations seeking literature and additional supporting materials like posters and bumper stickers, promising to distribute whatever they sent along. Almost immediately, I started receiving material. They'd send a couple dozen fliers, or a fistful of stickers or buttons, with a note telling me I could buy more if I ran out.

I thought, *Buy more?* I didn't have any money to buy more.

One afternoon, I drove back to my parents' house from

Madison and found six big boxes waiting for me on the porch from an organization called Human Life International. They'd sent a whole box of life-like plastic models of an eight-week-old fetus. The tiny eyes, fingers, and ears were very much developed. They'd also sent about a hundred copies of a very insightful, very informative book called *Pro-Life Answers to Pro-Choice Arguments*, in short, every visual aid I could imagine to help me make the argument for life to my peers at school. There was also a handwritten note from the priest who ran this outfit, thanking me for taking such an interest.

"God bless your efforts," he wrote.

It was like I'd won the lottery. All of this amazing material couldn't even fit in my beat-up hatchback. I'd somehow managed to recruit some friends from other campuses to help me man the vendor table, and it was during one of my stints at the student union that I struck up a conversation with the guy in charge of our campus chapter of the College Republicans. I still didn't think of myself as a Republican at this point, but I listened intently to what this guy had to say—partly, I'll confess, because he was cute!

Our College Republican chapter was putting together a group of students to hand out campaign literature on Election Day. The kicker was we'd get a full day of excused absences—and seventy-five dollars, to boot. I liked the way these College Republicans rolled, so I signed up. Right away, I was glad that I did, because that Election Day was a revelation. I loved talking to people about these important issues. I didn't pretend to have all the answers. Heck, I hardly had *any* answers, but I asked a lot of questions. I was young and completely open about my lack of experience in this arena. People seemed to respond to that about me, enough so that a couple months later, when the Bush-Quayle team was headed to New Hampshire for the 1992 primaries, the College Republicans asked me to come along. They'd seen me doing my thing on Election Day, and told me I came across as active and personable, like someone who might be able to connect with student voters. "We could use someone like you in New Hampshire," I was told.

There was no seventy-five dollar per diem, like there'd been for my Election Day canvassing, but I could get a ride to New Hampshire with other volunteers from my area, and there'd be a place for me to stay, so I'd only be out the money for meals and snacks. They sent me to work a rally with Vice President Quayle, which was terribly exhilarating. The people just went crazy for him, and I felt this thrilling rush of adrenaline to be in the same room as the Vice President of the United States.

I must have made more of an impression on these young Republicans than I thought, because the leader of the Bush-Quayle youth campaign recruited me to be a youth delegate at the 1992 Republican National Convention in Houston. Here again, I had no idea why they were looking to me for this, or what it might mean, but it was another adventure, so I jumped on it.

It was in Houston, I should mention, that I finally signed on the dotted line and became a card-carrying Republican.

And it was also in Houston when this new passion—politics!—was suddenly implanted into my heart, and I knew it was the one I wanted to pursue.

When the convention finally rolled around that summer, I spent most of my time with other student delegates from around the country. We all stayed in the same hotel, as many as fifteen of us to a room some nights, so most of us left together for the convention floor each morning. We all had our floor passes, and moved around that place like we belonged. And, suddenly, we did. I'd never been to a national political convention before, so I had nothing to compare it to, but everybody said there'd never been a youth presence at one of these things like the one they'd assembled that year in Houston. They did it right—and, on the back of that effort, they galvanized a whole new generation.

Including me.

A lot of what I did during that week was gather my peers from the youth delegate ranks to offer notes and comments to the media. Specifically, there was this one reporter from CNN who kept seeking me out after every speech, wanting to get my young-person take on whatever was being talked about onstage. And I recruited other young people for her to interview as well. In this way, I played something like the role of impromptu press secretary, lining up interviews for this reporter. Without the luxury of cell phones or text messaging, we had a designated meeting spot, at preappointed times. We were all moving about on the convention floor, or in and out of the local hotels, so it's not like this reporter could have tracked me down.

I actually got on television a time or two, only for a few soundbites, but it felt like a big deal to me. Before the convention wrapped, I was also interviewed by a reporter from one of the major news magazines, and a few local newspaper reporters from around the country. Here I'd been thrust into the middle of this momentous, tumultuous scene, and I'd somehow managed to make an impact. Yes, it was only the tiniest, flimsiest sliver of an impact, but *national journalists* were soliciting my opinion, other youth delegates were following my lead, and Republican Party organizers were pulling me aside and asking me what my plans were for the rest of the campaign.

It might not have been much, but it was something, and when I got back that fall I sought out my good group of friends and talked their ears off about the experience. I came back feeling so good about myself, like I stumbled onto something that felt so compellingly right. This was where I was meant to be, I'd decided. This would be my path—a career in politics was my future.

Of course, I had no idea what a career in politics might look like, or what it might mean, or where or how I might start, but the fire was lit.

"How could this happen . . . ?"

As we anxiously waited for the ad to go through postproduction, our team put together a whole media buying strategy. This was quite a contrast to the primary. Suddenly, we had money to spend on the campaign, but we were careful not to get ahead of ourselves. We had a commercial in the can we had not yet seen, and we were trying to figure the best way to get it in front of likely voters.

We'd already spent a bunch of money on the TV spot, but at this point no one from the campaign had seen even a rough cut of any ads, so I was beginning to feel a bit anxious about it. I had already been anxious when we left the studio that day, but now I was anxious upon anxious. I'd had a great deal of confidence in Fred going in—mostly because I'd been told by Senator Cornyn that he was the best in the business, and because I talked myself into believing he could help us close the gap in the polls—but I had come away thinking I never should have even read that stupid line. I'm no control freak, but here I'd ceded a bit too much of it, and now a part of me felt like I was waiting for some other shoe to drop.

And then, suddenly, one did.

One of our campaign staffers got word that a reporter from The New York Times *had seen a copy of the "I'm not a witch ad." It had been leaked and already gone viral. That's right—the* world *saw the ad before I did.*

Within one day, it became the most-watched video on the Internet . . . all before I'd seen any footage, let alone approved the final cut. In fact, I hadn't even wanted to use it. My plan was to go with the others we shot.

I couldn't think what this might mean for our campaign. It couldn't be good—I knew that much.

Immediately, Matt Moran tried to get Fred Davis on the phone. "How could this happen?" he asked. "I thought no one would see that commercial. We haven't even seen that commercial. How did The New York Times *get a copy?"*

Fred's team very patiently told Matt to calm down, but Matt was adamant. Fred said all the right things, and struck all the right notes, but none of this changed the fact that this ridiculous commercial had somehow been slipped to the media.

This was not our finest campaign hour, I must admit. And I had no one to blame but myself. I'd allowed this to happen, by trusting a group of people I hardly knew and going against my better judgment. By following a script I knew was all wrong. By going down a path I had no interest in taking. And now that the spot had been "leaked" to the media, the runaway train would only pick up steam. A bad situation would only get worse. Already, we were getting dozens of media calls back at headquarters, looking to get their own copy of the commercial, and fishing for a comment.

Before the ad had run on even a single station, it was making all kinds of noise—and it was the wrong kind of noise.

I huddled with my campaign team to consider our next move. Fred joined us on some of these sessions, and his thing was to capitalize on the publicity his ad was generating. It didn't seem to matter to him that it was mostly negative publicity. There's a saying in advertising that any publicity is good publicity. Frankly, I don't think it applies as well to politics, but Fred seemed to disagree.

Eventually, reluctantly, I told him we could go ahead with the spot, on a kind of trial *basis. Here was my false logic: Fred Davis was an expert at this sort of thing. He was one of the best media consultants in the business. He'd worked with people I admired—and people whose support I needed now more than ever. Among those people was Senator Cornyn, the NRSC chair.*

It was a wrong-headed move, made for all the wrong reasons, but it was mine.

CHAPTER FOUR

Finding My Way

Following that career-shaping summer of 1992, I returned to my parents' house in New Jersey. It felt to me like I'd been plucked from the moving sidewalk of my life and taken on a grand, formative adventure . . . launched into a whole new trajectory. A lot had changed for me.

However, I wasn't immediately able to return to school. After my first two years at Fairleigh Dickinson my financial aid award was cut, so I moved back home with my parents and took a nanny job. The following semester, to save on my room and board, I bunched all of my classes into a solid two-day schedule, to cut down on the commute.

It was a whirlwind-type schedule, and I enjoyed every minute of it. I found that with so many different responsibilities, and sometimes having to be in two places at once, I needed to learn to budget my time, and it forced me to develop some good habits. I had good friends up in Madison, good friends back home in Moorestown, and my days were filled with interesting people, interesting ideas, and interesting opportunities.

The plan was to finish up my last year of school on a part-time basis, now that Fairleigh Dickinson's full-time tuition was out of reach. I'd continue to bunch my few classes into a two-day schedule on the Madison campus, and look ahead toward graduation in May 1993. It would be a scramble for me to finish all my coursework by May, but it seemed like a realistic deadline. I'd been a student long enough.

It was time to get started on whatever might happen for me next.

To help pay the bills, I took a second full-time nanny job, which meant my time was no longer my own—at least, not *fully* my own. The hours were evenings and weekends. What little free time I had I filled with activist-type activities. Whenever there was a rally or a conference, I made every effort to attend. I'd gone up to New Hampshire with no strong feelings on politics, one way or the other, and then afterward to Houston. After hanging around with the good people in the Bush-Quayle camp, and sharing ideas, I came to realize that this was where I belonged. They knew my heart—a beat or two before I knew it for myself, if such a thing is possible. This last phrase might sound a bit corny, I know, but that was my takeaway from this experience. It was like I'd been out wandering in the weeds, living my politically uninvolved life and basically minding my own business, and now that I'd been let in from the cold I wanted to learn as much as I could, as quickly as I could. I think a lot of college students have a similar experience—when they first discover their "career calling." And even though my views were still taking shape, from here on out they would do so through a political lens.

• • •

I must confess, I was a bit heartbroken when the Bush-Quayle ticket failed to win a second term. I felt almost the same way I had sixteen years earlier, when I was seven years old and Gerald Ford had fallen short—like I hadn't done enough, like maybe if I had tried harder things might have been different, like it was all on me. I took it personally.

One of the events I attended that year as a student leader was the annual gathering of the American Conservative Union, the country's oldest and largest grassroots conservative organization. Every year, they held an influential and well-attended conference in Washington, D.C., called CPAC—the Conservative Political Action Conference. It's a highlight of the national political calendar, and the New Jersey College Republicans were organizing a group to head down.

The mood of the room at CPAC that year was on the somber side, since not too long ago President Bush had been riding high in the polls. His reelection seemed all but certain. Now that he'd lost the White House to a Washington outsider—a smooth-talking liberal from Arkansas with an outspoken First Lady who wanted to "socialize" our health-care system—there was a lot of digging in of heels, and hand-wringing about how to shift the pendulum back in our direction. There was also a kind of resignation, as folks seemed to settle beneath the liberal breeze blowing through town.

I met a lot of interesting, influential people at that conference. Leaders of powerful organizations, elected officials and loyalists who'd been in politics long before I was even born. One of them asked what I was planning to do after graduation, which was then only a few months away. I hadn't really thought that far ahead, and I said as much. I told her I'd applied for a job as a volunteer coordinator at a nursing home, and that I'd been invited back for a second interview, but that was about it. I was scrambling at school to complete all my requirements on time, and it now appeared I might need to make up a few additional credits once the spring semester ended, possibly through an internship approved by my faculty advisor. She told me this just might be my lucky day because she knew of an internship prospect I might want to consider.

The job was with a woman named Rebecca Hagelin, who is now a senior fellow at the Heritage Foundation, a leading conservative think tank. As a well-known author and public speaker, and the former director of communications for Concerned Women for America—a job I would later fill, in my own way—Rebecca was (and still is) well regarded among the D.C. in crowd for her frank commentary and savvy political instincts. She'd just partnered with a women's organization called Enough is Enough, whose mission was to educate people about the societal dangers of pornography.

A couple months later, two days after graduation, I packed my beat-up VW and drove to Rebecca Hagelin's house in Northern Virginia, just outside of D.C. The job was an unpaid internship, but it came with room and board—in Rebecca's basement. To this day Rebecca and I joke that she taught me how to write a press release, while I taught her how to load a dishwasher.

(Hey, when you come from a family of eight, you need to use every last inch of that precious appliance real estate—or you'll be doing dishes by hand all night long!)

The only problem with this scenario was that my graduation from Fairleigh Dickinson was only ceremonial. I was six credits short, and still owed about eight thousand dollars for the last semester's tuition. That amount of money was unimaginable for me at that point. Even with the second gig, there weren't enough hours in the day for me to earn it on a nanny's salary, so I was up against it, working evenings and weekends, in hopes of catching up.

By this point, I'd already arranged with my faculty advisor to receive academic credit for the internship I was about to begin with Rebecca Hagelin. This internship would earn me those needed six credits, which would finish off my undergraduate requirements, and that was enough to allow me to walk with my class during the commencement ceremony. I'd receive my actual diploma when I completed my internship and the final paper that went along with it. This kind of thing happened all the time, I was told, at Fairleigh Dickinson, as elsewhere. In fact, a lot of my friends were "graduating" under similar terms, so I wasn't too worried about this arrangement.

That is, until I had reason to worry. The final six credits would not be applied until that tuition bill had been paid in full. This, along with my other student loan payments, was a large debt for a nanny.

What ended up happening was I was invited to walk with my class, as planned. My family had come to Madison for the ceremony. It was a big deal. But when I opened the leather portfolio they handed me on the podium, there was an outstanding bursar's bill in lieu of a diploma. There are pictures taken of me that day, in my cap and gown, proudly displaying the portfolio and the bill. In spite of the obvious humor here, I hated that I was now looking ahead to years of student loan payments; it didn't matter that the payments would be small and somewhat manageable—because small payments on a large debt are better than no payments, and my diploma rested on it.

Still, I went through the motions of celebrating along with my friends and family. I told myself I'd do whatever I had to do to complete my internship with Rebecca Hagelin, write my final paper, submit all the necessary paperwork, and pay off my tuition bill as soon as I could.

Anyway, that was the plan—only it didn't exactly work out that way.

I was supposed to stay in Rebecca Hagelin's basement for three months. I ended up staying nearly twice that long. In that time I learned more from her about politics—how to prep for an interview, how to frame an issue—than I could have learned in another four years at school. She became my proverbial Jedi master.

I'd sit in her office as she was making calls to reporters, and she'd fill me in on what she hoped to get out of each call, and how she meant to go about it. Once, she was reaching out to a reporter who was planning to run a story a day or two ahead of when *she* wanted him to run it. As she was dialing, she said, "Okay, this guy loves to get an exclusive, so I have to keep that in mind." Then she laid it on thick for the reporter, and asked him to hold off running his story until the morning of her press conference when she wanted the coverage to appear. "I'll give you the interview ahead of time," she said, "and I won't talk to anyone else."

The reporter agreed to her terms, she explained to me later, but only because he believed he was getting something in return.

She was a terrific mentor, completely willing to let me in on her thinking, in every aspect of her work, and I went to sleep each night extremely grateful for the opportunity to work with her. At some point, though, it was time for me to move on into a paying position, and Rebecca helped me with that, too. She made an introduction for me about a job at the Republican National Committee on a Thursday, and by Friday I got a call to come in for an interview. They'd already seen hundreds of résumés for this one opening, but they said mine was the only one with such a variety of experiences. I'd spent some time the past couple summers working as a telemarketer, so I had some marketing experience. I had some campaign experience from working on the Bush-Quayle effort. I'd done some policy and media-relations work through my internship with Rebecca. I even had a tiny taste of broadcast media experience, if you counted my ad hoc coordinating duties down in Houston.

They were looking for a young person to join a sustained media effort for the Republican National Committee, working under the future Mississippi Governor Haley Barbour, who at the time was the chairman of the RNC. They had very specific criteria for this one specific job, and apparently I was the only candidate who met all of them, so they hired me on the spot.

I felt like I'd just hit a home run in my first at bat in the Majors. A real job, with a real salary at such a noteworthy organization. It was a small salary, mind you, and there wouldn't be enough left over each month after expenses to allow me to make much of a dent in what I owed the bursar's office at school. However, it was enough to get me started and make small payments, so I jumped at it.

Instead of returning home to New Jersey the next day, which had been the original plan, I moved out of Rebecca's basement and into my first apartment—in Washington, D.C., where I was due to begin work the following Monday. The job was on the production and distribution end of a television show the RNC was introducing named *Rising Tide*, which was targeted toward independent voters. The idea was to reach them with a televised program designed to appeal to their interests and sensibilities. It was, I was told, one of Chairman Barbour's creative initiatives, and he would serve as host. He'd open the show each week with a roundup of what was going on in Washington, distill the news for non-politicos, and help them to frame the issues of the day. It also featured an interview with a prominent newsmaker or lawmaker, such as Senator Bob Dole or Representative John Boehner, who'd share inside information with the viewers.

There was nothing like it on television, and it was the first time the RNC had reached out in such a specific way to this younger demographic, a group that a lot of people thought had been neglected by both major parties in recent years. Republicans in particular hadn't had a whole lot of success in galvanizing America's youth since Ronald Reagan was in office, and this was seen as a way to turn that around.

My job was to get this show on the air all across the country. In some cities, like Chicago, where the program was broadcast on WGN-TV, it was a relatively easy sell. In others, like New York, we couldn't find a major station to take us on, so we worked with local party leaders to help us place it on a cable access channel . . . any place we could get it aired. In this scattershot way, we managed to cover just about the entire country, in big markets and small. It was a real grassroots campaign, and we built it from the ground up. Each week, we added even more markets, and each week our viewership grew. The numbers weren't huge, mind you, but they grew steadily. We were getting good feedback and, most important, we were registering new voters in significant numbers.

The show would air live on Thursdays in some areas, but as soon as the broadcast ended, one of us would run the master over to the closest dubbing house and make hundreds of copies. These days, this kind of initiative could take place on the Internet—you'd hit Send and you'd be finished—but back then all of this had to be done by hand. We'd stuff those beta videotapes into overnight mailers and send them out nationwide, so stations could have them for a weekend run. It was a very labor-intensive effort, with a whole lot of running around.

I'd bounce around from the control room to the set, helping out wherever they needed me, whether it was making sure there was an aspirin waiting for our nerve-racked but brilliant director, Brian Young, at the end of each show, or running the teleprompter at just the right tempo to keep pace with Chairman Barbour's drawl. I remember one time during a live show the teleprompter went down. Unlike our current commander in chief, Haley Barbour didn't miss a beat. Rather he took the opportunity to go off script with memorable phrases like "We're gonna make the Democrats run like scalded dogs."

I don't think it's a coincidence that the GOP captured both houses of the U.S. Congress in the 1994 midterm elections, or that Republicans took the House of Representatives for the first time in forty years. A lot of analysts and historians were able to point to the weekly *Rising Tide* broadcasts as one of the reasons Republican candidates did so well with voters that year, and it was very rewarding to see our efforts pay off like that.

The trouble was, Chairman Barbour left the RNC a few years later and the program fizzled without his leadership. I left in 1995 to become the press secretary for Concerned Women for America (CWA)—the advocacy group that Rebecca Hagelin had once worked for. I was still based in Washington, D.C., and now it was my job to appear on CNN or the Sunday morning talk shows, representing what was the largest women's organization in the country, lending my voice to their chorus. It turned out I was comfortable on camera, so one interview or roundtable appearance invariably led to another, and when I wasn't on the air I was writing press releases and coordinating interview requests for our like-minded leaders.

I had been working impossible hours, and I barely had time to breathe, but I was loving every minute of it.

In a short time, I grew into an experienced talking head on issues de jour. And it wasn't just that I was experienced; people told me that when I appeared on television I came across as relaxed, personable, and passionate about my beliefs. And that's probably because I *was* passionate about my beliefs. Plus, I was so used to "performing" in front of my siblings, or the kids in the neighborhood, or theater audiences at school, or in summer stock, that it felt pretty natural—and, after growing up in such a large family, I was used to raising my voice in order to be heard. Going into my stint as a spokesperson for Concerned Women for America, I'd moved a long way from the days when I was attending church only because it was part of the deal to sleep over at my friend Eileen's house or to meet the minimum requirements to receive the sacraments. As a teenager, I considered myself an agnostic, and from there I went into a kind of questioning phase, opened my mind to all kinds of beliefs, all kinds of people. I'm grateful God intervened in my life when He did and it was my heart's desire to reach those searching as I was. I was invited to appear on a new program on MTV, focusing on young people and sex. It sounded pretty interesting to me, but CWA wanted no part of it. They thought that type of station represented all the base elements of our society, and that to appear on one of their programs would be a kind of pandering. They had a point.

However, the MTV audience was precisely the group I wanted to reach. Most likely they weren't watching *NewsHour* or the Sunday morning political talk shows. They were watching music videos, and I thought we'd do well to hit them where they lived. So about a year later, on good terms and with CWA's blessing, I ventured out on my own, forming an advocacy group called the Savior's Alliance for Lifting the Truth—or SALT, for short. The phrase came from a Bible verse that summed up our mission.

It started with a handful of volunteers but before too terribly long I was able to hire about four staffers to run the office. I traveled the country, giving speeches to youth and church groups, on college campuses and in public forums. In this way, it was really more of a ministry than an advocacy group—a *grassroots* ministry, if you will. We eventually had chapters in high schools and on college campuses across the country; we even had two NFL players as our celebrity spokesmen—Kyle Brady, of the New York Jets, and Justin Armour, of the Denver Broncos. Our mission was to train and mobilize young people to reach their lost or hurting peers—and in time we did just that. "Our aim," I wrote in an article "is to organize a generation of leaders who will defend truth in their God-given arena."

I started appearing on *Politically Incorrect*, the late-night roundtable hosted by comedian Bill Maher, which featured a revolving-door panel of guests from the worlds of entertainment, politics, academia, religion, and pretty much every segment of popular culture. It was ostensibly a comedy show, but it came to be known for rigorous debate and probing commentary on any number of hot-button issues. I was on a panel with Al Franken, now the junior senator from Minnesota, who back then was a stand-up comedian and a regular on *Saturday Night Live.* I mention Senator Stuart Smalley, oops, I mean Franken, to show the kind of guests sought by Bill Maher and his producers. We were meant to be loose-lipped and irreverent enough to be entertaining, while at the same time serious and plugged-in enough to be engaging.

By all accounts, I held my own among this fast-talking group, defending my deeply held positions with good cheer. The producers said they got such a positive response from my initial appearance, that they kept asking me back—and each time out I would weigh in on some new moral or legal or political dilemma.

I also agreed to do the MTV interview the folks at CWA had turned down, and this turned out to be a seminal moment in my career as a conservative activist. The comments I made on this one show, which was called *Sex in the 90s*, came back to bite me years later when I decided to run for the United States Senate.

On MTV, my goal for this audience was to reframe commonly held assumptions about sex. I wanted to help raise a standard of behavior and present a perspective to the MTV audience that was different from what they were being fed. I wanted viewers to think about what it *really* meant to save themselves for marriage. I know this was counterculture, but I wanted to put it out there. They were free to accept or reject my position, or to do their own thing, but I wanted to put it out there for them to consider.

Of course the producers went right for the jugular, "What about masturbation?!" I put out the idea that sex is intended to be a beautiful act of self-giving, not mere self-gratification. Sex is such a profound, wonderful experience in which two people completely give their bodies to each other: It should be a sacred and vulnerable act. Anything other than that, including masturbation, would cheapen that experience. The church simply presents a higher standard, a more aspirational approach. People are free to take it or leave it.

During the 2010 campaign, reporters loved to ask me if I regretted making those comments. It was a different time in my life and I had a different purpose. My goal was to reach confused young people. I recognized my former self in them and wanted to let them know there could be a happier future out there for them. I was merely giving voice to a tenet on sexual purity that I believed MTV's audience needed to hear.

Besides, my purpose wasn't to rack up a stack of national television appearances. This was a means to an end. And an effective one at that. I received many letters from people who had seen me on television and told me how my words had changed their lives. One young girl was up late worried about an abortion she had scheduled for the next morning. After she listened to what I had to say about fetal development on *Politically Incorrect*—specifically that there is a heart beating at eighteen days—she canceled her abortion and got help from a group whose Web site I mentioned. She later sent me a picture of that baby, who must be approaching his teens by now.

Another letter was a response to one of my way-too-candid appearances on *Politically Incorrect* in which I shared my own confusing journey toward Christianity. The teenage boy who wrote the letter was apparently suicidal. He heard me share how lost I once was, but he clung to words someone once shared with me: "If you want to know if God is real, ask Him to prove Himself to you. He loves you that much that He will let you demand He reveal Himself."

The boy took those words to heart and prayed. He sent me a letter about how my openness and willingness to be so transparent sent him on his own faith journey, and told me he was now getting the help he so desperately needed.

So do I regret making these statements? I could say I am tempted to say yes, because of all the commotion they caused in the 2010 campaign. But I know at least two people are alive today as a direct result of what I said, and the commotion is a small price to pay for the chance to take part in helping to save someone's life.

And even though I took a lot of heat for the MTV appearance, when the clip resurfaced during the 2010 Delaware Senate campaign, the joke wasn't *only* on me. Sure, there were a couple of juicy one-liners aimed my way but it's possible that the buzz over this *Sex in the 90s* clip started to backfire on my opponent. One night Jimmy Kimmel made a joke about this whole thing on his late-night ABC talk show, *Jimmy Kimmel Live*, however, he painted my opponent, Chris Coons, as the "pro-masturbation" candidate. Works for me.

I'd started SALT back in Washington, but after a while I gave some thought to moving our efforts to Los Angeles, where I'd be better positioned to make more appearances like the ones on MTV and *Politically Incorrect*, outside of the typical pundit circuit. I wasn't ready to make the move just yet, but I weighed the pros and cons. On the plus side, my sisters Jennie, Eileen, and Liz were out there, and I had it in the back of my head that I might pursue some type of steady job in television. SALT was a nonprofit, meaning we raised some money through donations, but most of our contributions came in the form of the honoraria I received for my speaking appearances. Still, however I sliced it, there was barely enough to cover our bare-bones expenses, so television seemed like a natural extension of the work I'd been doing.

Another reason I was considering this move to L.A. was because when I lived in Washington I always found myself hopping on a plane for the long flight from D.C. to L.A. for some television appearances.

I eventually did end up moving out to Los Angeles and found opportunity around every corner. I remained a regular on *Politically Incorrect*, and even more opportunities came my way. I'd been in development talks with Paramount executives, and was up for the role as a new host on ABC's *The View*. I even flew to New York to meet with Barbara Walters. As I crossed the ABC newsroom, Diane Sawyer whizzed by carrying a thick stack of papers. I wondered which breaking news story she was racing to file.

Then I saw Barbara. She was leaning on the doorjamb, shoes kicked off, talking to a staffer. She greeted me with a welcoming smile and her casual way immediately put me at ease. I followed her into her office and took a seat in the chair across from her desk. As we spoke, she was so disarming I quickly forgot I was speaking with a broadcast icon who pioneered the way for so many women. No wonder she can make celebrities and world leaders open up like few others can. The interview went so well they drew up a proposed contract, but ultimately the job went to Lisa Ling. It all worked out for the best, because shortly after that interview, something happened to take me out of circulation for quite a while.

My sisters and I received news that my father's sister, Aunt Christine, had died after struggling heroically with breast cancer. We all dropped everything to fly to Texas for her funeral.

I was at Jennie's when we got the news, so she quickly packed a bag, then we headed to my place so I could grab some clothes before heading to the airport for a late evening flight. We were in Jennie's little red late-model Subaru when a woman in the car behind us apparently fell asleep at the wheel. As we headed toward the exit ramp, her car smashed into us from behind. If we had just been heading straight when she'd rear-ended us, we probably would have been okay, but our car was veering toward the right. The impact sent us spinning into several lanes of oncoming traffic. I know it sounds cliché to say everything went in slow motion, but it did. There was an incredibly horrible surreal sense as we spun in a circle. Even the sounds of crashing metal were muffled, and sounded somehow distant. After the first hit, we were hit by another car, and another, and another. With each crash, there was a fleeting sense of relief that we'd survived, followed instantly by another heightened panic, knowing we'd be hit again. It was an awful roller-coaster experience.

There was a long, terrifying moment when we thought we were about to die, crossing all those lanes of speeding cars, spinning wildly. Feeling that it might be our last moments, we told each other, "I love you." I can still picture that scene in the front seat of the car. It was horrifying, and for a few fleeting seconds it felt like it was happening to someone else, to some other pair of sisters rushing to the airport for their aunt's funeral. Somewhere in the middle of that long, terrifying moment, my eyes locked on the gaze of a woman approaching in a big old Mercedes. We were out of control, crossing the freeway at a kind of perpendicular angle. She was driving in her lane, barreling right toward the driver side where I was sitting. There was nothing either one of us could do to save ourselves, or each other. I started praying, and Jennie joined me. In my head, what I was thinking was this: "Jesus, your will be done. I hope to see You in heaven, if this is my time to go."

According to Jennie, I yelled, "Pull a miracle! Pull a miracle!" He must have been listening. Somehow the Mercedes hit our car just behind the driver's seat where I was sitting, and sent us spinning further, colliding with several other cars, until finally the rear of our car crashed violently into the median.

I turned to Jennie to see if she was okay. She turned to me in the same instant, and we flashed each other these wide-eyed *Oh my goodness!* looks. Then one of us said, "I think it's over. It's over. We're alive!" We leaned into each other and hugged.

We were both dazed and disoriented. We stumbled out of the car, and went over to one of the drivers who'd hit us to see if she was okay. The police and EMT vehicles soon reached the scene. One of the rescue workers said, "The people in the red car, what happened to them?"

"That's us," my sister said, as we approached.

The EMT team couldn't believe it. They'd been inspecting the crash site, looking for bodies, and we just wandered up to them like nothing at all had happened. "There's no way anyone walked away from that car," we heard one of the police officers say.

Well, we did.

"You were wearing your seat belts?"

"Yes."

"If you hadn't, you would have been thrown right through the front windshield."

A little shout-out to the use of seat belts here, as they saved our lives. . . .

The woman who'd hit us in the first place and sent us spinning was taken away to a nearby hospital and later released. I don't know what happened to the lady who'd been driving the Mercedes. There were no fatalities, which was pretty incredible, considering the wreckage. The EMTs wanted to take us to a hospital to get checked out, but we were afraid they'd admit us, and we didn't want that kind of delay. In spite of a piercing headache, I was thinking we could still make our flight to Texas in time for the funeral. And Jennie agreed.

So, to urgent care we went, where they put us in neck braces and treated us for concussions, various cuts, bruises, and bruised ribs—and Jennie had a bruised tailbone, as well—so we were both pretty banged up; but all in all we felt that for the magnitude of the crash, we were in pretty good shape.

They told us it was probably foolish to get on a plane so soon after suffering head trauma; the change in air pressure was potentially dangerous, especially if there was any internal bleeding. But we felt strongly that we really wanted to get to Texas to be with the rest of our family. Believe it or not, we made it to the airport on time. And then our flight was canceled! We were rerouted to Denver, where we had to catch a connecting flight to Texas. When we got to Denver, the connecting flight was promptly canceled. Everything that could go wrong on this trip did go wrong, and then a few things more besides. It was like a scene out of that John Hughes movie with Steve Martin and John Candy, *Planes*, *Trains*, *and Automobiles*. The automobile part hadn't worked out so well, and now the plane part was turning out to be a mess; all that was missing was a train derailment.

All those takeoffs and landings were excruciatingly painful. Plus, I was more out of it than I thought at the time. The doctors were able to determine later that there had been some bleeding on my brain, which explained my extreme discomfort with all those changes in cabin pressure. By the time we finally landed in Texas, my face was swollen to where it was unrecognizable. We must have made quite the pair, Jennie and me, in our matching neck braces and swollen faces.

We looked so bad by the time we arrived in Texas the next morning that my mom insisted she take us to the emergency room. After all that hassle and hustle and heartache we ended up missing the funeral anyway. The funeral director was really gracious about it, because he knew how important it was for us to have a chance to say our good-byes, so they didn't remove Aunt Chrissy's body for burial until we could make it there, which happened only after they put me through a battery of tests at the hospital.

I loved my aunt dearly, and I felt I needed to be there with the rest of my family, so I wasn't about to let anything keep me away, even a six-car pileup and a plethora of flight delays and cancellations. It turned out I was banged up pretty good. And it took a good long while for me to recover from my injuries. I was soon diagnosed with a condition called syringomyelia, which resulted from damage to my spinal cord in the crash, and which meant I might wind up in a wheelchair. The condition also impacts the central nervous system. There's no cure, and it's not something that results in a full recovery; all that can be reasonably hoped for is to try to manage its progression, which is something I will always have to do.

I spent my thirtieth birthday getting my umpteenth MRI. If you've ever had one yourself, you'll know that it's the kind of procedure that forces you to reflect. It can be suffocating. You have to lie there on a gurney, stock-still, while the scanner takes a complete 360-degree picture of your body. If you move a muscle, they have to start all over, so there's nothing to do but lie there quietly and think. It occurred to me, while I was in the middle of this one MRI, that this was not what I expected my life to look like when I turned thirty; this was not how I thought I'd be celebrating.

And yet I had every reason to celebrate. I was alive, after all. I lay there in the MRI machine and contemplated all that had been going on. Was I really where I wanted to be at this time in my life? Was I happy in Los Angeles? Did I get the same rush walking onto a studio lot as I did walking up the Capitol steps?

"I could have done without all the attention. . . ."

It was Saturday night, October 10, 2010.

And by "Saturday night," I mean late on Saturday night. It was well past most bedtimes, although when you're in the middle of a U.S. Senate campaign the night is still young at 11:30 P.M.

I was huddled with the usual crew—my sister Jennie; my campaign manager; Matt Moran; Patti Simpson, our deputy campaign manager; and Barbara Dolan, one of our schedulers (and my aunt!). We were going over the agenda for the next day and reviewing our calendar going forward.

We were all a little fried, a little frazzled. We'd taken a hit in the mainstream media over the past couple weeks, owing mostly to our miscalculation on how to respond to those old Politically Incorrect *clips. The silver lining, though, was that our base seemed to grow on the back of the dubious attention. More and more, we were hearing from people across the state of Delaware and across the country that our core message was hitting home with those who chose to look past the diversions.*

Jennie looked up from her notes and said we should probably look at the fallout from our response ad as a kind of push. "I think it helped us and it hurt us," she said. "Hopefully, in the long run, it'll go in the plus column."

"Maybe," I said, "but I could have done without all the attention."

At this, my staff could only agree, but it appeared we were in for a whole lot more of it. Matt set down his cell phone in such a way that the rest of us could tell he'd just received a message of some importance. It seemed to me he was trying to bite back a grin, although it could have been a look of concern. Clearly, something was going on. Finally, he said, "I think we should turn on NBC."

So we switched the channel to Saturday Night Live *and continued with our meeting. There was so much going on that I promptly forgot the weird look of worry or wonder that had just crossed Matt's face, and turned my attention back to the events of the next day.*

And then, a familiar image flashed on the screen, accompanied by the familiar sounds of a piano. Dread came over me. I knew right away what it was—our ad was about to be parodied on one of the biggest stages any of us could imagine.

I braced myself for my second spoof on Saturday Night Live. *We'd tried to keep our sense of humor, about this and anything else that threatened to trip us up on the way to Election Day. But this . . . this was* Saturday Night Live, *a television icon.*

We sat there, watching, no chatter, no crosstalk. All eyes were fixed on the screen.

I knew this was coming. I didn't know it on any kind of good authority. Not like that. But I knew it in my bones. I could tell from the tone and tenor of the campaign, and the viral-type response to Bill Maher's clips, and our half-baked commercial that we'd wind up here, in some way or another. It'd already made the rounds on Leno and Letterman, so this was the inevitable last stop on my virtual late-night comedy tour.

The joke was on me, and I was ready for it. Like I said, I knew it was coming . . . and here it was.

And do you know what? It wasn't nearly as bad as it could have been. It was actually pretty funny. Kristen Wiig's hair looked a whole lot better than mine. Plus, the SNL *writers came up with a couple of great lines. The best was probably when she said that the people of Delaware deserved a candidate for "the human Senate" who can promise, first and foremost, that she's not a witch. "That's the kind of candidate Delaware hasn't had since 1692," she said, which got a big laugh—at the NBC studios and in our campaign office.*

As soon as the clip was finished, I tweeted my concession that the skit was indeed funny. Our phones lit up. Our in-boxes filled. Our cell phones vibrated with texts and calls of congratulations from friends and supporters. It was a badge of honor, folks were saying, to be lampooned by Saturday Night Live, *and I could now join the ranks of presidents and other world leaders.*

One text said that you haven't really arrived on the national political scene until you've been ripped by Saturday Night Live, *so I tried to see this as a good thing. I did. I tried. I really, really tried.*

CHAPTER FIVE

Finding My Voice

Without really realizing it, and without really meaning to, I'd become well known on the pundit circuit. To tell you the truth, I hadn't even realized there *was* a pundit circuit when I started out—although, in all fairness, it all kind of came into focus at around the same time.

Think about it: When I was growing up and becoming more politically aware, there weren't a whole lot of media outlets for meaningful, in-depth commentary on either side of the spectrum. We took in our news and analysis in tiny bites. There were the Sunday morning talk shows, of course; there were the usual suspects of political analysts and former elected officials who were trotted out by the big-three networks during each election cycle, or who followed a major address or event; there were the established political columnists on the staffs of leading newspapers and national magazines. Stations went off the air after midnight and played the national anthem as their sign-off. There wasn't the 24/7 news overload from television, radio, and the Web driving information at lightning speed. If you had cable, there was CNN and C-SPAN, and that was about it. Now we've got FOX News and

MSNBC and satellite radio and countless Web sites and bloggers and podcasters. There's no end to it; at any hour of the day, you can search your dial or the Internet and fill your head with invective and insight from any number of "professional" issue-mongers.

The impact on how we share information, how we *talk to each other* as a society, has been immediate and enormous. Now, in the space of a generation, we've become accustomed to getting our news and analysis in heaping spoonfuls, drawing from a bottomless bowl. And it's not like we'll run out of things to talk about any time soon, or run out of expert or practiced talking heads with deeply held opinions we ought to consider.

As I emerged from the fog of the months following our car accident, I realized that I'd become one of those talking heads or, at least, close enough to being one of them that folks were paying attention. Invitations were coming in from all over the country, asking me to appear on television or contribute an op-ed piece or guest column. I loved the opportunity to speak my mind and my heart in front of all these different groups, in all these different forums; it felt to me like I was doing good work, and shining a light on the important issues of the day.

In addition to my semiregular appearances on *Politically Incorrect*, I was showing up on CNN with some frequency in those days, and on MSNBC, because back then they were still somewhat objective. I was being interviewed by Bill O'Reilly and Sean Hannity, reaching bigger and bigger audiences. I wouldn't go so far as to say I was a ubiquitous presence on television, but I was certainly a presence. From time to time, I'd even get recognized out in public, which was always a very humbling experience—and an uplifting reminder that I was being heard, at least in some small way.

I wanted to deepen my message beyond the soundbites and talking points and develop a stronger foundation for my convictions. With this in mind, I applied to a summer seminar at the Phoenix Institute, a leading consortium of learning annexes, with a special focus on the intellectual, spiritual, and psychological components of classical Judeo-Christian thought. Courses were conducted by top-tier professors from some of the world's most prestigious universities, and it just so happened they were running a program with Oxford professors at the University of Oxford in England.

It sounded wonderful—what a challenge—so I applied. The program wasn't cheap, nor was the airfare to England. Yet, I'd saved just enough in recent years to cover the few thousand dollars in travel, tuition, and living expenses. My previous student loans were now close to being fully paid, and I thought this was a sound investment in my future. And it was—only I didn't recognize it as such at first.

The program was called, "Postmodernism in the New Millennia." To develop critical thinking, we were required to write in the *disputatio* format. As described by Professor Bruce Griffin, my tutor (which is what professors are called at Oxford), "this format demands that you furnish the three best reasons *against* your case before you are allowed to set forth your reasons *for* your case. So, for example, if you wanted to argue for capitalism, you needed to give the three best reasons in defense of communism *before* you could make your case."

When I went to hand in my first paper, the professor told me I had to *present* it. I was completely unfamiliar with the Oxford way of doing things—and, therefore, completely unprepared for a presentation. When I managed to finish, I sat down thinking I'd been articulate and thoughtful and that I'd made really good points. I was expecting an A, but after I got my grade and my feedback I had to think again. I got a C! And, even worse, the professor wrote that my arguments were "predictable!" Predictable? What did that mean?

For our next exercise, we had to synthesize the theories of Blaise Pascal, the seventeenth-century French mathematician and philosopher, with postmodern philosophers, using mathematical equations (and a bit of quantum physics) to support our arguments. It felt to me like I was in so far over my head I could scream—but, instead of screaming, I called home.

After waiting my turn at the pay phone in our dorm, I dialed the country code and then the phone number and hoped my mom would pick up on the other end. When she did, I blurted out every piece of worry and frustration I'd been experiencing since I arrived on campus. I said, "I don't know what the heck I was thinking. I made a big mistake."

My mother interrupted me. She said, "Chris, something drew you to that program. You were always a determined kid, and something made you get on that plane and get yourself over there."

It didn't sound like she was about to offer me any sympathy so I said, "What's your point, Mom?"

"My point," she said, "is that this is a good experience. There's something in you that wants to meet this challenge.

Worst-case scenario, you wasted your money because you didn't do well in the class. Best case scenario, you tap into something you didn't know you had."

Here I'd been thinking I wanted my mother to tell me it was okay to come home, but she put it back onto me. Since she'd never gone to college, she placed great value on our education. Looking back, it was a perfect piece of parenting. Even at the time, I was grateful for her faith in me, and before hanging up the phone I thanked her for being a whole lot smarter than I am. I knew what I wanted to hear from her, but she knew what I *needed* to hear from her . . . and the difference was everything.

After that one phone call, I doubled-down and threw myself fully into my assignments. For this Pascal exercise, I holed up in the famous Bodleian Library, where they probably had a copy of just about every book ever written, and read everything I could find on the subject. Walking into that library, with the tall dome ceiling that echoed even a whisper, I thought of all the famous scholars who had studied in that very room. I felt like I had tapped into something really powerful. There were handwritten manuscripts scribed by monks dating back to the thirteenth century right there on the shelf. And as I pored over all of these wonderful resources I kept thinking of what my professor had said. I'd consider the material, and reconsider my response, wondering if it was too predictable. I thought, *Okay, what would Professor Griffin* not *expect me to say?*

It was such a positive, liberating exercise, coming on the back of that encouraging phone call to my mother, because it reinforced for me that I had an untapped strength and determination. As long as I put my mind to it, as long as I didn't doubt myself, I would do just fine. And I did. Professor Griffin came up to me at the end of the program and congratulated me. He said, "You rose to the challenge and exceeded expectations."

In the end, I found my voice as a student and thinker. All along, I'd been out there on the lecture and pundit circuits, speaking from the heart on matters of conscience, but my time at Oxford, where I had to rise to the demands of the program, gifted me with a new approach to learning, and to sharing what I was learning with others.

I'd continue to speak from the heart, but from here on in I could back up those feelings with critical thinking.

The experience prepared me for yet another academic challenge: I was invited to participate in a graduate fellowship at the Claremont Institute in California. Other Claremont fellows include heavyweights such as former Secretary of Education Bill Bennett. It was an honor to be invited to study among such respected thinkers, especially because there were only ten spots in the incoming class. I asked Professor Griffin to submit a letter of recommendation on my behalf and I began the rigorous application process. Fortunately, at the time, the program was based solely on professional merit and potential, and undergraduate transcripts were not required. This was a good thing for me because there was still a bursar's hold on my records. When I completed the course of study at Claremont, I'd be awarded an Abraham Lincoln Graduate Fellowship in Constitutional Government, which sounded pretty good to me.

Although undergraduate transcripts were not required, I took the opportunity to reconnect with officials at Fairleigh

Dickinson to pay off my tuition balance and finally collect my diploma. I wanted to get my academic house in order—and it was a good thing, too, because there now appeared to be a whole new wrinkle in my standing at FDU. It seemed the faculty advisor who had supervised my internship with Rebecca Hagelin was no longer at the school, and that the papers I had written, along with the corresponding paperwork confirming my participation in the internship program, were no longer on file. Even more troubling, my particular course of study from ten years earlier wasn't even part of the school's present course offerings, which basically placed my *uncredited* credits into a kind of black hole.

Aaaaghhh! I thought. *What a mess!*

When I called the school, I was directed from the bursar's office to the dean of students' office to the president's office. I spent a lot of time on hold. And, in the end, I hadn't really gotten anywhere. I hung up the phone more unsure than ever about my undergraduate degree. I did, however, take this opportunity to finally pay off my tuition balance. By 2003, I'd built up a small cushion in my savings, enough to finally take care of the remaining college bills—so at least that part was settled. But paying off my FDU tuition bill didn't clear up the matter of these final few credits from the internship, which I was now hearing might not have counted toward my degree. Still, I was thrilled to be able to put myself back in good financial standing with FDU.

As long as I'm on this subject, let me put a pin in the narrative for another few lines so I can close out the story of my undergraduate career, which by now had been dragging on for way longer than necessary. As you can imagine, this hole in my résumé began to weigh on me as I moved from a place of activism to one of active leadership. Once I became a candidate for elected office in 2006, it became an issue. I didn't want to go into a heated political contest with an asterisk on my record. Wherever possible, I made it a special point *not* to identify myself as a Fairleigh Dickinson *graduate*. I did, however, mention with pride that I had attended the university, but I had started to highlight my graduate fellowship at Claremont.

Ultimately, I received a letter from FDU president J. Michael Adams, who graciously suggested that we work together to clear up the mess. I was extremely grateful for his approach. We came up with a way for me to receive those few outstanding credits. It turned out that my completion of that years-ago internship had never been in dispute, only that the credits could not be counted since I was not considered to be in good financial standing at the time. Furthermore, now that I was back in good standing, the credits could not be counted because they no longer corresponded to one of the school's programs. He told me that I would have to take a few exams and submit myself to questioning from a panel of FDU faculty members—in much the same way a doctoral candidate might be required to defend his or her dissertation.

I happily complied and was finally awarded my undergraduate degree. I couldn't have been more delighted—not only to have the mess sorted out and the question mark removed from my résumé, but because it's a significant life achievement to be able to call yourself a college graduate. It's a special point of pride, even if it kind of happened at a snail's pace for me. I'd gone through the motions once before, in 1993, walking in the commencement ceremony with my friends and fellow students, and I counted that as the real accomplishment, but even after all these years I allowed myself a second rush of personal pride. It might have taken me a while to set things right, but I got there eventually.

There, that should clear *that* up. (I hope!)

Dialing back to 1999, out in Los Angeles, I started thinking seriously about moving back to Washington and going into business for myself as a marketing and media consultant. I'd developed a ton of media experience by this point, as well as established a number of contacts on Capitol Hill throughout the government, and with newspaper and magazine editors across the country. I knew my way around an issue or a campaign. Already, I could count on a handful of clients who had indicated an eagerness to work with me in this area if I should ever decide to go this route.

The clincher on this decision was the Republican sweep in the 2000 elections. I saw it as a real turning point in American history—and in my own. It wasn't just the dawn of a new millennium; it was that for the first time in my adult life we were looking ahead to a Republican administration, a Republican House, and a Republican Senate. I didn't want to miss out on the party, I guess you could say.

I found a terrific apartment on C Street on Capitol Hill, through a woman at my church. Even after moving to Los Angeles, I'd maintained my D.C. ties because I was still spending so much time in Washington. A good friend mentioned that she was moving, so I called her to see if I could take over her lease. Luckily, the rent was within reach.

I just loved that apartment! And the neighborhood! Ari Fleischer, President Bush's press secretary, lived on one end of the block; John Ashcroft, the U.S. attorney general, lived on the other. The only reason I could afford to live in the middle of such a power center block was because the apartment had been handed down within the church for so many years, and the lease had never been surrendered, so my rent was about seven hundred dollars. It was a real bargain—and a real find. We had two floors in a gorgeous four story townhouse with exposed brick and a big old fireplace. My roommate was a phenomenal young woman named Kristen Werkhoven. She was finishing her master's degree at Georgetown, while working for Condoleezza Rice at the White House and also holding down a full-time job on the night desk at C-SPAN. It was an inspiration, watching Kristen work so hard, so diligently. She was such a focused, committed person, but she was also a whole lot of fun to be around. She had so much energy and so much enthusiasm. She made quite a picture, my roommate, with bleach-blond hair and big green eyes. She loved Britney Spears, which I always thought was the funniest thing, given the weight and seriousness of her graduate studies and her work in the field. Really, it was quite a contrast to how she carried herself in her career, where she quickly became a respected foreign policy analyst.

With my limited clientele, I couldn't afford Capitol Hill office rent, so I was a little limited in my search. Finally, I found a teeny-tiny office on the corner of Second and Pennsylvania— and by "teeny-tiny" I mean to say that it was *really* teeny and *really* tiny. The reason it was so small, I soon found out, was because it used to be a storage closet. (Literally!) There was room enough for two desks and a single visitor—and even then, that would have been pushing it—but I grabbed it, in spite of its size.

That's where I found myself on the morning of September 11, 2001, a date that unfortunately has become one of those "where were you" memories that will weigh in the hearts of so many Americans for the rest of their lives.

Specifically, I was on my way to the office, which was just a few blocks from my apartment, when I was overcome with a sense of unease. It was hard to explain or understand at the time, and it's even harder to explain or understand with nearly a decade of perspective, but something didn't *feel* right. It was like I was being swallowed up by a bad, bad feeling.

I tried to ignore it, and continue on to a press conference I was expected to attend, but the more I set it aside the more it gnawed at me. The sky was a brilliant blue. There wasn't a cloud in sight, nothing at all to darken or dampen my day; I couldn't think what it was that was troubling me so, but I couldn't ignore it any longer. So I turned around and went back home.

I walked in my front door, tossed my bag on a chair, and reached for my Bible. I sat down at my dining room table and started to read—about peace—and just then the French doors of my kitchen burst open. The brick walls of the apartment seemed to shake, picture frames rattled, and a vase on one of my shelves wobbled so hard I thought it would topple to the floor and shatter.

The rattling stopped almost as quickly as it had started, so I figured whatever it was had passed. I still hadn't connected my uneasy, ominous feeling from earlier that morning to this sort of miniearthquake that had just happened. I continued reading, but before I could turn the page there was a loud noise—more of a thundering *whooooosh*. It cracked *heavier* than thunder, if such a thing is possible, and the sensation was completely unfamiliar.

Only later did I realize the sound I heard must have been the shock waves of the fighter jets breaking the sound barrier as they *whooooshed* over my roof—a sonic boom!

Seconds later, my phone rang. It was my then-boyfriend Michael, who was working for Pennsylvania congressman Curt Weldon. As soon as I picked up the phone he said, "We're under attack!"

Michael, a very passionate young man, was enthusiastic about his beliefs. When I heard him exclaim, I thought he was speaking politically, so I said, "All right, what did the Democrats do *now*?"

"For real! We're at war!" he exclaimed.

Michael was in a high-level briefing in the Capitol Building, sitting next to Leon Panetta, President Clinton's former chief of staff, who would go on to become the director of the CIA and Secretary of Defense under President Obama. In the middle of the briefing, Panetta received a message on his cell and then turned to Michael and said, "We're under attack. The Pentagon's been hit. The Capitol is next. You better get out of here."

Michael was calling to give me the same warning.

"Christine, the Pentagon's been attacked."

I went numb as Michael spoke. It was as if I could feel the blood drain from my body. I was sick to my stomach over what I was hearing. Heartsick, too.

"Just pack a bag and get ready to go," Michael said. "I'm coming to get you."

My first thought was to call my family to let them know I was okay, but after hanging up with Michael I could no longer get a signal on my cell phone or my landline. Kristen was out of the country so I knew she was okay. I felt helpless waiting for Michael and thought about heading out to meet him on the street. But with all of the chaos unfolding outside of my window I knew finding him would be impossible. There was nothing for me to do but pace about the apartment. I flipped on the TV for information and saw the World Trade Center. It was now burning. I looked out my third-story window to see what was going on down on the street below. Already, I could see people frantically running down the sidewalk, heading out of town. Women in skirt suits, carrying their briefcases in one hand and their high heels in the other, were sprinting barefoot down the street. Hundreds of Hill staffers were spilling onto the sidewalk, bursting through every door of every building in my line of sight, like ants streaming down from an anthill.

It occurred to me that I probably knew a great many of these people outside, running for their lives, but for whatever reason the only person I could think of was my mother, who was probably so frightened by now. Both Eileen and Liz lived in New York at the time, and Liz often had meetings in the World Trade Center. I wanted to know if they were okay. I was trying desperately to call home, but I couldn't get through. As I was frantically hitting redial, Michael showed up, and we piled into his black Ford Focus to join the exodus out of the city.

Traffic on Maryland Avenue was moving at a crawl as we inched toward Michael's parents' house in Silver Spring, Maryland, but once we reached a safe distance from the Pentagon the magnitude of the morning began to sink in. There was no way to get my head around it, and as we passed the rest of that day in the relative safety of Silver Spring, glued to the television, it remained out of reach. No one could say with any certainty what was happening, or why it was happening, or what might happen next. The air was filled with tension and dread and mourning.

Looking back, I can't remember if any of us slept that night. I don't think so. I can't imagine so. But Michael was asked to make his way to his office the next morning, so we piled back into his car at first light and made the return trip along those same uncertain streets. We drove directly to the parking garage beneath the Rayburn Office Building so Michael could go straight to work. I walked from there, but once we got out of the parking garage and started moving around I couldn't think of where to go. I didn't want to go to the office or to my apartment, so I just walked and walked. The streets of Capitol Hill were as eerily quiet as a ghost town. It felt like a sci-fi movie, where I was moving about the desolate streets in search of other life forms.

I walked down Independence Avenue toward the Pentagon. I must have walked for miles without passing another person, other than an armed military guard here and there. It was jarring to see guards pacing and patrolling the streets of Capitol Hill, carrying huge pieces of weaponry. This was something you'd expect in a war-torn third-world country, not America, and certainly not on Capitol Hill.

There were no cars parked along the streets, no pedestrians scurrying to meetings. The only sound to pierce the heavy silence was the steady *clank clank clank* of a pile driver I later learned was located more than eight miles away.

After walking awhile, I came upon the bicycle path across from the Pentagon and turned numbly to look at the damage. Flames were still coming from the sides of the building. The scene was relatively calm, compared to the panic of the day before, but there was nothing peaceful about it. It had been just about twenty-four hours since these orchestrated attacks on the United States, and I stared across at the scene in disbelief. I couldn't begin to make sense of what I was seeing, what our nation was facing, what the next moments might bring.

Later that day I was asked to travel to New York to appear on a televised townhall forum to talk about this calamity. My hotel was just a few blocks from the World Trade Center, so I walked about, to absorb the gravity of the scene before I went on TV to talk about it. Everything, the streets, storefronts, windows, and sidewalks were covered with a layer of gray ash. As I walked, each step would kick up this ash as if it were freshly fallen snow. *These are people's ashes, fathers, mothers, brothers, sisters.* I remember thinking to myself. I felt as if I was trespassing on their graves.

The next day on the show when I commended President Bush for his bravery and strong leadership, no one in the audience scoffed or booed or hissed. When I said his address was courageous no one on the panel challenged me.

On that September 12, America stood united. No one questioned whether or not our military troops should get every resource they needed to do their job. No one would have even fathomed the notion that these wicked terrorists deserved the same Constitutional rights as the people they murdered. That September 12, America would have been appalled by any future administration that even considered giving these terrorists the due process afforded by our Justice system, as the Obama Administration would later propose. On that day it would have been inconceivable.

A couple years after moving into my apartment on C Street, I had an opportunity to buy it, even though it wasn't in great shape. The whole time we lived there, Kristen and I were careful not to upset the good thing we had going. When the plumbing didn't work, or the pipes were cold, or the tiles in the bathroom needed to be replaced, we tried to fix things ourselves or do without; we worried that if we called our landlord over every little problem, he'd find a reason to raise our rent or send us packing.

The opportunity to buy came because, sadly, our landlord passed away. The person who was handling his estate got in touch with me and offered to sell me the duplex. Apparently, as a tenant I had the right of first refusal now that the estate was planning to sell. In some cities, these rights are known as "key rights." A letter came, offering to sell me both units of the four-story townhouse at a price of $325,000.

My first instinct was to buy it. I'd been saving for a down payment and was planning to buy a house in the area anyway. Normally, I wouldn't have been able to touch a house like this one, not in this neighborhood, but with the rental income from the second unit I thought I just might be able to swing it. The place needed some work, though. There was a full-blown hole in my bathroom wall, and in the second unit's ceiling, so even though a part of me wanted to consider buying, I wasn't sure if it was worth the asking price.

So I invited my friend Erik who was in real estate to weigh

in. When I told him what the landlord's estate was asking for it he said, "Are you kidding me? I could flip this house for at least six hundred thousand as is, without touching a thing."

Then, for good measure, he added, "Put some money into it, and it could sell for over a million."

By the time we finished, we talked about a joint venture. He'd put up the equity, and I'd put up the key rights, and we'd be partners. It sounded almost too good to be true. We looked at the potential deal from all angles and it seemed like a sound move.

The house was really perfect for me and I was glad I'd be staying put. I'd just started doing some work in Wilmington, Delaware, and was planning to continue to commute. I figured it was a reasonable distance, about an hour and a half from D.C. by train. I'd walk to Union Station from my apartment, and then take a taxi from the Wilmington station to my office. From time to time I'd leave my car in Wilmington for the week, and drive it home on Friday evenings, because I didn't really need it on Capitol Hill, where I could pretty much walk or take the Metro everywhere.

In addition to my right-of-first-refusal rights, I was also supposed to be the point person for the renovation work we had planned, since I lived there and my partner on this deal did not.

The night before we were scheduled to close, I couldn't sleep. I was disturbed rather than excited about the deal—at least, not the way I should have been excited about such a great opportunity. So I did what I'd always done in times of stress or uncertainty: I prayed. I thought about a piece of advice given to me when I was considering making a move toward television: *Not all good opportunities are the opportunities you are meant to take.* In other words, just because it sounded good didn't mean it was the right thing for me. I ran the numbers in my head again and couldn't imagine what was making me so restless and uncertain. I could live there and let the equity increase, or, we could fix up the place and sell it in just a few months, and I could easily walk away with around $200,000—more money than I'd ever seen in one place. But as I got to my knees by the side of my bed I began to think about it a little differently.

"Dear God," I said, "once again, I just assumed this opportunity is from You and I thanked You, but I didn't ask You about it. If I'm not supposed to do this, I won't. But, I need to know Your will."

As soon as I spoke these words, it was like I could breathe for the first time in a long while. Something had been choking me, and I hadn't really realized it, and now it was like its grip had been loosened from around my neck. I felt certain that I was not supposed to buy that house.

I've told this story to several people over the years, and half the time they say to me, "Christine, how do you know that what was choking you wasn't the uncertainty you were feeling, and that relief meant He gave you His blessing and was telling you it was okay?"

To this, I have no ready answer. I only know what I know— what I *knew*. And what I knew, in just that moment, was that I was not supposed to buy that house.

I called Erik the next morning and said, "Erik, I can't go through with this. I don't think this is what I'm supposed to do."

As it happened, my would-be business partner was a solid

man of faith. Like me, he put great trust in the power of prayer, so he understood where I was coming from. But that didn't mean he couldn't ask a question or two. He said, "Are you sure, Christine? Are you absolutely sure?"

I said, "I think I'm meant to put down roots in Delaware, and if I buy this house, that probably will never happen."

To this day, I don't know what got me thinking in just this way, but now that I was, I kept coming back to it. I knew I was supposed to buy a house in Delaware. It's like I was being drawn there. Erik tried to get me to see the practical side of going through with the closing, but he'd been through enough faith exercises to know that sometimes you just can't know why you're meant to do a certain thing, or why you're *not* meant to do a certain thing. You just know that you're meant to do one or the other; *and* you just know not to question it.

"What the heck is auto-tuning . . . ?"

Right away, I caught myself longing for a simpler time in the political process, for those prehistoric days before You-Tube, because that's where our ill-fated first ad ended up. And by right away, I mean **right away**. Within hours after its first "official" airing, there were a handful of spoofs already making the rounds on the site, and I had to wonder how they got there so quickly.

According to several reports, the ad itself was already the most watched clip online—and this was before it had even aired a single time on television as a paid commercial! It's amazing how quickly it spread, like video wildfire, and I didn't know what to think of this. (Frankly, I didn't want to think about this at all, but I had to.) On the one hand, I'd convinced myself that the underlying message of the ad was actually okay, perhaps even strong, although it was diluted by the opening line, which I was now regretting like you wouldn't believe.

What was I thinking?!? I could have kicked myself going down that path, but there was no point in second-guessing or wishing it away. The line was the line. The ad was the ad. *What's done was done. What troubled me, though, was that nobody was talking about the actual message we were trying to get across. The heckling only had to do with the opening. The rest was largely ignored, swallowed up by everything else.*

We were in the habit, back at our campaign headquarters, of meeting each night as a group whenever possible to go over the events of the day and prepare for the next day.

Jennie cracked open her laptop and said, "There's something you have to see."

"It's about the ad, right?" I said, with a sigh of resignation.

She nodded.

"Please, I really don't want to. Let's just move on."

Already, as a "jaded" political veteran, I knew to avoid what they were saying about me in the press, good or bad. Reporters, columnists, pundits . . . I didn't want to start believing what they had to say—a piece of advice I learned from my friend Kyle Brady, the pro-football player, back when he was part of the SALT. I didn't want my head to get too big or too small. I didn't want to be falsely encouraged, or unfairly discouraged. It takes you off focus either way.

But Jennie was persistent. "You'll want to see this," she said.

Sure enough, it was another one of these YouTube-type spoofs—only this one had been "auto-tuned." I'd never heard the term before, so I said, "What the heck is auto-tuning?"

Turns out auto-tuning is an effect that can turn the

spoken word into a song through pitch adjustment, and Jennie had come across a video where someone had done just that.

The altered video started with a catchy, bouncy tune, which immediately set a more positive, upbeat tone. Our piano music was soft and somber, like something you'd hear in the background as someone read a sonnet, so this new version immediately had a different feel to it. There was new footage as well. This one begins with a clip with a young woman turning on her TV late at night, looking distraught. Next, the video cuts to a guy sitting at his computer—his demeanor is stressed and worried. Then as he clicks to the commercial, his mood appears to brighten. Then it cuts back to the woman on her couch. As the message plays, you could see a tear come to her eye. The video concludes with a clip from Mr. Smith Goes to Washington, where Jimmy Stewart pleads with the government to listen to the people.

The underlying message struck me as heartfelt, and certainly a lot closer to what we were trying to communicate in our original ad. Whoever put it together wasn't out to trip me up or to ridicule me. I'd stumbled, and here it took an anonymous techie who believed in my campaign to get me thinking about how I might make it right. To draw out the real message of the ad:

I'm not a witch,
I'm nothing you've heard,
I'm you.

None of us are perfect,
but none of us can be happy with what we see all
    around us . . .
Politicians who think spending, trading favors, and
backroom deals are the ways to stay in office. . . .
I'll go to Washington and do what you'd do.
I'm You.

CHAPTER SIX

Home

My heart and my gut and my prayers were all telling me I was meant to buy a house in Delaware. But a funny thing happened on my way to the real estate market. I ended up finding something far more valuable than a place to live: I found forgiveness; I found a purpose; I found a home.

The search alone was a significant marker in my relationship with my father, who by now was doing *much* better than he had been in some time. He was making all kinds of extra efforts to be the kind of parent to my siblings and to me that he hadn't had a chance to be when we were kids—and as my adventures in house-hunting began to take shape, he began to play a huge supporting role.

As a first-time home buyer, I don't think I could have navigated my way without my father lighting a path for me, and in the end he did far more than show me the way; he helped the two of us get past the distance in our relationship and onto firmer ground.

I love my father and I've come to admire his growth and his willingness to change and power past his many hard times. By 2003 he'd become the kind of grandfather to my nieces and nephews that reminded me of my maternal grand-father, spouting pearls of wisdom, making time, offering a safe harbor of unconditional love—basically, the kind of man he was all along but was trapped beneath his addiction.

One of the great blessings of my life—indeed, of *our* lives—was that my dad took an active role in my planned move to Delaware. It was a chance for the two of us to work together on a shared mission, and he took to it wholeheartedly. He drove down from New Jersey almost every day, it seemed, and while I was at work in Wilmington, he'd canvass all these different neighborhoods and talk to merchants and officials and residents, trying to get a feel for each neighborhood that caught his attention. I'd meet up with him after work and we'd compare notes. Each day was like a reunion, because underneath the excitement of looking at all these wonderful houses and meeting the good people in these great small towns and imagining myself among them, I was also making repairs with my father. We were putting down roots and reconnecting in so many ways.

From time to time, my sisters would join us on one of our search missions, and we'd take turns marveling at how diligently our father was going about his end of the house hunting. It turned out he thrived on this sort of thing—who knew? After a while, my father zeroed in on Wilmington's Little Italy section, and following one or two tours of the neighborhood my sisters and I all happily concurred. The only thing to do at this point, we all agreed, was to find the perfect house. Easier said than done, right? Well, with my father on the hunt, it was a whole lot easier. My dad did all the legwork, and by his count he probably saw every house on the market in that charming neighborhood, until one day someone suggested he talk to someone named Vinnie.

"Everyone knows Vinnie," he was told.

Vinnie turned out to be a seventy-nine-year-old widow named Vincenza, who was still living in the house she'd grown up in. She was like the matriarch of her community, and when we went to see her she couldn't have been more gracious or more welcoming. She told us all about growing up on her street, which was once filled with families from the same village in Italy. Their homes had been destroyed in the war, and they all moved to America together. We so enjoyed our visit with Vinnie, and the more she talked, the more I wanted to move right in, but I still needed to find the right house at the right price. Finally, as we prepared to leave, Vinnie mentioned that her sister had just passed away, and that her family was planning to put her house on the market. The house was just a few doors down from Vinnie's, and she said if we were interested we could go over and take a look.

Were we interested? You better believe it!

That very afternoon, we went over to see this charming two-story row house. I felt at home in it right away. It had the exact layout of my grandparents' home on Twenty-ninth Street in Philadelphia, my mother's childhood home. The backyard was tiny—about ten feet by ten feet—but just like the Philadelphia house it had grape vines, a fig tree, and a peach tree. The clincher came when a neighbor came by with a bag of fresh tomatoes grown in her backyard garden, which she offered to me as a kind of pre-housewarming gift.

The house was just about perfect, except it needed a lot of work. It wasn't exactly a fixer-upper, but my father estimated I'd need to put in about twenty thousand dollars, so I factored that into the price and made an offer.

Paulina, Vinnie's niece and my soon-to-be-neighbor, negotiated a price, and we came to terms we both liked. It was one of those deals where both sides felt really good about the transaction. I'm a big believer in "win-win" type deals, especially when you're buying a home, because you don't want to start a new path in a new place with any lingering feelings of mistrust—at least, *I* don't want to start off in that way, and here I was grateful that I didn't have to.

The first item on my father's to-do list was to fix the floors— even I could see they were in bad shape—so we arranged for two contractors to come by to give us estimates. One guy wanted $2,800; the other asked for $3,000. That seemed like a lot just to get the floors sanded and redone, so my father suggested we do it ourselves. And we did. But it ended up costing far more than the professional estimates after factoring in the cost of our rental equipment and covering up our mistakes. (We had to redo a couple spots and buy replacement floorboards for where we went a little crazy with the sander.) But I wouldn't have traded the extra expense or the extra effort for anything. Why? Because my father and I weren't just rehabbing my new house. We were repairing and rebuilding our relationship, which had been broken for far too long.

So that explains the "forgiveness" that found me as I looked to buy my first house. The "purpose" came next. Once I was settled in I became close to my neighbors, Holly and John Hosler, who were also new to the area yet already very much plugged in to the community. We'd spend most evenings sitting on my porch rockers discussing all manner of things well into the night. It was during this time that I became involved with a growing grassroots movement of like-minded, good-hearted souls who were becoming increasingly dissatisfied with the liberal leanings of the state's Republican Party. You have to realize, even though I'd worked in Delaware for a while, I'd only lived there for a couple of months. I hadn't had time to learn all the ins and outs of local politics, not just yet. Up until this time, my political interests had mostly been national, big-picture stuff, but the more discussions I had with my new friends and neighbors, the more I was reminded of a time-honored truth: All politics are local.

And apparently there was a growing rift among Delaware Republicans. Ever since the good old days of solid Republicans Governor Pete du Pont and Senator Bill Roth, the party's conservative base now had been all but snuffed from the scene. And here in my own backyard (my *new* backyard!) folks were out to change all of that. Ideologically, there was no longer any significant difference between Delaware Republicans and Delaware Democrats. Center-right independents felt that they had no political home. I heard story after story from local Delawareans that proved they had been shut out of the political process in their home party. And yet there were many Conservatives throughout the state, fighting to be heard, and I fell in alongside.

One of the more compelling (and instructive) freelance assignments I worked on during this period was a passion project in every sense of the phrase. I was hired as an independent marketing consultant by Mel Gibson's production company, Icon Productions, to help with the prerelease campaign for *his* passion project, the controversial movie *The Passion of the Christ*. It ended up being a huge success but there were some tense moments in there when it looked like *The Passion of the Christ* might never see the darkness of a mainstream movie theater.

All of the dialogue was delivered in Aramaic, Latin, and Hebrew, which critics said would make the story difficult to follow, even with the benefit of subtitles. People in Hollywood thought it was foolhardy to seek a major theatrical release for such a difficult film, but Mel Gibson was determined to deliver what he thought was an important message. He took a big, bold risk for something he believed in.

I certainly admired his passion, and his commitment, and I was thrilled to sign on as part of his marketing team. It was a tough sell, getting this movie out on time, with a thin promotional budget and even thinner prospects for mainstream success—that is, if we believed industry forecasts predicting that the movie would be a bomb. The movie had yet to find a distributor, and we were only weeks away from our targeted opening date—Ash Wednesday, the beginning of Lent, which in 2004 fell on February 25.

I remember sitting in on a conference call with about a dozen members of the marketing team to discuss the release and our stalled attempts to find a distributor. This call was led by the movie's executive producer, Steve McEveety, whom I would come to know as a brilliant, principled man, and a devout Catholic. My specific role in this effort was to coordinate our outreach to churches and youth media, which meant pitching to MTV and Comedy Central and all those young adult–oriented cable channels, but on this one call we were all putting our heads together to see how we might move forward on our tight schedule. The general mood of the call was that we should push back the movie's launch to give us more time to build a selling campaign, and to find a distributor.

"Tell Mel that Good Friday is just as spiritually significant as Ash Wednesday," one of the consultants suggested, believing we could put the extra few weeks to good use.

Another consultant took up the same argument. "We need more time," he said.

But Steve didn't see it that way. Not at all. In fact, he all but bristled at the idea that we should delay the premiere. All along, Mel Gibson had said that the Ash Wednesday opening was significant. As I understood it, this was part of his vision for the whole project—that *The Passion of the Christ* was a dramatization of the Stations of the Cross, and he therefore wanted audiences to have an opportunity to reflect on the themes of the film during Lent, a time that was already filled with spiritual significance. To release the movie at any other time of year, he said, would have been to miss the point, like throwing a dart at the calendar and picking an arbitrary date, so, Steve weighed in strongly.

He said, "Mel didn't hire you to tell him what he *can't* do. He hired you to *do* what he *needs* to be done. The film's opening on Ash Wednesday. That's a given. And now, if you don't mind, I'm going to excuse myself from this call and leave it to all of you to figure out how to make that happen."

Now, I'm paraphrasing here, but his point was clear—and

his message was heard. If we'd all been in the same room to-gether, instead of on a conference call, I'm sure I would have seen everybody's jaw drop, that's how determined Steve was in his reply.

As soon as Steve got off the phone, we turned our focus to making that Ash Wednesday opening a reality. We all had our areas of expertise, and we could have gone around in circles, trying to figure ways to get a Hollywood distributor to take on this film that was being dismissed by the insiders. And we would have gotten nowhere. We had to think outside the box.

So we stepped outside of the production mind-set and into a political approach.

We decided we should look at this like Ash Wednesday was our Election Day, and we were really far behind in the polls. How did we get out the voters on Election Day?

It was essentially the same question we'd been considering for the entire call, but once framed in a different way our ap-proach seemed to change. Together, we hit upon the idea that since Christian conservatives already had a vested interest in the material, we should ask them to buy in now, and commit to supporting the movie ahead of its release. This way, we could reach out to distributors and let them know there was a fixed number of people who were going to show up in their theaters.

Out of this, there emerged a sort of "vote for Christ in Hol-lywood" push that helped to launch the movie. That wasn't the phrase we used in making our pitch, but that was the message behind it. Everyone on that phone call contributed to the plan as it was taking shape, and by the time we ended the call we could go to concerned Christians and say, "Hey, you want better films in Hollywood? You want stories of spiritual significance, stories that reflect your values? Well, here's your chance to put your money where your mouth is. Mel Gibson, Bruce Davey, and Steve McEveety are trying to do just that, but they need your help. They need you to buy a ticket."

On our still-tight timetable, a Web site was launched to help coordinate prerelease sales, and the effort took off. We set up promotional opportunities for Mel Gibson and Jim Caviezel at churches and schools around the country. We tried to recruit activists to help promote the movie at the same time they were advancing their own agendas. Basically, we ran a grassroots campaign, the same way we would have built up support for a candidate or an issue . . . from the ground up.

The day we launched the Web site, there was so much traffic it crashed within hours. That's how big this thing had gotten, in a relatively short stretch of time. Folks eagerly wanted to show their support so there was a sort of virtual stampede as they went online all at once to preorder their tickets. It was just too much for our system to handle—and too much for any of us to believe. It was phenomenal, really. By the end of that first day, we'd sold hundreds of thousands of tickets, which now meant that Icon Productions no longer had to go searching for a distributor. The tables had turned. Now the distributors were coming to Icon, asking for exclusive rights.

The great lesson of this effort, for me, was twofold: One, it almost always pays to think outside the box, because *inside* the box can be a stuffy, stifling place, where good ideas go to suffocate. And two, it absolutely always pays to stick to your convictions, and your vision. Say what you will about the difficulties Mel Gibson might be experiencing now as I write this, but back then he showed himself to be a man of great character and purpose. He had a clear idea of how to make and market this film, and he would not stray from that purpose. He would not let conventional wisdom shake him from what he knew to be right and true. He knew this movie needed to be a resource for reflection during Lent. He knew he shouldn't wait until Good Friday to put his message out into the world.

And he was proven right. The movie opened on Ash Wednesday, as planned. It earned over $83 million in its opening weekend, the fourth-highest opening weekend for any domestic release in 2004. It went on to gross over $370 million in the United States, and over $600 million worldwide, making it the highest-grossing non-English language film in history.

Not bad for a movie no distributor wanted to touch, don't you think?

Another personal and professional highlight came in 2004 when a friend of mine, Chuck Holton, asked if I'd like to accompany a group of journalists on a cultural exchange–type trip to Jordan. These days, Chuck works as a military correspondent for CBN; his timely and perceptive reports appear regularly on *The 700 Club*. I'd met him at the Congressional Correspondents' Dinner one year, when we were seated next to one another.

The trip was sponsored by the Kingdom of Jordan, ostensibly to show Western journalists that they were one of our allies in the war on terror. I'd done a good deal of on-air work as a pundit and analyst, so Chuck reached out to see if I wanted to join them. The trip turned out to be a real eye-opener for me. I expected to be confronted with the vast cultural differences that continue to divide us from Middle Eastern culture. But I did not expect it in such a poignant way. Part of our trip was to tour Jordan's natural wonders, so a visit to their serene hot springs was planned. The bus ride there was an event itself. As we bumped along gravel roads I took in the scenery as it played out before us. It truly was like no other place I'd ever seen. We'd have to stop as shepherds led large herds of sheep across the roads. As we passed a cement wall, I could see rundown huts just behind it, with small campfires in the yards, and clothes drying on lines. I pointed in the direction of the camp and asked our guide, "What's that?"

"Oh, that," the guide fumbled. "That's nothing."

I pointed again, "Over there. The people around the fires, and the huts."

It was a Palestinian refugee camp. And our host happened to be Palestinian. He told us how his grandmother still hung her old house key by her front door in hopes of one day returning to her homeland.

I am very pro-Israel in this situation; they've always been a strong ally of ours, and it is only right to remain loyal to our allies. Israel is the only true democracy in the Middle East and as a sovereign nation they have the right to defend their existence. Yet, in this moment, I recognized that caught in the cross fire of the Palestinian-Israeli conflict are *people*, regular people with families who love them, just like my family.

It wasn't just about ideology or politics. I could see how these refugees were living, and it struck me that there were *people* caught in the middle. Good people. Hardworking people. I hadn't meant to put our guide in a tough spot, and after a while he came to trust that I was here in good faith to observe what was happening in this part of the world, so he became more honest and open.

We continued our trip to our next destination, the hot springs. It was considered off-season, and our guide hadn't expected to see locals there. Yet they were there, wading in the springs. And although it didn't register as anything out of the ordinary just yet, all of the bathers were men.

Our plan was to go swimming, but when we got there, our guide changed his mind.

"No, no, no," he said, very insistent. "Not this time."

One of the women on the trip was able to read between the lines of the guide's hesitation. She said, "It's because you don't want us women to be in bathing suits, right?"

He hesitated and then realized he could probably be a bit more forthcoming, so he nodded yes. Then he said, "This is the reason. The women must not be in bathing suits."

"No problem," another piped in, "we'll go in with our clothes on. That should be okay, right?"

Reluctantly, he agreed that this would be okay, so we went into the water with our clothes on. I was wearing long pants and a T-shirt, and the other women were all similarly attired. We refreshed ourselves for a good long while.

As we cooled off in the water, I noticed a young woman standing on the grassy shore, off to the side. She was wearing blue jeans, and a jean jacket buttoned all the way to her chin. She had a scarf wrapped tightly around her neck and head, covering all but her eyes. Judging by her body frame, and by the small sliver of skin I could see around her eyes, she appeared to be quite young, probably in her teens. Even covered head to toe like that, her attire was still quite a contrast to the burkas I'd seen on the other women. I took that as a kind of nod to Western culture. She watched us so intently.

Finally, after watching us unwind in the springs, she approached the edge of the water. It was like she was being pulled along by a different way of seeing the world, a different way of being. Without meaning to, we were flaunting our freedom right in front of her—men and women, swimming *together* in the water, *laughing*. Clearly, she wanted to experience whatever it was that we were experiencing. Just as she stood and prepared to step her foot into the water, she was tackled by a group of men and dragged up the slope of land, away from the water's edge.

The men were all yelling—in Arabic, I presumed. They sounded angry, scolding. Looking on, from a distance, it was terrifying to witness. I started to think they might be hurting this young woman, so I approached our guide and asked him if there was anything we should do. He was completely honest in his response. It was almost like he felt relieved to have a chance to explain what we were seeing. "These men, they are not hurting her. It is nothing like that. They are saving her."

He went on to tell us that if this young woman had indeed touched the water, she would have been impure, because the water was made impure; men and women had been bathing in it together. Furthermore, it was not appropriate for a woman to laugh out loud the way we had been. In that part of the world, if a woman was made impure, she would be banished— even worse, she could be killed.

Somewhat numbly, our guide reported that these Jordanian

men had rescued this girl from her own curiosity, which could have brought about her death. It seemed to weigh heavily on him.

And then, in a rare moment of candor on the bus ride back to our hotel, he shared a story he hoped might illuminate the situation for us. Just a week or so earlier, he said, he'd been walking home from work when he noticed a small stream of blood trickling along a dirt road. He heard a commotion off in the distance, and followed the stream in the direction of the noise, and as he turned the corner he came upon an unsettling celebration. What he saw was a small parade, and at the center of the procession was a man who was receiving cheers and congratulations. The reason? He had just restored honor to his family by killing his daughter, right there in the public square. Apparently, his daughter had been seen by her neighbors holding hands with a local boy, and they suspected there must have been more. So the father had no choice but to kill her. It was her blood filling the street, along with the sounds of apparent celebration from friends and family. This was what is called an honor killing, or honor crime.

I was greatly disturbed by our guide's explanation; he too appeared deeply saddened by the events he was describing. When I got back to America, I began to read up on these so-called honor crimes that are committed in the name of purity and honor—not only in the Middle East, but all over the world. In Jordan, this young woman (a girl, really!) had come within a half step of being killed for shaming her family and her village. This was not the takeaway the Jordanian government wanted for their visitors, but I took it home with me just the same.

Toward the end of our tour, we visited a Bedouin encampment out in the Wadi Rum desert, where we were hosted by a family of nomads. They were very generous to us, serving a feast of olives and cheeses and putting us up for the night in large tents furnished with intricately woven rugs and divans with coverlets.

That night, I couldn't sleep. I didn't want to miss any part of this rare experience. At around five o'clock in the morning I stepped outside my tent to take in the surroundings. Everyone else was fast asleep in their tents, even our hosts, so I slipped quietly from the camp into the ink-black night. Once I stepped just a few feet from camp, there were oceans of stars overhead in the clear night sky, but they did little to light my way. The night air was pleasantly cool and mild, but there wasn't even the slightest breeze. There was no sound but my own breathing.

I was transported to an ancient time. Away from our camp there were no signs of the modern world, no electrical wires lining the sky, no paved roads. Only miles and miles of flat sandy desert with barren red rock mountains far off in the distance. It was a breathtakingly beautiful scene, a transcendent moment. It caught me completely by surprise, but as I took in the quiet, splendor and majesty of that setting, I started to feel like I was back in biblical times. This was the land where Jesus was baptized by John the Baptist in the Jordan River. Jerusalem, the city of King David, was just to the north. At dinner the night before, our hosts—men, women, and children—still dressed much like their ancestors were when Abraham and his family migrated to the area.

It was all a wonder to behold . . . It was almost too much

to take in. To think that I was standing in the cradle of religious history was almost overwhelming. It felt to me like I was experiencing the transcendent timelessness of God.

And then, as I stood there, soaking in this wonderful moment, I heard from over the horizon the resonant, unmistakable sound of the Islamic call to prayer. I looked around to see where these haunting chants were coming from, but the night was still dark. There was no movement, only sound—the mournful sound of prayer. I could see no other encampments, no tiny villages over the hills. And yet from all sides there rang the ghostlike echo of the Islamic call to prayer. I looked around again but there was nothing to see. There was only the lift and cadence of these ancient words, voiced by several muezzins in a kind of discordant unison, filling the darkness beneath the eternal stars.

It was a majestically haunting experience.

CHAPTER SEVEN

A Public Life

Back home in Delaware, my consulting business was beginning to take off. There was money coming in from a steady base of clients. The SALT was no more; in its place was O'Donnell & Associates. I'd been juggling several freelance clients and things were on a roll. Work leads to work, and here it led to plenty. Following my efforts on the launch of *The Passion of the Christ*, for example, I was hired to help coordinate the publicity tour for a tie-in book written by Father John Bartunk, a priest who'd served as a theological consultant on the film. I also did some work on behalf of a Russian artist named Natalia Tsarkova, the Vatican's first female portrait painter, for the unveiling of *La Madonna de Luce*, her painting of the Luminous Mysteries. The painting had hung in the private library of Pope John Paul II, before it was shown to the public. It was my role to plan the unveiling and generate some media attention for the piece. The Senate had just passed a resolution honoring Pope John Paul II after his passing, so we held our unveiling in the Capitol building in the spirit of that resolution. (On the same day, just to add a sense of significance to our moment, the Supreme Court nomination hearings were being held on the Senate floor just a few doors away.)

I also did some public interest work for the World Education and Development Fund, which included setting up a U.S. Senate briefing on the link between education and a long-term illegal immigration solution.

In all, I was doing good work, sometimes for good money, and on behalf of good people. Was I making a difference? I certainly hoped so. Was I making any money? Some—enough to hire a full-time "associate," and treat myself to something nice every once in a while. Was I helping to champion causes and issues that were important to my clients, to me, and to the whole wide world? You better believe it.

All was right in my little corner of Delaware, but soon after a couple of chance encounters set me in an entirely new direction. The first came from a local political junkie named Tom Nicastro, who was the good friend of my neighbor Paulina (the woman who'd been so helpful back when I was buying my house). I'd known Tom peripherally since I moved to town, but I was surprised to hear from him on this; he took me aside in the summer of 2006 and suggested I consider running in that year's Republican U.S. Senate primary. It was about the last thing I expected to hear. He strongly believed that the party's transparent rejection of core Republican principles would be its undoing. (Our state party refused to adopt a platform outlining its positions. More on this later.) He suggested that because of my experience working with various national organizations based in Washington, with legislators on Capitol Hill, and my profile in the media, I'd be well positioned to throw a scare into the party establishment.

Betty and Peter Chillano, my grandparents. Grandpop was so proud of that uniform.

Before power red, I wore power pink and always sported that hat.

My dad helps me put the star on our Christmas tree. This was my second try after picking a "Charlie Brown" tree. We had to cut the top off of this one to make it fit.

Kindergarten class picture. Can you tell my mom cut my bangs? She'd line us all up one by one: snip, *next*, snip, *next*, snip, *next*.

Left to right: Liz, me, and Evelyn. My grandmom made our costumes by hand. She even stitched the wigs in this photo. My dad suggested we say "Here comes the judge, Here comes the judge!" instead of "Trick or treat." But because we were too young for *Laugh-In*, the joke was lost on us.

The neighborhood kids, 1976. Our township wasn't officially celebrating America's Bicentennial. So Mom organized the neighborhood kids and we held our own parade. There were plenty of old ballet costumes and bikes to decorate to fill the streets.

O'Donnell family, Christmas early seventies. (Clockwise, left to right) Danny, Carole, Jennie, Liz, Eileen, me, my mom, and my dad in the middle.

Left to right: Playground friends, my mom, and me (in back with arms raised). We're standing on top of the jungle gym made from old tires that was part of the Lenola School playground that my mom coordinated—under budget!

Proudly showing my "Dorothy Hamill" haircut and my Brownie uniform in the second grade. I remember feeling so grown up when this picture was taken.

My parents and me in a photo booth in 1980. I love arcade photo booths—but does anyone ever get a good shot? That challenge is part of the fun.

My mom and me at the Italian Market in Philadelphia. Every year my mom spends her birthday buying and cleaning the fresh fish for the traditional Christmas Eve seven fishes feast. Days of preparation go into a meal that's gone just about as soon as it hits the table!

Lining up for the Fairleigh Dickinson University commencement ceremony in 1993.

Moorestown High School Senior Class photo, 1987.

Courtesy Disney

Comedian turned U.S. Senator Al Franken and me during a 1998 episode of *Politically Incorrect*. Backstage he told my sister and me that I was the girl you "hate to love." Pun intended. He got over that, because by 2010 he dutifully campaigned against me for the man Harry Reid called his "pet."

Jordan, 2004. In route between Kerak and the Hot Springs, our bus was delayed as shepherds herded their flocks across town. We took the opportunity for an unscheduled stop to meet the locals and experience authentic culture. Here, I'm with the shepherds.

Courtesy Chuck Holton

Conservative Republicans were frustrated that in 2006 the Delaware GOP nominated a man so far to the left that he later became a campaign coordinator for

Barack Obama. So, they recruited me to run a write-in campaign in the 2006 U.S. Senate race. This is my parents and me leaving the polling place after I cast my vote…pencil in hand!

Congresswoman Michele Bachmann and me at a dinner in Washington, D.C., spring 2010.

Caesar Rodney (Luke) and Paul Revere (Marc) with me at the 2nd annual Wilmington Tax Day Tea Party on April 15, 2010, at the Wilmington Riverfront. The tireless work of the folks who started this movement tilled the soil for our September victory.

Delaware State Fair, July 2010. Who doesn't love campaigning at the State Fair? Where else can you get fried Oreos alongside a plate of scrapple? (Don't knock it 'til you try it.)

Peach Festival parade, 2010. A volunteer from another campaign said to one of our supporters, "She must pay you guys a lot to walk with her. She always has a huge crowd." He was getting paid to walk with his candidate, so he was surprised to learn our supporters were walking with me simply because they wanted to!

(AP Photo, Rob Carr)

Rehoboth Beach, Delaware, 2010. We won Sussex County by a significant margin, thanks in large part to the team pictured here with me at WGMD's studio on the *Bill Colley Show*.

(AP Photo, Rob Carr)

Dover, Delaware, 2010, on stage at the Elks Lodge on primary night, surrounded by friends and family.

(AP Photo, Rob Carr)

Primary night, 2010. CNN just called the race and the team breaks out in cheers. Immediately we began receiving e-mails from people across the globe telling us our team's victory was an inspiration to those who'd ever felt oppressed or stepped on.

(AP Photo, Rob Carr)

The morning after the primary. Jennie, me, and my mom taking a break between interviews in our makeshift green room, the lobby of the Fairfield Inn in Dover! It had been transformed into a buzzing international media hub as reporters from Japan, England, and France were crowding around to get reaction.

(AP Photo, Rob Carr)

October 2010, Widener University debate. When the media rushed the podium afterward, I clarified my remarks that "Separation of Church and State" is nowhere in the Constitution and said it was appalling that my opponent, Chris Coons, couldn't name the five freedoms that *are* protected by the first amendment. Reporters must not have heard me because, otherwise, it certainly would have been irresponsible journalism to cover my comments the way they did.

I'M YOU

Do I really need to put a caption here? If you are the one person reading this book who does not know what this is, boy, could I hug you right now! But, just in case, this is a still frame from our now infamous first General Election campaign ad.

10.30.2010

The Steel Magnolias Support the Troop Rally, Middletown, Delaware. It was an honor to share a stage with such brave troops and their families. Also, a lifelong Democrat who leads a statewide veterans' organization publicly endorsed my candidacy on this day. It was one of those truly humbling, inspirational days that reminded me why I'm in this in the first place.

CNN debate at University of Delaware, 2010. I was probably saying something like, "Pick one, Chris. You can only have one position on how you'll vote on the Lame Duck tax

increases." At this point, he had no fewer than five public positions. George Stephanopoulos was one of the only mainstream journalists to call him on this.

During this Wilmington Rotary Club debate, I questioned Coons for raising taxes on seniors and disabled residents, and then spending it on things like a men's

fashion show. Denying it, he said, "I don't know where you get your information…" So I pulled out the budget spreadsheet from *his office* detailing those expenditures. No response! And of course, this was ignored by the local media.

Farmers for O'Donnell Rally, Sussex County, Delaware. Agriculture is one of the leading industries in Delaware, and it's been twenty years since Delaware farmers have had a Congressional representative championing their needs in Washington.

Milford Riverfest. Milford was the center of the maritime industry for nearly two centuries; towns like it are what make Delaware so special. Every community still has its own unique "Main Street."

At Buckley's Tavern in Centerville, Delaware, with Tennessee Senator Lamar Alexander. Buckley's is one of the old-time establishments that enhance the small town feel of our state. One local reporter called Delaware "the biggest small town in America."

(AP Photo, Rob Carr)

The Goldsborough Family. Their family-run farm has been a consistent source of support for generations. Now, overregulation, Cap and Trade, and the death tax threaten to take that all away.

Republican National Committee Chairman Michael Steele made sure the RNC engaged our campaign as soon as we won the primary. Chairman Steele held a rally in Dover, Delaware, as part of the RNC's "Fire Pelosi" tour.

(AP Photo, Rob Carr)

(AP Photo, Rob Carr)

Several of our campaign stops were at local bowling alleys. Thanks to the creative efforts of Patty Hobbs and Donna du Pont, each stop was loud, crowded, noisy, and a lot of fun!

General Election, 2010. Surrounded by family at the podium. Although we didn't win the election, I was proud we accomplished a lot. The Delaware political establishment will never be the same.

(AP Photo, Rob Carr)

(Courtesy ABC News)

Washington, D.C., January 2011. On ABC's *Good Morning America*, commenting on the President's 2011 State of the Union speech with former interim DNC Chair Donna Brazile. No, we didn't both get a memo to wear red. And yes, that is "the" blazer!

His timing left me no room to think things through; the filing deadline was only weeks away. I was flattered, but Tom's notion seemed so outrageous, so *out there*, I could hardly give it serious consideration. Don't get me wrong: It was nice to be thought of in just this way, but I caught myself thinking, *Seriously? Me?* Tom was absolutely serious, and he kept pushing me on this, but I just couldn't see how to make it happen, just from a practical standpoint. Even with the recent boost to my savings, I'd only just begun to rebuild my account after paying off my undergraduate bills. There was no way I could have come up with the filing fee, which was just under ten thousand dollars. I was no millionaire; I was barely even a *thousandaire*; there was no way I could have afforded to be a U.S. Senate candidate.

The greater, more compelling argument against running was that the deck would be stacked against me. It would be stacked against any outlier candidate, from either party, but on the conservative side of the aisle this was especially so. In recent years, Republican primaries had pretty much become nonexistent in the state of Delaware. And if someone did step up to run in the primary against the party's anointed, that person would be vilified and bullied out of the race. Mike Castle, Delaware's lone congressman, and Priscilla Rakestraw, the Republican National Committee woman, were both decidedly liberal. At times, Priscilla would demand that our party never support a pro-life candidate for statewide office despite the pro-life plank in the *national* Republican platform.

As if that wasn't bad enough, as far as card-carrying conservative Republicans were concerned, certain party leaders weren't exactly rolling out the welcome mat for new members or for new ideas. When I moved into town, one of the first things I did was reach out to the Wilmington Republican Committee. They never called me back. Every year, I reached out to them again, and I've yet to hear from them. As I write this, I've been the Republican candidate for the U.S. Senate not once but *twice*—and I still can't find out where the Wilmington Republicans meet. It's like it's some secret society that gets together at an undisclosed location, and only lets you in if you know their secret handshake.

I appreciated that Tom was thinking of me on this, but it seemed to me out of the question so I had to set it aside.

The story does not end there. A few days later, I was in a meeting on Capitol Hill listening to Pennsylvania Senator Rick Santorum explain why those of us who advocated for a strong national defense should support oil exploration in ANWR. I was sitting with Sara Blackburn, the talented young woman I'd hired to work with me on a number of projects over the years. During a break in the senator's presentation, she turned to me and said, "Christine, you should run for Senate."

This was getting strange. For the second time in less than a week, someone I admired and respected was suggesting I make a bid for an office I would have never thought to seek on my own. I couldn't understand it. "What's *that* about?" I asked. "You're the second person to say that this week."

"Maybe that means there's something to it," Sara said.

Something to it or not, I was wary. I'd never thought of myself as a candidate for political office—certainly not the United States Senate. I was much more comfortable as the behind-the-scenes strategist, at least insofar as the political stage was concerned. It might have started with Tom and Sara, back to back like that, but then as talk grew of this idea, I kept hearing more of the same. They were all suggesting that with my national contacts, with my media platform, with my experience working in Washington, I was uniquely positioned to bring a much-needed voice to the primary campaign.

At least, that was the idea.

It was really late in the game by this point. Really, *really* late in the game. But after talking to others, I went from thinking, *There's no way I can run,* to thinking, *Well, why not?* That year voter turnout would be about thirteen thousand total in the Republican Senate primary. That's not a big number. By my count, there were enough frustrated Republicans throughout the state that if we turned them all out we could win.

Still, the primary was only about six weeks away, so turning out our conservative base was by no means assured. We might not have left ourselves time to get our message out. As it was, there was barely enough time to file. Like I said, we were late to the party on this one—so late that it appeared for a few frustrating days that I wouldn't be able to raise the filing fee and get our paperwork in on time, and we'd have to let go of this idea and save it for another day.

I had a meeting scheduled with Father John Connor, a priest I had come to know through my work with *The Passion.* I told him my motives and what I was planning to do: to stand up to the party committeewoman and represent the principles of our party, but in order to do that, I needed to raise nearly ten thousand dollars by the next day.

"Ten thousand dollars?" the priest asked.

"Well, almost. It's just under that. That's the filing fee," I said. "I don't have it."

"Maybe not," he said, "but I think I can help you."

I had no idea what he meant, so I pressed him to explain. It turned out Father Connor had a good friend named Eustace Mita, one of those truly inspirational people who you rarely meet in life. I went to see him later that day—only our mutual friend hadn't called ahead to make an introduction. Unaware of this, I met him in the foyer of his office and said, "Hi, Father Connor sent me."

"That's nice," Eustace said, "but why?"

I thought, *This is not good.* But it was. It truly was. Eustace turned out to be a wonderful man, truly committed to the cause, and once I set out the reason for my visit, he was happy to help in whatever ways he could. Right then and there, he made some phone calls and helped me raise what I needed to cover the filing fee. After thanking him profusely I raced to file the paperwork.

I was just in time. The deadline to file was noon; the clock said 11:59.

Talk about cutting it close.

The decision to run in the primary came with some adjustments at work. First and foremost, I had to drop my freelance clients—in part, because they were nonprofit organizations and I feared they might be accused of a conflict of interest, but also because I did not think I could run an effective primary campaign in a we're-gonna-make-a-powerful-statement sort of way and still give my clients the attention they deserved.

This was no small thing, because those clients accounted for the bulk of my monthly billings, so money was

tight around the office for a while. The cushion I'd been building became a little less cushiony; my future, a little less certain.

I'd left myself less than six weeks to raise money and get
the good word out—no time at all, really. It was the epitome of
a grassroots effort. We did what we could, with the time that
we had, to let people know that we represented a chance for
Delaware Republicans to reclaim their party from its liberal
position, and to restore traditional Republican values to the
statewide political debate. I went to meetings, held rallies,
handed out flyers, pounded the pavement . . . But, in the end, it
was one of those too little, too late situations. We might have
known, going in. More to the point, we *did* know, but we ran
anyway to call attention to the way Delaware's GOP establishment seemed to run roughshod over its conservative base.

And I like to think we did just that. I finished third in the
primary, but we made a whole lot of noise along the way. In
fact, I made so much noise, my supporters kept after me to
think about continuing the effort as a write-in candidate for
the general election. What I heard was that my candidacy had
struck some sort of chord throughout the state. The folks who
got behind this effort did so with great cheer. They, too, had
been shut out by the Republican Party in the state. They, too,
had grown frustrated that there was no party platform at the
state level. (The more I think back on this last item, the more
it strikes me as an outrage. I mean, the Delaware Democrats
have their own platform. Most state parties have their own
platform, and the ones that don't seem to at least fall in line
with the national party. Not so in Delaware.) They, too,

looked on at their party's new left of center U.S. Senate nominee—a guy who two years later would become a state coordinator for the Obama campaign—and wonder how we'd drifted from our core values. They relished the idea to forge ahead and make even more noise.

After hearing from so many supporters in this, I decided to continue the effort as a write-in candidate; I was all over it. Why? Well, because we'd come this far and felt like we'd built up a head of steam, for one. And mostly because I wanted to see if we might at least upset the balance of power in the state to where our voices would be heard going forward. Did I expect to win? No, of course not. But I couldn't ignore the groundswell of support that had come my way in the past six weeks, either.

We ended up breaking records, even for a write-in candidate, and rattling a whole bunch of cages. We collected somewhere over 4 percent of the vote. The reason for the uncertainty is that the results are no longer posted on the Delaware Department of Elections Web site and they decided to discount any votes that had been cast with my name misspelled. Voters who took the time to go to the polls and mistakenly voted for "Cristine O'Donnel" or "Christine O'Donell" or "Kristine O'Donnell" had their ballots tossed. It didn't matter if their intentions were clear; if the form wasn't filled out according to the *interpretation* of our election laws being applied by the Department of Election officials, it was discounted. The *letter* of the law actually provided for misspellings, as long as intent could be determined, so the officials monitoring our count simply chose to ignore it; subsequently, the Delaware state legislature changed the law.

(Oh, by the way: If the state of Alaska had played by these rules during the 2010 Senate election, Joe Miller would be representing that state, so this goes to show there are any number of ways to skin a cat, or skew a result.)

Still, even with the lower number, more votes were cast for my write-in candidacy than had ever been cast for any independent candidate in state history. Further, more people voted for me as a write-in candidate than voted for *all* the independent candidates on Delaware ballots that year combined.

It was pretty amazing, the impact we had on this race . . . with virtually no time and no money and no hope of making a serious dent in the minds of the electorate. And yet, some powerful things happened that Election Day, I later learned. In some districts, at some polling places, the heavy demand caused the voting machines to run out of the tape used for write-in ballots. A few machines even broke down. People had to wait in line for over three hours just to cast their vote, but rather than throw up their hands in frustration and go home, they did just that; they waited. Election officials would canvass the line, telling people that if they weren't voting for a write-in candidate they could proceed to the front, but nobody moved. Instead, they stood patiently, waiting for someone to insert a roll of register tape so they could vote for me.

None of us saw these results as disappointing. Rather, they were an unmistakable sign that we were on to something. The people of Delaware had been stirred by the possibility for change. They voted for me because they believed I represented them, when no one else did. It was their achievement, not mine, because they were fed up with top-down establishment governance.

And so the phones in our makeshift campaign offices began ringing off the hook. No condolences . . . in fact, it was just the opposite. People wanted me to get started right away on 2008. The messages continued to pour in, only now they had a whole new flavor to them; now they were hopeful, positive, forward-looking; now they cast me as a kind of agent of change.

If six weeks wasn't enough time, well then how about two years, Christine? That ought to do it.

Call after call came in, letter after letter, urging me to consider seeking the Republican nomination again in 2008, but I couldn't think that far ahead, not just yet.

Meanwhile, things had slowed to a crawl at work. The economy had started to turn. Nonprofits were slashing their budgets left and right and up and down, and when that happens consultants are one of the first items to disappear from the company ledger. I did manage to land one midsize client for an ongoing project that ran from spring 2007 until the end of the year, but that barely brought in enough to pay the bills. Also in that period, there were a few mini-projects, or quick-turnaround gigs, but nothing else to really build a business on.

I don't set this out to complain, only to set the scene. In the back of my mind, I was preparing for a Senate run in 2008, but it would have been nice to get onto some firmer financial footing before I started campaigning. I'd pretty much run through the savings I'd accumulated ahead of my hasty 2006 campaign, and I was scrambling to get out in front of my bills so I'd be well positioned for another run. Already, I'd met a few times with our then state GOP chairman, Terry Strine, who was supportive and encouraging. He reminded me, as I knew full well, that as state party chairman he would need to remain neutral if another candidate entered the field, but at this point no one else had indicated their intention to run.

All of this was taking shape when I went to Washington one day for a series of exploratory meetings to lay the groundwork for another U.S. Senate try. When I left my last meeting, I reached instinctively for my cell phone to tap back into the rest of the world. When I did, I found about a dozen messages telling me that Randy Richardson needed my help. It was the strangest thing. I'd never heard of Randy Richardson, but the people who were reaching out to me on his behalf, many of them friends and volunteers who'd worked with me on our write-in campaign, were all telling me to get in touch with him as soon as possible.

Randy's story was really the story of his daughter, Lauren Richardson, who'd nearly died from a heroin overdose in the summer of 2006, at the age of twenty-one. She was still breathing when her body was discovered, but doctors soon declared that she was in "a vegetative state." Up until this time, Lauren had been kept alive with a feeding tube, and now, according to a court order, this support had to be removed.

However, it was also discovered that she was pregnant at the time of her overdose, so Lauren's doctors shifted their focus and ran a bunch of tests and determined that Lauren's unborn baby was unharmed by the trauma and was doing okay. By some combination of God's grace and a medical miracle, doctors were able to keep Lauren alive through her pregnancy, and she eventually gave birth to a healthy child.

Contrary to the earlier medical determination, however, Lauren's condition had greatly improved. Her father said she was now responsive. By the time the baby was born, he said, Lauren was aware of her surroundings and able to communicate. But the courts were acting on the doctors' initial diagnosis, which had said that Lauren was in a vegetative state with no chance of recovery.

Now that the baby had been born, however, the focus shifted yet again to Lauren, and all the way back to the prognosis offered by her doctors at the time of her overdose. Once again, measures were put in place to remove her feeding tube.

Randy and I agreed to meet at Holy Spirit Church that was centrally located between us. There was a thirty-four-foot statue of the Blessed Mother out in front so it's easy to find. His direct point of contact with me came through our mutual friend Bess McInniney, one of the volunteers from our write-in campaign in 2006; she was one of the many people who'd left me those frantic cell phone messages.

Randy had exhausted all of his options by this point. He'd sold his business to cover his mounting expenses. He was distraught when I first met with him. And soon, so was I. It was the most maddening thing, to think that the court could intercede in this way, basing a present-day course of action on medical records from the time of the accident. He'd been working with the Delaware Pro-Life Coalition to fight this, and the reason I'd gotten all these calls was because he'd just won a twenty-one-day injunction. He and his team were reaching out to me because they now had three weeks to convince the judge not to remove Lauren's feeding tube. They wanted to tell their story in the media, hoping to get some support.

It was a cold, rainy January day so I decided to dress comfortably in blue jeans; my hair was in a ponytail and I had no make-up on. I wondered if my choice of practicality over presentation did not offer him the assurance he was seeking. As he later tells it, I was right. He explains that initially, he wondered what Bess had gotten him into. But after I made a few calls, then came back in the room to let him know a town car was on its way to take us to New York to appear on the Hannity show, his doubts about my abilities disappeared.

My heart broke for the whole family. I couldn't imagine what they were all going through; it was a devastating, impossible mess, but from here on in it would be my mess, too. Whatever else was going on in my life at the time, whatever decision I might make about the campaign, I couldn't look away. If these good people thought I was in a position to help, then that's what I would do. Anyway, I would try.

We had twenty-one days to save Lauren's life. The first thing I did was meet her. She was at an assisted living facility. Standing in the doorway of her room, I peeked inside. This was not at all what I expected to see. There were no noisy, beeping machines, or tubes going this way and that. I know there must have been at least one tube (obviously), but I didn't see it. The room was quiet. Lauren was sitting up in bed, her dark blond hair neatly brushed, her covers placed just so. You could see she was loved and cared for. I imagined her as any of the girls I knew growing up on my street. In my mind I imagined her riding bikes with my friends and me, down the middle of the street we played on, I saw her splashing in the pool with us in the summer. She was just like us. I smiled at her and walked across the room toward her. Her green eyes followed me. She was completely responsive.

I grabbed a chair, pulled it to her bedside and sat down. I said, "Hi Lauren, my name is Christine. I am here because your father asked me to intercede on your behalf, and possibly use my media contacts to bring public attention to your story. Is that okay with you?" She acknowledged this with a kind of grunt of understanding. "Okay, then, that's what I'll do."

We couldn't fathom the court's position. Clearly, this young woman wasn't in a coma. She wasn't brain dead or in a vegetative state. It's not like they were talking about disconnecting her breathing tube, or that she couldn't breathe on her own. What was at issue was her *feeding* tube. They were going to starve her to death. It struck me then, and still, as an extension of the pro-life position I'd taken all of my adult life on the abortion issue—only here was a chance to work for the sanctity of *all* human life, not just the life of an unborn child.

The first call I made on Lauren's behalf was to a producer I'd worked with on Sean Hannity's show. I told her the story, and she was intrigued. *Outraged* and intrigued—enough to agree to set up an interview as soon as possible. Then I called a woman I knew at the White House bioethics office. She, too, was willing to help in whatever way she could. Within a matter of hours, I was able to reach back out to Randy and say, "Are you available to do an interview tonight?"

Things happened quickly after that. A town car came to pick us up in the church parking lot, and we were whisked up to New York to appear on Hannity's show that night. On the drive up, we were frantically working our cell phones, trying to arrange for some video footage that would show Lauren at the assisted living facility being responsive and engaged. We wanted to get the world to see that this young woman was very much alive. She wasn't brain dead. This wasn't a right-to-die case, as it had been depicted in the courts and in the media. No way. It was a right-to-kill case. It was a flashpoint for pro-life Americans who wanted to make the all-important point that all life should be protected, not destroyed.

They formed an organization called Life for Lauren, trying to call attention to her story. The Alliance Defense Fund graciously agreed to put together a strong legal team, pro bono. Randy had to sell his business, but after paying for Lauren's long-term care there was little left. Our team worked like crazy on this thing. We finally won the intitial twenty-one day hurdle, but the fight was far from over. We continued working round the clock, sometimes eighteen hours a day, for several months. Ultimately, Lauren's parents came to an agreement that would spare her, and are working together to care for her.

As I write this, she's still very much alive, although her health took a turn for the worse just before Christmas 2010. Up until then, she'd made steady improvements all along, and is now living at home with her father. Her daughter is thriving and living nearby with Lauren's mother and they get to see each other often.

I share her story in these pages for the way she unknowingly played a significant role in my decision to finally seek the Republican nomination for the 2008 U.S. Senate race.

In the months that had been filled with the Richardson case, another Republican candidate entered the field and started making appearances around the state asking, "Where's

Christine?" As if I was in hiding, or taking their support for granted—even though the reality was I'd been consumed by Lauren Richardson's plight. The campaign groundwork I started to lay was interrupted and now things were different. My involvement *had* kept me away from state politics during a crucial time in the run-up to the 2008 nominating convention, so I started to think maybe the timing wasn't right for me on this go-round.

To this guy's credit, he did come by my house one evening with his wife to tell me his decision. He'd been a supporter in my previous campaign, so we certainly knew each other. We were on the same side on a number of issues. He politely but firmly told me that it would not be good for two Christians to be competing against each other; whoever prevailed in the primary, he suggested, would be weakened for the general election.

He went on to tell me that God had told *him* to run, implying that if I decided to seek the nomination I would be disobeying God.

He then suggested that since I had been sort of missing in action these past couple months, challenging him at the nominating convention would be pointless. And, finally, he concluded his visit by telling me he'd already raised thirty thousand dollars—which put him well ahead of my fundraising efforts.

Actually, it put him just about thirty thousand dollars ahead of me, because I'd yet to make a push in this area. Even more troubling, my personal finances weren't looking so good. My work on the Richardson case was pro bono and without an income I'd fallen several months behind on my mortgage. I was tapped out. The decision whether or not to run was now complicated by whether or not I could *afford* to run.

My first thought was that this guy was right. Maybe I should step aside and leave him a clear path to the nomination. I figured I might as well press the point a little. I said, "I have to know one thing. Are you going to challenge a certain party leader's insistence that we only support liberal positions that contradict the party's national platform?"

In my head, this was a pro forma question, to which I fully expected an emphatic, "Of course!" But what I got back instead was . . . well, it was a little weird, a little wishy-washy. This guy started talking about how it was his strategy to "infiltrate the party from within." Then he said, "Once I have a seat at the table I'll be able to reveal my true position."

This struck me as an absurd response, especially considering that he was making it to me of all people. After all, the whole point of my previous campaign had been to stand up for justice on behalf of the conservative Republicans in our state, who had been systematically excluded from party ranks for years. After all, our convictions are not something we should be ashamed of, or have to hide from our very own party leaders.

(Jump ahead to 2010, when this same guy came to a private, off-the-record pastors' meeting where he was seen furiously taking notes, which I'm told he later gave to my opponent.)

I didn't see any merit to this guy's strategy, but underneath I also thought the timing might be off for me to make another run at it, so I told my challenger that I would consider what he had to say. I said, "Whatever happens, you have my word that I won't run unless I absolutely believe it's the right thing for me to do."

That week I attended a screening of a documentary enti-tled *Expelled: No Intelligence Allowed*, hosted and cowritten by Ben Stein, the actor, comedian, commentator, lawyer, and one-time speechwriter for Presidents Nixon and Ford. Since my work on *The Passion of the Christ*, I was invited to a lot of screenings, and this one seemed interesting. It was about what may or may not have been a mainstream conspiracy to keep God out of our science laboratories and our classrooms, and it turned out to be a real game-changer for me. It seemed to echo what I'd just gone through with the whole Life for Lau-ren effort I'd been working on for the previous few months.

The latter half of the movie presents a cogent case for in-telligent design. Intelligient design is the idea that the com-plexity of the universe suggests an intelligent creative force and not a random series of evolutionary events. The filmmak-ers showed historical footage of a hospital in Nazi Germany where Hitler had authorized the systematic killing of the dis-abled. It then showed how in their twisted minds they thought they were helping to create a master race and further along the evolutionary process by exterminating the disabled, as they were doing in this one hospital. (By *no* means am I saying that all evolutionists are Nazis.)

As Stein inspects the present-day site, he asks the woman in charge if she'd ever thought that the sane people were the ones on the operating tables, while the doctors charged with killing them were the ones who were insane. To this, the woman could only shrug her shoulders and disagree, defend-ing these long-dead Nazi doctors, saying they had a purpose, carrying out Hitler's mission.

As I watched this scene, a lump swelled in my throat. It

was wicked how these people could be so heartless, so thoughtless and unfeeling in pursuit of an ideal. I saw echoes in the Byzantine laws on the books in Delaware that allowed the courts to permit the euthanizing of Lauren Richardson only because of her own disability. In the minds of some, this young woman did not deserve to live, simply because it cost too much to keep her alive. Once I made that connection I knew I had to run. These types of laws aren't just in Delaware and their existence is a telltale sign of the growing culture of death in our great nation. I had a chance to stand up for what was right. I had to run.

And, just to drive the point home, Ben Stein ended the movie with a clarion call to viewers to stand up and be counted. He challenged us with a call, echoing Rabbi Hillel, one of the most famous scholars in Jewish history: "If not you, then who? If not now, then when?" Stein reminded us that we *may* pay a heavy price for speaking up. He asks, "If you don't get involved, will anyone be left to carry on this struggle? Anyone? Anyone?"

Sometimes a movie, or a book, or even just a two-line quote speaks to you at just the right moment, saying just the right thing you need to hear and maybe even answering a question.

CHAPTER EIGHT

The Delaware Way

Before I could focus my full attention on a 2008 Senate run, I had to get my own house in order. Literally. For the past couple months, my work with the Life for Lauren effort had been pro-bono, there'd been no money coming in. Consequently, I'd fallen several months behind on my mortgage payments. Even though I chose to make a personal sacrifice in order to help Lauren and her family, I was struggling and found myself in a difficult position, not unlike many families struggling in today's economy. Providentially, I had doubled up my mortgage payments when money was good, and because the value of my home had increased, I had over fifty thousand dollars in equity. That amount could get me out from under the weight of my debts, pay off my mortgage and penalties, and still put away a nice little sum to tide me over for the next while.

So now I had two options: I could sell my house and clear my debts, and possibly even use some of the proceeds as a safety net if I decided to run for office; or I could set politics aside for the time being and take on some new clients, get current on my mortgage, and try to build up my savings. It was a one-or-the-other-type deal. I talked it over with my friends and family because this was not a slam-dunk decision either way. I was torn—really, really torn. It's not like I was seduced by the lure of public office or firm in my conviction that I was the *only* person for the job. At that point, I honestly didn't know if the former supporter-turned-mole, who showed up at my door proclaiming that he was doing God's will, would do a good job of it. In the end, I felt compelled to choose the political road, remembering—among many other things— the hopes, needs, and dedication of the Delawareans who had supported me during the 2006 write-in campaign and now were urging me to run once again.

Despite the strength of my conviction to take the political road, I wasn't so determined to be the next U.S. Senator from the First State that I would seek the nomination at all costs. I would take a more cautious approach. First, I'd challenge my opponent for the convention nomination. If I didn't prevail at the convention, that would be my answer. I wouldn't "primary" him—meaning, I wouldn't force a statewide primary election if he and I were the only two candidates in the field.

Keep in mind, the screening of that Ben Stein movie had taken place in the spring, so I hadn't exactly left myself a lot of time to ramp up before the convention in early May. With his thirty thousand dollar head start, my opponent could afford to mail out full-color tri-fold brochures; we could only send a black-and-white photocopy of a personal letter from me to nominating convention delegates, outlining my desire to run with my goals for the state and for our nation. My opponent had a slick, full-service, superefficient team to send out his mailing. We had what I called "a stuffing party," attended by my large extended family gathered together in a kind of makeshift assembly line. Even my four-year-old nephew joined in, diligently placing stamps on each envelope. At the convention, my opponent passed out professionally printed position papers, done up on glossy, full-color stock; my position paper was a sheaf of single pages, generated on a portable bubble-jet printer in a motel room the night before.

We didn't have bells and whistles, but we had a message, one that we believed in. My team and I would dedicate the few resources we had to getting that message out wisely, reaching as far as we could.

What I hadn't anticipated, though, were the extra efforts that opponents would take to undercut my candidacy. Truth be told, here I'm not referring to the former volunteer who was also seeking the nomination. No, the real dirty tactics flowed from the long arm of the Delaware Establishment, who clearly wanted me to sit this one out. Apparently, I'd already made an enemy of the incumbent Democrat, Joe Biden—one of Delaware's favorite sons (although he's no favorite of mine). He'd been entrenched as our senator since I was a toddler. He ran for president in 1988, as he was doing in 2008 yet again, while at the same time mounting a halfhearted reelection campaign to defend his seat in the U.S. Senate; it was like he wanted to have his cake and eat it too—like the Senate would be a consolation prize if he didn't make it to the White House.

It was that obnoxious sense of entitlement that seemed to permeate the Delaware political machine. Following one of the early 2008 presidential campaign debates, I made the "mistake" of criticizing Senator Biden in an op-ed for a comment he'd made in the debate calling for a no-fly zone in Darfur. I was in my usual role of commentator, and I suggested that as chairman of the Foreign Relations Committee our esteemed senator should be aware that the genocide in Darfur was taking place on the ground, with machetes, in which case a no-fly zone would be perhaps ineffective. The Biden camp ended up clarifying the senator's statement, issuing a retraction of sorts, stating that if our military were to get involved in Darfur, it would have to begin on the ground.

Still, I wonder if Biden's supporters didn't take my remarks as constructive criticism. A couple weeks after I made these comments I was audited. (Really!) Not only that, other people close to me were audited and received notice the same week as I.

Coincidence? Perhaps.

There was another disturbing event that threatened to derail our campaign before it had even begun, but also took the legs out from under the leader of the Delaware GOP—Terry Strine—the guy who'd recruited me to run in 2008 and offered me the party's support if and when I had the field to myself. Well, perhaps somebody thought Terry was guilty by association (guilty of *what*, I have no idea!), because at the very same nominating convention where I ended up winning the nomination, he was unceremoniously ousted from the executive committee. It was a complicated coup orchestrated by the grand dame of Delaware's Grand Old Party, Priscilla Rakestraw, that resulted in Tom Ross as our new party leader. Coincidence? Or, a run of really, really bad luck for those of us on the conservative side of the political spectrum who happened to believe in things like life and liberty, and the pursuit of political office?

I once heard a priest say, "If you're going to love your enemies, you first must have the courage to make some." Let's face it: I was making enemies left and right—and here the phrase had particular meaning for the way I seemed to anger folks on both sides of the aisle, on the left and on the *ostensible* right. It was beginning to feel like nobody from the Delaware political establishment, Republican or Democrat, wanted to see me run. The only folks who seemed to want to hear from me on this were the hard-working, hard-charging volunteers and supporters who'd signed on for the 2006 write-in campaign—which made sense, of course, because they were the very reason I'd decided to make another run.

I focused on the good people who were turning out to show their support, the folks who were inspired by our message, and I came to the conclusion that as long as what we were doing was pleasing *them* . . . well, then that was enough. Heck, it was more than enough; it was plenty.

The exciting thing about that 2008 campaign was that we were out in front of an exciting new movement. People who had never taken part in the political process were standing up and joining us, but the party elite acted like they would have much preferred it if these folks remained on the sidelines. The state GOP didn't lift a finger to help our campaign—kind of odd, don't you think? I mean, here I'd been dutifully nominated by party delegates at our state convention, I had no primary challenger, and there was an infrastructure in place that would have been an enormous help in getting our message out across the state, but it felt to us in the trenches as if our state officials were sitting this one out.

For example, we were assured that the GOP was going to write a fund-raising letter on our behalf, but no one we knew in Republican Party circles had ever received or even seen such a letter. One of our staffers actually found a bundle of letters in a closet at their headquarters, after the election. We thought this was interesting. The letter had indeed been generated, so the party could take itself at its word, but it had never been mailed. It's almost the same thing, right? (Sarcasm intended.)

Meanwhile, Senator Biden was spending $4.9 million on his senate campaign—ads, billboard, staff . . . the whole *shebang*. He was out there shaking hands, kissing babies, doing what he had to do to reinforce the Biden brand across the state, for a full two months before Barack Obama tapped him to be his running mate at the Democratic National Convention in August. And those coattails arguably doubled his statewide expenditures, to an already almost 50 to 1 spending advantage *before* the VP propaganda and earned media blitz. That said, I don't think he spent too much time worried about his reelection—at least, not at first. After all, he was going up against an inexperienced outsider who didn't even have the full support of her own party, while he himself was completing his sixth term and could call on a base of support, so he must have figured this thing would be a cakewalk. But then, he started to act as if he must have figured wrong, because we started to get some ugly reports about his tactics. We heard from quite a few different people who'd been planning to hold fund-raisers on our behalf, who'd received personal phone calls from Senator Biden, urging them to reconsider their support of my candidacy. These calls weren't from members of

Biden's staff, we were told, but from Biden himself. One of our supporters called to tell us of the quasi-demanding phone call he'd received. He couldn't have been more excited to tell us about it. He said, "This is a real compliment, Christine. It means he thinks you're a threat."

Maybe, I thought, but it would have been nice if our esteemed senator could have responded to our threat in a different way.

Keep in mind, Delaware is small, and Delaware's political circle is even smaller. It didn't take more than one or two degrees of separation for it to be known who was helping this would-be intruder on the backroom deals.

Another supporter reported that he'd been visited personally by Senator Biden *and* Representative Mike Castle, our *Republican* congressman (and former two-term governor). Their message was clear: *Don't have this fundraiser.* Our supporter was told in no uncertain terms that there were consequences to going against Biden and Castle. This type of strong-arm politics was to be expected, I guess, but to be undermined by my own party? It was maddening. Everyone working on our campaign was sacrificing, because they believed in our message. People had set aside their jobs and their personal lives to volunteer for us. They thought it was important to stand up against the machine—both the political establishment in our own state, and what was going on at the federal level. They saw that there was a unique opportunity here, and there was. Since I was our party's *endorsed* candidate for U.S. Senate, who just happened to be running against the Democrat's vice presidential candidate, it presented an opportunity for the Republicans. Whether they thought I had a chance against Biden or not, it was an opportunity for another voice to be heard, to speak out about this man's constant gaffes and inconsistencies. Instead, they turned away. Really, our state party demonstrated they were not interested in such opportunities. I found out later, after I made my own connections to the McCain/Palin team, that numerous invitations had been extended my way, only to be rejected by our state party supposedly on my behalf. Of course the messages were never passed on to me.

This looked bad for all of us, to be divided in such a public way. Mississippi Governor Haley Barbour was coming to Delaware for a GOP fundraiser, and of course I wasn't invited. Recall, I used to work for the governor back at the RNC, so I got together with him the day before the event, and as we parted he said, very amiably, "Well, I'll see you tomorrow at the fundraiser."

Caught a little off guard, I said, "Okay, see you then!"

Then I turned to our team and said, "We better find out what fund-raiser he's talking about."

We had to do an end-around to arrange for tickets, but we finally got them, and what happened when I got there was a revelation. Actually, what was most revealing was what *didn't* happen. Our new chairman, Tom Ross, stepped to the platform to introduce Governor Barbour, and in his remarks he acknowledged every party bigwig, every elected official, and every candidate for every conceivable office, all the way down to the state legislature . . . all except me, that is.

It was such a transparent rebuke—and pretty darn insulting, in my own home state, in front of my old boss, a guy who was also being talked about as a future presidential candidate.

Well, Governor Barbour made it right when it was his turn to speak. He didn't have to, but he did; I figured it was because he must have seen what was going on. He stood right up there and gave me my own little shout-out. He said he was grateful to see his old friend Christine O'Donnell in the audience, or words to that effect. He even took it a little further, saying that I'd done a great job back when I worked for him, that the party should be proud to have me as their candidate, and that he had no doubt I'd do a great job in Washington if I was elected.

Normally, when you hear accolades like that at a fundraising event, they're followed by applause, even if it's only perfunctory applause. But here there was mild applause at best. It reminded me of that old Zen koan: *What is the sound of one hand clapping?* It's the same as when people are afraid to applaud because they don't know what kind of grief or backlash might come their way if they do.

All the while, our campaign was making some real progress. Despite the pushback from within our own party, our events seemed to grow bigger each time out. Crowds were more and more enthusiastic. Our offices were being swamped with calls from supporters and volunteers. Clearly, we'd tapped into something the Delaware elites had ignored too long. We knew all along it'd be tough to beat an entrenched politician like Joe Biden, *especially* once he received the vice presidential nod and was elevated to name-above-the-title status, but if everything had broken the right way we had a shot. It might have been a long shot, but it was a shot just the same, and as Election Day approached there were some polls showing that we were closing the gap. In Delaware, it doesn't take a lot to move the needle in a statewide campaign. There aren't a whole lot of us, and the state is small—almost to the point where you *can* shake the hands of each and every voter. I was going to every chicken barbecue, every Latino festival, every parade. We were traveling up and down the state, every day, and the mood of the state seemed to be trending in our favor. We were hearing from conservative Democrats, for example, that they didn't much see the point in voting for Biden *twice*, so we were picking up some support in interesting new places, so much so that on Election Night we found reason to hope against hope.

We had two screens up at our headquarters as we awaited the returns. On one, we were tuned to Fox News, which was streaming news and images from all over the country. On the other, we had the feed from the Delaware Department of Elections Web site, which was reporting our statewide results as they came in, in close to real time. At one point, the results flashed on the Web site showing Biden in the mid 50's and me in the mid 40's. Even though some districts had not yet reported, we were proud we were breaking the 40's. This was darn respectable considering the little over $100,000 we'd raised to Biden's millions. We might have been snubbed by our party, or written off by the liberal media, but we could feel what was happening on the campaign trail; there was a real momentum buildup heading into the election, so these numbers were especially validating. And the good news behind the numbers was that the only one of Delaware's three counties that had yet to fully report results from *all* districts was Sussex County.

Now, Sussex County had been good to us in the 2006 write-in campaign. We had a strong showing in several districts down there and thought this bode well for 2008.

There was this sudden surge of speculation about what might happen if Biden was elected vice-president, but *lost* in his reelection campaign for U.S. Senate. And then, just as our headquarters was filling with possibility, it was like someone pulled the plug on us. Literally. All of a sudden, the state's Department of Elections computers went down. It was the strangest thing. No one in our group could remember such a thing ever happening before. And no one could say with any certainty if this was another one of those head-scratching "coincidences" or just a patch of bad luck. The computers were down for an hour or so, but it felt like forever, and in that time our prospects went from bright to dim to dark. When the computers were back up, and the Web site was once again reporting results, the screen showed that results were now in all over the state, and that Biden had collected 64 percent of the vote to my 36 percent.

We were deflated, defeated. We worked so hard only to be crushed by the Delaware political establishment. And the results came hand-in-hand with the realization that Obama would be elected president, which meant my opponent *wouldn't even serve* the U.S. Senate term he'd just won here at home. It felt like a kick in the stomach, like we'd spent all this time and energy running against a phantom presence.

There were a whole lot of good news/bad news elements to the 2008 campaign (although I didn't really care about them just then). First, the good news: We broke records. We received the most number of votes that anyone had ever collected against Joe Biden in a general election—and here he'd been seeking his seventh term. We made a dent in the status quo, laying a foundation for the future. That, to me, was the true measure of what we'd accomplished. Nobody likes to be stepped on, beaten, or even ignored when they're out there fighting for the greater good, but sometimes you have to take your hits if you hope to make a difference. Here, we'd taken our hits, but we could look back with great satisfaction that our message seemed to resonate with so many people. We'd assembled a core of hardworking, dedicated folks. Now, the bad news: we all had to turn tail and go home. The wind had been knocked out of us, and for weeks after the election I'd hear from our key staff, telling me how dejected they were feeling, how disappointed.

Even I had my doubts. This shook my faith and I began to wonder, *What's the point? Did God send me on a fool's errand?* This result seemed to *prove* the establishment was unshakable; if you dared to challenge them, you'd be crushed. I'd started getting feedback from others saying they were impressed with the 2008 results, especially given all we were up against, but that wasn't much of a consolation. Then, as I was feeling so low, things took a turn for the worse. I was looking at a mountain of bills. The economy took a nose dive, and there were few prospects for income—especially since I'd put my consulting work on hold for so long. New clients were tough to come by. I'd already sold my house before starting on the campaign in order to get on my feet for the Senate run. There was no money coming in, and quite a lot of it had gone out during the campaign.

I still had strong relationships with a number of nonprofit groups that had worked with me in the past, but they had no room in their budgets for a public relations consultant or media strategist. Even if they'd *wanted* to hire me, they couldn't.

Still, I needed work. I couldn't wait for the economy to turn back around. I needed to pay bills. I'm grateful, in fact, that when things got bad for me, I was able to find a job cleaning houses for ten dollars an hour. I did some laundry, some babysitting . . . whatever work I could find to bring in some money.

At the same time, I was rummaging through my closets, selling everything from jeans to jewelry on eBay and Craigslist. My thinking here was that if I could do without, and if someone else might want it, I'd try to sell it. I sold a diamond ring—not an engagement ring, of course, but a really nice ring. I sold a pair of earrings.

My circumstances forced me to reevaluate everything, and break down all of my expenses against my new hourly rate. I asked myself, *Do I really want to wash someone's windows or do their laundry for ten hours, just to get cable?* The answer came back a resounding *no*, so I canceled my service and started using the library. The library offered free Internet access, and for entertainment I could take out DVDs, so it met my basic needs. In a way, this was a good thing, because it broke me of the bad habit of coming home exhausted each night and flipping on the television for some mindless entertainment. Now, I'd spend my time reading or watching a documentary or taking a walk. I became more efficient online, too, because the library limited you to two hours on the computer, so I was careful not to waste time. I concentrated on what was really important: checking all my e-mails, following through on my job searches, and monitoring the online news sources.

I moved into a small apartment to shave my monthly expenses even further. Like a lot of Americans, I had no choice

but to downsize. I sold a bunch of furniture. When I finally ran out of valuables or collectibles to sell, I started combing local thrift stores, hoping to find some hidden gems at a bargain-basement price that I could move on eBay for a small profit. One of my best "finds" was a pair of designer boots that I bought for three dollars and sold online for fifty—a huge pay-day for me.

At one point, I had a kind of epiphany. I was scrubbing someone else's bathroom floor, plagued by an overwhelming sense of failure. I kept thinking, *Why did I even run in the first place?* I couldn't shake this thought. If I hadn't put everything on hold for the campaign, I would have still had a bunch of great clients, or at least more savings to get me through the downturn. I wouldn't have had to sell my house. Then came the epiphany: I'd made all these sacrifices for a reason. I had to tap into what little faith I had left and trust that all things work together for the good, no matter how bleak they seem at the moment. Even if I never ran another campaign, or worked for another political client, I would have added my voice to an important chorus. There was a whole lot of discontent and confusion out there, and we'd tapped into it—at home in Delaware and across the country. We made a start—maybe even a good start, even though we ultimately lost.

We'd paved the way for others to follow.

I wasn't exactly struck down by a thunderclap of clarity. I'd known these things all along, on some level, but it took re-alizing them in just this context—*scrubbing someone else's bathroom!*—for me to get that the 2008 campaign had been a good and noble sacrifice. I was able to lift my head high again and move forward. Of course, I still had no money, no prospects, and no idea what I might do next, but I started going to church again, talking to my supporters, and embracing the fact that our campaign had seemed to kick-start a new dialogue in our state.

Despite winning the vice presidency, Biden did not officially resign his Senate seat until after he'd been sworn in for his seventh term on January 6, 2009, which was allowed by state law. Delaware Governor Ruth Ann Minner, a Democrat, then appointed Ted Kaufman, a longtime Biden aide, to serve as his successor. Kaufman let it be known he would serve only two years, which led to speculation that Beau Biden, the vice president's son, would seek his father's seat in a special election in 2010. My team was not ready to give up, we had a series of small meetings and fundraisers, and then officially filed the paperwork for another Senate run. This was in March 2009, although at that time I still wasn't sure I'd go through with it—in fact, more and more I was thinking I was done with politics.

I was enjoying my low-maintenance lifestyle. I'd destroyed my credit cards, and was trying to live as frugally and simply as possible. In a way, it was cleansing.

I was still going through my audit during this period (part of the cost of doing business as a political challenger in the state of Delaware, I guess). I was meeting regularly with the IRS agent who'd been assigned to my case, and very much mindful that my financial life was no longer my own. Even so, my future opponents saw that I had earned so little that year, they suggested I was *holding out*. They said it was impossible for someone to live on that kind of money.

Little did they know that, coming from a family of eight, I'd been taught by the very best. My mother knew how to stretch a dollar so thin you could see through it. Each week, I'd go to the supermarket with a predetermined amount in cash, no credit cards, and I was careful not to bring along my debit card, so I wouldn't be tempted to go over budget. Then I'd walk up and down the aisles. I'd tell myself, *Okay. You need eggs. You need milk. You need chicken and bread. You don't need Peanut Butter Cap'n Crunch.* What I'd learned from my mom was that you could make a whole chicken go a long way. You could make a chicken salad. You could use the bones to make soup. You could get by on fifteen dollars a week.

In March 2009, I filed my candidacy, but by now I was no longer committed to the idea of running again. In fact, I'd all but set my mind against it, and by late September doors opened for a marketing opportunity in the field of higher education. Politics was about the farthest thing from my mind and I was ready to start a different career in an entirely different direction. But as summer turned to fall, and the 2010 special election was now just about a year away, I started hearing more and more from friends and supporters, urging me to jump-start my campaign.

One late summer afternoon, I sat down with a dear friend, Krystina Hamilton, a young woman I'd gotten to know through a Bible study. After spending so much time together, in such a personal and intimate setting, Krystina knew my heart, so when I filled her in on my latest thinking, that I didn't have it in me to make another run, and that I was seriously thinking about getting out of politics altogether, she didn't comment. Later, she told me that she'd held back because she understood that I needed a break, but that she was sure I was an activist at heart, and that I would come back to it in my own time, in my own way. While I was thinking I would walk away from politics for good, she knew it was only a respite.

Things were looking up for me by now. Money was coming in, albeit in a trickle, but coming in nonetheless. One night as the sun was setting I curled up on my couch to check my e-mail (which I was doing at home once again!). There was a note from my good friend Luke, who had been a strong supporter of my previous campaigns and frequently kept in touch. He was shocked to hear that I was all but certain I wasn't going to run again—stunned, in fact. He insisted that I join him and a political consultant friend in New York. I had nothing else on my calendar, so I splurged on the train fare and headed up to New York the very next day. The three of us talked for hours, while I brought up every obstacle that had been worrying me.

Finally, Luke said, "All I'm hearing from you is excuses."

He was right—and I had a whole bunch more.

At the end of our meeting, Luke shared a cab with me to Penn Station. It was an eventful cab ride—not quite up there on the epiphany scale with my bathroom-scrubbing moment, but close. He said, "Christine, I know the last campaign was tough on you. It took a real toll, and you need time to recover, so take that time. But no matter how bad you're feeling today, you have to know you won't always feel this way. Remember, you started something special. It would be a waste of your hard-earned political capital if *you* weren't the one to complete it. Think how you will feel this time next year when there's a wishy-washy candidate running for that same Senate seat, espousing everything you're against. Your core values, the values we all hold so dear, won't even be a part of the discussion."

Luke's words played over and over in my mind on the train ride home. I leaned my head against the cool glass window and watched the rest of the world whiz by. It was dark and I could see lights on in the homes we passed and I thought of the families inside. So many of them were facing the same financial struggles as I had, but more was at stake for them. They had kids; I was single. There's a big difference. The policies coming from D.C. were only making the economy worse. I thought again about how I would feel this time next year, if no one was speaking up for them. *"You won't always feel this way."*

Instead of going straight home, I stopped to visit my parents in New Jersey. I wanted to run these ideas by them. My father was ecstatic to hear that I was even *considering* another run. He was ready to start making signs and planning rallies right then and there. My mother, though, was less than thrilled. She told me it had hurt her terribly to have to watch me endure what I went through in 2008, and she didn't want to see me sign on for more of the same.

"It's not that I don't think you'd be great or that what you're doing is not important," she said. "But you're my daughter. I just can't watch what they did to you."

She pointed out, wisely, that this time around I wouldn't just be taking on Delaware's political establishment, but the White House, too. She certainly had a point.

That night, I slept at my parents' house, in the bedroom I once shared with my four sisters. Like I'd done so many times before, in that very same room, I knelt by my bed and prayed.

"Dear Lord," I said, "I don't know what to do. I don't ever want to run from a challenge that You have placed before me just because it's hard. If this is something You have called me to do, I promise to see it through. But I need to know that this is the right move. I need the promise that Your strength will be perfected in my weakness and that no matter what happens, everything will work out for the good." My life was taking a new direction. Money was coming in again. Things were looking up. And I'd have to walk away from that if I stepped back in. I crawled back into bed, wrapped myself in the large down comforter, and fell asleep.

The next morning, I stumbled down to the kitchen for coffee. My mother, who always gets up before everyone else, is in the habit of lining up extra mugs for us whenever we stay over—and mine was waiting for me. She'd set out my very favorite, with a picture of the Morton's salt girl twirling her umbrella, which now seemed to have been an omen, because there'd be a rainstorm of allegations and accusations raining down on me and my candidacy before too long.

After my third cup of coffee, I logged on to my parents' dinosaur of a computer to check my e-mail. And—lo and behold!—my in-box was stuffed with notes and comments about a Rasmussen poll that had just been released, showing me within single digits of Beau Biden, the presumptive Democratic nominee, with a two-to-one advantage among the much-needed Independents, and not too far behind Representative Castle, the Republican front-runner.

This was an astonishing result. I hadn't announced any sort of formal campaign. Many Delaware Republicans, as I knew well, were very upset with Castle; I'm not a big fan of labels, but

I must say I enjoyed the one they'd slapped on him. Because of his liberal voting record, they called him the King RINO—a "Republican In Name Only." But the numbers were especially significant because the names "Biden" and "Castle" were constantly pumped in the headlines while I had been working so hard to disappear.

And what's more, Beau Biden's favorable ratings couldn't have been higher as he was the "favored son," nobly fulfilling his duties with the Delaware Army National Guard in Iraq while also serving as the state's Attorney General. One of the e-mails I opened that morning came right to the point: "So when can we have your announcement press conference? I think it should be this week!"

I had almost forgotten my prayer of the night before, but this was my answer, loud and clear.

Meanwhile, there was a middle-class movement taking root in Delaware and in America's heartland, a groundswell that had been jump-started by activists who believed in a reduction of the national debt and the federal deficit and who placed great importance in the time-honored values of God and family and the United States Constitution.

Meanwhile in Delaware, Republican refugees were finding a home in the para-party groups that were forming all over the state. (And by "para" I mean parallel.) In just a short time, these groups were organizing, forming, and building the grassroots network the Republican party no longer maintained.

The Tea Party movement earned its name as bloggers and analysts looked to thumbnail a group of tax revolt–type protests around the country, as voters seemed to rail against the recent bailouts of American banks engineered by the Bush and Obama administrations. And now, in the fall of 2009, as I considered another run, I looked on with great interest as other populist campaigns promised to upend the "business as usual" approach to American politics. Most notably, there was a congressional race taking shape in New York's 23rd Congressional District, in the northern and central parts of the state, where the winner of the Democratic nomination, a Plattsburgh attorney named Bill Owens, was being opposed by Republican state assemblywoman Dierdre Scozzafava (another RINO); there was also a third-party candidate in the field, an area businessman named Doug Hoffman, who had initially sought the Republican nomination before receiving the Conservative Party nod.

This was where things got interesting, because Hoffman's campaign gathered a ton of support and attention, most notably from conservatives across the country who were tired of RINOs who watered down our party. Just before the election, polls were showing Hoffman with a slight lead, and the seat was so important to Democrats that Delaware's own Joe Biden, now as vice president, traveled to Watertown, New York, to campaign for Bill Owens. Suddenly, the weekend before the election, Scozzafava withdrew from the race and threw her support to her *Democratic* opponent, effectively killing Hoffman's chances, but at the same time shining a light on how his independent candidacy had galvanized the Republican Party base in that part of the state and exposed RINOs for their eagerness to abandon party principles on a whim.

Pundits across the country weighed in on the importance of this one contest. I even wrote an op-ed about it called

"Whigged Out Republicans" for the *Philadelphia Bulletin*. In it I stated that the "big tent" of the Republican Party was getting so crowded the pegs were about to pop out and the whole thing would collapse and Republicans would go the way of the Whigs.

New York Twenty-Three seemed to be a harbinger of things to come—as indeed it was, because it was only a couple months later that a little known Republican state senator from Massachusetts named Scott Brown shocked the political world and the whole of New England by coming out of nowhere to win a special election to fill the seat of the late Senator Ted Kennedy. It was a stunning piece of political theater, produced in large part by Tea Party activists in what had traditionally been a Democratic stronghold, and I looked on from my place on the political sidelines and thought, *Hmmm . . . maybe it's time to get the band back together and make another run.*

CHAPTER NINE

Making Trouble

There were two serendipitous tipping points in my decision to finally seek the 2010 Republican nomination for U.S. Senate—the bright, neon signs I'd been looking for that would shine unmistakably and irrefutably as the answer to my prayers.

The first one found me on a plane to Houston. Now that the core group was back together, we were signing up new volunteers a hundred at a time. We had the right parts of the engine, but not the fuel (money) to make it run. So I was headed to Houston for our first major fund-raiser hosted by a fiery redhead named Chari Hust. As I was preparing for the trip the day before, a friend casually suggested I try to meet up with Joanne Herring, a prominent Texas socialite, while I was in Houston. This was easier said than done. Joanne Herring was a well-known, well-connected political activist, and had assumed a significant role in foreign affairs. Julia Roberts portrayed her in the movie *Charlie Wilson's War*. . . . In my mind, this was an inappropriate time to reach out to her. I thanked my friend for the helpful thought and filed it away for a time when I might have a bit more political clout.

The next morning, I took my seat on the plane and cracked

open my copy of *The Wall Street Journal.* There was an article about President Obama's new plan to stimulate the economy and help the environment by creating green jobs. The article really set me off, so I took out my pen and started making furious notes in the margins, dotting my i's with a heavy pen. I wrote a line or two for the remarks I'd have to give later that day, about how the "green jobs" described by the president were merely a code for more government spending, more dependency. "Government doesn't create jobs," I scribbled. "Entrepreneurs and business owners create jobs."

As I looked up from the newspaper for a moment, I made eye contact with the man seated next to me. He smiled and said, "You read the paper quite passionately."

We both laughed, and struck up a conversation. Soon, we'd moved from politics in general to the Delaware U.S. Senate race. My seatmate turned out to be Raza Bokhari, a well-connected political consultant himself, and he knew a good deal about our race back home. After a while, he said, "You know, you should really meet Joanne Herring."

I told him he was the second person in two days to bring up her name.

He said, "There's a reason for that. She's a lot like you. She's passionate about the same things you are."

As it happened—and here's the serendipity part—Raza had a lunch meeting scheduled with Joanne that very afternoon, to talk about the situation in Pakistan, and he invited me to join them. We went directly to her house from the airport, and we hit it off immediately. Raza was right, and so was my friend back home. Joanne and I *were* passionate about many of the same things, and I had to marvel at the happenstance that led to that unlikely visit, and that she would take the time to meet with me, clear out of the blue. Even more exhilarating was her pledge to help my campaign, in what ways she could. She was instrumental in some of my earliest fundraising efforts, introducing me to several key donors. She also introduced us to Mitt Romney and paved the way for his later endorsement, so it really was an invaluable meeting for our campaign.

The second chance encounter found me at another CPAC conference in Washington, D.C., the very same gathering I'd attended as a College Republican that had jump-started my interest in politics. Specifically, it found me at the conference gala where I was seated with Jason McGuire, a good guy I'd come to know over the years as a concerned activist and excellent organizer. As we took our place at our table, Jason asked very generally about my campaign. I hadn't made any kind of formal announcement, so the campaign was still very much in start-up mode. We'd gained some good ground on that trip to Houston, but without the right team in place it made no sense to go forward. There was too much at stake for me to go at it with anything but my best foot forward, and I said as much. I said, "We still need that one piece, someone who knows how to really mobilize a campaign and keep the politics local, but at the same time find a way to balance all of that with this wonderful national movement that's going on across the country."

"Oh," Jason said, almost playfully. "That's all, huh? Kind of a tall order, don't you think?"

"Not really," I said. "That person's out there; I know it. Like whoever helped organize what just happened in New York Twenty-three." Here I'd referenced the grassroots groundswell that had nearly elected Doug Hoffman in the special election this past fall.

"Well, if that's the case," Jason said, still somewhat playful, elbowing the gentleman sitting between us at the table, "this is your guy."

My "guy" turned out to be Matt Moran. Neither one of us knew it just yet, but he would soon become my campaign manager, the final piece in my best-foot-forward strategy. I turned to Matt and said, "Really? You're a campaign strategist?"

As I'd come to know, Matt doesn't talk a whole lot, so he just kind of shrugged and said, "Well, yeah. But I'm trying to get out of politics."

"What campaigns have you worked on?" I asked, trying to move the conversation along.

"New York Twenty-three," Matt responded. We hadn't even gotten our salads yet, and already I knew this was going to be one heck of a dinner.

Chari gave the biggest contribution by sending her firstborn, David Hust, to Delaware to help get things off the ground. And now that Matt Moran was on board, and with a much-needed momentum push from my new friends in Houston, it was time to put my best foot forward, at long last.

Now that we'd assembled our campaign team and were looking ahead to formally announcing my candidacy, I started to realize that my reasons for running were straightforward. They went way beyond the platitudes you sometimes hear from candidates who claim to be running a people's campaign, or who want to breathe some fresh air into our musty old government. In our case, this was all true, but at bottom I was running to give Delawareans back their voice.

Oh, we were out to win this thing, make no mistake—but, as important, we wanted to chip away at the roadblock that had been in our path for far too long. Significantly, that road-block was personified in the candidacy of Mike Castle, our nine-term congressman and former two-term governor who now meant to fill the U.S. Senate seat that had been occupied by Joe Biden for generations. For a time, it had appeared that the vice president's son Beau would be the front-runner for the seat once held by his father, but Biden had recently an-nounced he'd sit this one out. A botched pedophile prosecu-tion case as our States Attorney General reportedly forced him out of the race. (And incidentally, for his 2010 reelection, the Delaware GOP never ran a candidate against him . . . nor even fielded a candidate. Doug Campbell, a third party candi-date with virtually no money and no party backing was able to garner a respectable 21 percent. Can you imagine what could have happened if the Delaware GOP had made an effort?)

All this would certainly cast Representative Castle as the new early favorite. Yet more and more, people began to look at the too-long political career of Mike Castle as the textbook ex-ample of the career politician, and in this case, one who con-sistently undermined his own party's national platform. Many felt he seemed to be more concerned with the Delaware Good Ol' Boys Club than his constituents, to the point where he now stood as a kind of impediment to what should have been our true platform. Our own polling, which was consistent with Rasmussen and other respected polling outfits, showed that

Delaware independent voters tend to line up on the center-right. Issue by issue, they were aligned with Republicans far more than they were with Democrats. This was significant, because in the First State, there are almost as many independents as there are Republicans. So, if the Republican Party ran a candidate for statewide office with a platform true to the national party's own platform, and then orchestrated an effort to educate voters on those issues, the party could win over all those independents.

But Mike Castle had voted with the Democrats well over fifty percent of the time, on major initiatives. So if the party educated voters on these major initiatives, they'd be indicting Castle, not just the Democrats. Keep in mind, Delaware has only one congressman and for nearly twenty years, that was Mike Castle. So more often than not, Castle stood in the way of a successful Republican agenda in our state.

My thinking was, *Hey, let's honor and respect Mike Castle for his dedicated service, but at the same time let's call him on his record.* Going by his voting record and his stated positions on the barometer issues of the day, if he prevailed in the primary, it would essentially mean we'd have a choice in the general election between a Democrat and a Democrat-lite.

His presence on the ballot would have been destructive in our efforts to seat true Republican candidates in other races across the state. And more important, in the effort to reform the Delaware Republican Party, his presence in the Senate would have made things even worse. How? Well, when one of our Democratic officials would vote for a tax policy that hurt small businesses, the state Republican party would be hamstrung in its ability to speak out against it; they couldn't raise awareness on this issue, or harness support for an opposing view, because their own de facto party leader would have voted the same way.

Let's face it, having Mike Castle in place for as long as we had, with him leaning so far to the left for as long as he had, made it difficult for other Republicans in our statewide efforts. Every election cycle, we were losing races that might have gone our way in a different political climate. For the longest time, Delaware had been a kind of safe haven for conservatives. Governor Pete du Pont, Mike Castle's predecessor as governor, had been a great conservative Republican, and our state thrived on his watch. (Even liberal Delawareans would concede this point.) Senator Bill Roth, the man who gave us the Roth IRA, offered another strong conservative voice and vision. But since those two giants had left the political scene, we'd started giving away a whole bunch of elections; it'd been a real downward spiral, to the point where good candidates weren't even putting themselves up for election anymore, because they didn't see the point in fighting an entrenched establishment that seemed to want nothing to do with them.

That's precisely why I was running.

The 2010 campaign would be marked by an endless parade of confounding, head-scratching moments, dirty tactics from within my own party, and boldfaced lies and distorted truths that were hurled at me from all sides and would end up overshadowing our message—which I suppose was the whole point of their efforts.

From the very beginning—or, at least, from the moment our campaign was seen as some kind of threat to certain segments of the Republican establishment—certain party leaders rolled up their sleeves, gnashed their teeth, and came looking for me. I'd already set off our state party leadership with my 2006 and 2008 campaigns, but here it looked like I was about to ruffle even bigger feathers, on an even bigger stage.

Enter Karl Rove. Say what you will about Karl Rove, but he's no conservative, not in my book. As the architect of George W. Bush's presidential campaign, he deserves a nod for returning the White House to the Republican column, but from where I sat he was the chief RINO in the Bush administration. Since resigning from the Bush White House, he'd passed himself off as a conservative political analyst, trying to fool the faithful into believing he'd been one of us all along—with only mixed results.

I greatly admire President Bush as a leader with the courage to defend his country and to stand for his convictions . . . *most of the time.* But liberal influences within his own administration, led at times by Karl Rove, severely tarnished Bush's legacy among true Constitutionalists, and undermined our Republican-led Congress. Of course, the problem didn't begin or end with Karl Rove; dozens of moderate Republicans were also to blame, including Delaware congressman Mike Castle. Make no mistake, it was Karl Rove's camp that pushed amnesty for illegal aliens, and cut deals with liberal Democrats for overspending and for ever-expanding regulation. It was Karl Rove's style of Machiavellian, unprincipled realpolitik that destroyed the Republican brand. No question, one of the key factors behind the GOP loss of Congress in 2006 was the widespread disgust among conservatives with Rove's policies.

In December 2009, Karl Rove came to Delaware to do what he could to get Mike Castle elected—and to bury my campaign in the process. Rove invited Tea Party leaders to a closed-door meeting in Dover and headlined a fund-raising event for the Delaware GOP at the Baywood Country Club. Among the attendees of the closed door meeting was Russ Murphy, one of the leaders of the 9–12 Delaware Patriots, a grassroots advocacy group in our state that was founded to recapture the patriotic fervor that swept the country in the immediate aftermath of September 11, 2001. Russ reported that the meeting was little more than an opportunity for Karl Rove to thump his chest and "bloviate." At some point in the middle of his self-congratulatory remarks, Rove found time to urge the Patriots and Tea Party supporters in attendance to get behind Mike Castle in the upcoming Senate race, arguing that no other candidate could win in a general election. He didn't single me out—*that* would come later—but he made an emphatic point of saying that it was Castle's "turn" to run.

A lot of folks in that closed-door meeting tried not to chuckle, because Karl Rove seemed to have no clue that Castle's long tenure as part of the establishment was a big fat negative in the eyes of our state's true activists. In their estimation, and in mine, Castle's long tenure had been a little too long, and it had lately taken a decidedly liberal turn; rather than *qualify* him for the U.S. Senate, his "established" liberal voting record seemed to *disqualify* him in the eyes of many.

Rove's slap was more of a roadblock than an attack—but whatever you called it, it was the first obstacle of many facing our campaign. At the event at Baywood, Rove gave an impassioned speech about how, after the primary, we all needed to unite around the victor, regardless of how we'd felt before the primary. Over and over he stressed how crucial it would be to put our differences aside immediately after the winner was announced and band together to ensure that the primary winner would be elected in November.

I turned to Jason O'Neil, who was sitting to my left, and said, "That's good to hear. We're going to need him!" And he smiled and nodded in agreement.

Later that month, I began to hear reports of false and intentionally harmful comments being tossed my way by other Republican insiders. Some of these had more bark than bite to them, but I'd be bitten soon enough. By January 2010, before my official announcement event, I started getting phone calls from fair-minded reporters, whispering that the Delaware GOP was circulating a thick file on me, carefully highlighted to reveal dozens of apparent transgressions. Among these, I would soon learn, was a false claim that I lost my house in Wilmington to foreclosure, as well as a false report of a tax lien on that same property.

The file was filled with one outrageous lie after another, and I couldn't counter them quickly enough. Any reporter who took the time to look into any single allegation could see it for what it was—a fabrication. I hadn't lost my house to foreclosure. I didn't lose it in a sheriff's sale, as was also suggested. I'd fallen behind on my mortgage, and *chose to sell it* so I could pay off my loan and any accumulated penalties. The sale transaction was part of the public record, available for review by any journalist or concerned citizen.

Yes, it was certainly true that I was being audited. But the audit was *still going on* when these allegations first surfaced. As anyone who's ever been audited can attest, these things take time. There had been no final determination in my case. The people circulating this false information on me were just trying to kill my campaign right out of the gate, but I wouldn't go down without a fight.

While these charges were first breaking we heard from a well-known Republican Party activist who had been a friend of the campaign. He himself ran for office later that year and became a target of the Delaware GOP, but at the time he simply wanted us to know the extent of the crusade against me. He said, "The Delaware GOP is going around telling us that if we get behind you, our funding will be cut." And the threat was not only directed at my supporters; it was aimed squarely at me. Our friendly informant went on to tell us that my opponents were out to mess with my head, to mess with my reputation, to mess with my credit—only he used a much uglier word than "mess" to get his point across. He said, "If you go forward with your official announcement, they said they're gonna mess with you so bad, you'll never be able to run for office again. Not only that, by the time they're done with you, you're gonna be so toxic, you'll never even be able to get a job again."

So we moved up my May announcement to March to smoke them out and see what they had. Immediately following my official press conference, I received a letter from the IRS saying I had a tax lien on my home—the very same home I had sold two years earlier. A reporter called, saying she had received a copy of that same letter, on the same day I received it. Her response to how she got it so quickly was simply that she was "a good little reporter."

So I started making some calls to see what this supposed lien was all about. I followed up with the IRS agent assigned to my case, to find out the latest on my audit, and was told that my file was still under review. H&R Block had prepared my taxes for the year I was being audited. As a precaution, I'd sprung for H&R Block's audit protection program. They called it "Peace of Mind" insurance, but as a standard audit turned into a tax lien, I had no such thing.

The false reports of a tax lien on my home were curious, and more than a little troubling, because I no longer owned a home. In this way, and in so many others, the claims in the file being circulated to reporters made no sense. How could there be a tax lien when I didn't even own the property? How could there be a lien when the audit wasn't even completed? It was an absurd charge, but I wanted to try to get to the bottom of it, so I put in another call to an IRS representative. I walked him through these latest charges, and he assured me that it was simply a "computer error" and that it would be corrected. There was no lien and the letter had been generated "accidently."

Ultimately, the IRS audit determined that I owed approximately $1,100 in back taxes and penalties, which I promptly paid—however, false stories circulated for the rest of the campaign claiming I owed $11,000, ten times the actual amount. Inevitably, once one reporter saw that higher figure in print, other reporters down the line would invariably pick up on it. It's like that childhood game of telephone, where one misheard remark gets passed to the next person in line, and by the time you get to the end of the line the things being said have very little to do with what was said at the outset.

Karl Rove appeared to be leading the charge against me on this front, going on national television even after the primary, demanding that I "explain" why I had not paid my taxes. In fact, I *had* paid my taxes in full, both at the time of my original filing and the amount tacked on at the end of the audit. The audit had been a nuisance audit to begin with, and after three years the IRS could only come up with $1,100 in additional fees and penalties, which I promptly paid. But Karl Rove continued to ignore the facts and the supporting documentation I'd dutifully posted on my Web site.

The thing about political campaigns is that once these kinds of charges are thrown at you, they're like a red wine stain on a white carpet. You can't get rid of them, even if you're able to dismiss them one by one as fabrications and exaggerations. The cumulative effect can be damaging, damning. We supplied all kinds of documentation to reporters who'd run the original negative stories; we even included a copy of my canceled check to the IRS together with a receipt confirming that my bill had been paid in full, but nobody printed a retraction. I also made available copies of the statements from the IRS that detailed the fact that the erroneous tax lien had been a computer error. But those never made it into any follow-up accounts, so I started letting people know that I'd sold the house in question in 2008, to indicate conclusively that there could be no pending tax lien.

(And just to be clear, if there *had* been a lien on the house back in 2008 the sale would have never gone through.)

It rankled me to see myself painted as a criminal by my own party. And yet throughout the campaign the GOP leadership went out of its way and bent its own constitution to undermine my candidacy and leave voters with the impression that my picture should be plastered in post offices across the state beneath a big "Most Wanted" banner. During the campaign, the Delaware Republican Party savagely attacked my character, impugned my integrity, and falsely reported my actions. But I wasn't the only one under attack. The real victims were the Republican voters and the state's true activists. When Karl Rove, Mike Castle, Delaware GOP Chairman Tom Ross, representatives from the National Republican Senatorial Committee, and other party leaders came looking for me, these good people ended up in the critics' sights as well. This wasn't only about me; it was about *them*.

It was about *us*.

The entrenched party establishment didn't want GOP voters to have a voice on this one. They wanted to tell them how to vote. And now, as I look back at the unconscionable, bull-headed tactics of my *esteemed* colleagues on this, I can't shake thinking that it's this type of behavior—the politics of personal destruction—that discourages good candidates on both sides of the aisle from getting involved in our political system. Think about it: How would you like to be labeled a criminal, for the simple crime of running for office and trying to change America for the better?

Even after I lost the general election, Karl Rove was still beating the drums for all who'd listen, telling everyone I was a tax cheat and a deadbeat. Even though we sent all the documentation over to his office with a cover note telling him to stop saying I owed the IRS money, and to stop saying there was a tax lien on my house, he just ignored the truth.

At this late date, it was pretty much a moot point, but it made my skin crawl to have to watch this guy make the rounds on the talk shows, spreading these malicious lies even after the election was over, even after we'd beaten back each and every charge. He was like a Chihuahua who wouldn't let go.

Ah, but I don't mean to get ahead of the story of the 2010 campaign. I just needed to vent, I guess. (And, if you'll indulge me a bit later on in these pages, I promise to vent some more.) As it played out, these trumped-up charges were just the tip of the spear being hurled repeatedly at me by my own party, but there was also a full-on assault of slings and arrows unleashed by the media. Some of these were the results of my decade old words that were now being used against me. The first and best example of this was the comment I'd made some ten years earlier to comedian Bill Maher on his ABC-TV talk show *Politically Incorrect*, which led to one of the most bizarre pieces of political theater in recent memory.

The fallout from this one appearance threatened to overshadow my entire campaign. Recap: On the night of the Republican primary, Bill Maher appeared on CNN's *Larry King Live* to talk politics and whatnot. That night, I should point out, CNN was one of the first networks to officially "call" the Delaware U.S. Senate primary, so the conversation naturally turned to our campaign. Bill took the opportunity to slam some of my views; however, he also seemed to go out of his way to say nice things about me personally, reaffirming my belief that we were friends. Our "friendship" had grown out of a series of regular appearances I'd made on Bill Maher's late-night talk show more than a dozen years earlier, and ran to several events and promotional appearances I'd made on behalf of the show.

One of these extracurricular appearances stands out in my memory. For a brief while, Bill took his show on the road, doing a staged version of *Politically Incorrect* on college campuses around the country. Like many of Bill's so-called regulars, I agreed to participate, and one night things got a little ugly. A student started to heckle me during the Q & A portion of the show, and Bill rallied to my defense. He told the student that he was being rude, that I had been invited to this stage as *his* guest to speak my mind and share my views. Bill said he would not allow the audience to be rude to his guests. But the heckling student didn't seem to care. He just chuckled, rolled his eyes, and mumbled something like, "Whatever . . ." Then he proceeded to ask his question. Bill jumped right back in and cut him off. He told this kid that he'd lost his privilege to ask a question, and to step away from the microphone that had been set up in one of the aisles. Once again, the student chuckled and rolled his eyes, so Bill became even more adamant. He said, "Step away from the mic, young man. You will not be asking a question!"

Finally, reluctantly, the rude student stepped away, in a snotty huff.

Up on stage, I leaned over to Bill and whispered, "You *are* a gentleman!"

He whispered back, "Don't let it get out."

And so you can see why I might have felt fondly toward

Bill, and had reason to assume the feeling was mutual, which was why I agreed to appear on his HBO show right after the primary. I got an e-mail from his producer inviting me on, but I was booked at other events on the few dates she'd suggested, so I sent her a return e-mail and put her in touch with our press staff and assured her we would get something on the schedule as soon as possible.

Jump ahead to that Friday, September 17, three days after our primary win over Mike Castle and all the national media attention and speculation that came with it, and Bill Maher had a new show, HBO's *Real Time with Bill Maher.* We'd been told he was planning to address my candidacy in some way, so I tuned in, assuming that we were in for a dig or two but that overall the tone of Bill's remarks would be respectful and funny.

We were all in for a big surprise—and it wasn't a happy one. Bill led his show making some snide comments about my campaign and me, repeating some of the half-truths and full fabrications that had swirled around our effort since the beginning. I was stunned. More than that I was hurt, because it felt like a betrayal. No, Bill and I had never hung out, or exchanged texts or e-mails. (That said, we *did* exchange Christmas cards for a couple years, back when I'd been a semiregular on his ABC show.) By this point, though, we'd been in each other's swirl for a good long while, and spent a substantial amount of time in each other's company, and I'd thought we were friends. At the very least, we'd been colleagues, with a good working relationship. That's why I'd tuned in—and, frankly, it's why I turned off the television before Bill even finished his monologue.

It turned out I missed all the fireworks, because what happened next set the tone for the rest of our campaign—and not in a good way. Bill jokingly told his viewers that he would show a clip of me from our old *Politically Incorrect* days each week until I came on his show. He put it out there like a joking threat, like he'd hold this forgotten footage of me hostage until I met his demands and agreed to debate the issues on his program.

(Incidentally, I got the following text from a friend as the first clip hit the air before the you-know-what hit the fan: *OMG! . . . your HAIR!?!?* I had to laugh, because my hair was big and curly, but in my defense this was before I'd discovered the ceramic straightening iron.)

When I heard about this "threat" afterward, it struck me as just an extended bit—it was a *comedy* show, after all. In fact, I only heard of it indirectly at first, as reporters chased after me with their microphones, asking me if I was planning to cave to his pressure and debate him on his show. I'd already agreed to do Bill's show, but that was before he'd taken this childish turn. Now that he was insulting me, I was of course having second thoughts. And, now that he was *threatening* me, those second thoughts were running into thirds and fourths.

That first clip he showed was from an appearance I'd made back in October 1999, where I mentioned the now infamous blind date I'd once had.

Back in 1999, nobody had seemed to care, but now that I'd just become the Republican U.S. Senate candidate from Delaware, they would care a great deal, and the clip was played and replayed all over the Internet, and on media outlets all over the world, leading to the strange sequence of events I've been doling out in small doses throughout the book.

But again, I am getting ahead of myself. Back to the preprimary campaign.

Each week, it seemed, we were kicking things up a notch. More and more people were turning out for our events. However, we weren't quite where we needed to be in terms of our media coverage. Yet, underdog outsider-challenger candidates across the country appeared to be gaining ground against entrenched candidates in their local House and Senate races. We knew it was only a matter of time before some of the positive attention that had been attached to *those* campaigns would attach to *ours*.

It did soon enough.

On a gorgeous summer evening in late June, I was driving back to headquarters with a young woman named Molly Griffin, our summer intern. We'd thought we were done for the day, but then a call came in from "the Batcave," which was what we called our headquarters. Apparently, Mike Castle had just cast one of only two Republican votes for the so-called Disclose Act, a bill that had been presented as a measure to protect free speech but was effectively a grassroots gag-order. Even worse, this bill had what I called an Establishment Protection Clause. Any group over ten years old with over one million members was exempt from the bill's restrictions. So basically, if you already played the "I'll scratch your back, you scratch mine" game, you didn't have to comply.

Mark Levin, a national talk radio host, was furious and

had just called to invite me on his show as Castle's opponent to discuss the issue.

It was a thrilling opportunity—and, with Mark Levin's widespread and loyal following, it was just the kind of "pop" our campaign needed.

The only problem with this request was that we needed to do the interview immediately. As in *right away*. Mark's show was broadcast live in certain parts of the country, and this was breaking news, so Molly pulled the car over to a safe spot while I quickly dialed the number to the production studio. It didn't matter to us that we were in a car, on a cell phone; we couldn't let this opportunity pass. To anyone who happened to pass by, it might have looked like we were having car trouble, and that I was on the phone with AAA, while in reality I was broadcasting my views and concerns to millions of radio listeners all over the country.

Meanwhile, Molly fired up her laptop and popped in her mobile Internet receiver, in case I needed her to access any facts or figures from the Internet to support my positions, but if you've ever tried to search the Web with one of these devices, you'll know it's not able to retrieve information fast enough to keep pace with a live radio interview. Still, it was an impressive measure of Molly's preparedness that she even thought to try.

It turned out I didn't need any Internet support. It was easy for me to challenge Mike Castle on his vote because I believed he was on the wrong side of this issue, and after a lively discussion with Mark Levin, and several calls from listeners, we ended the interview.

As I pressed the button on my phone to end the call, I

looked across the front seat to Molly and said, "That was fun, huh?"

By the time we got back to the Batcave, Krystina and David Hust were rushing out to meet us. They had some great news they couldn't wait to share. In the few minutes it had taken us to drive from that spot on the side of the road back to headquarters, we'd received more than twelve thousand dollars in online donations from Mark Levin's listeners. It was a crazy number for a bare-bones campaign like ours, and we were all jumping up and down with excitement. Realize, twelve thousand dollars might not seem like a lot for a U.S. Senate race, but in a small state like Delaware it takes fewer votes to win a U.S. Senate *primary* than it does many county council *general elections*. Even though Castle raised over a million dollars at this point, this twelve thousand dollars was meaningful money to us—enough, certainly, to help us sway a lot of voters.

That night, as Mark Levin's show continued to roll out across the country through different time zones, the online donations kept rolling in. By the next morning, the total was approaching thirty thousand dollars, the precise amount we needed for the first of many direct voter outreach efforts. But it was not just the financial boost that made the Levin program a turning point in our campaign; it was the opportunity to be heard by so many fellow Delawareans. Up to that point, our race against Mike Castle had received scant media attention. Many Republican voters didn't even know there was a primary. How could they? The Delaware GOP certainly wasn't telling anyone. (Just to give you an idea of the power and reach of a national radio interview, a Rasmussen poll released shortly after my impromptu appearance on Mark Levin's program showed me in the lead in the November general election against the Democratic candidate.)

As a direct result of that interview, one of Mark Levin's listeners called our office to offer his support. His name was Bill Barron, and he organized what turned out to be the largest meet-and-greet of our entire primary campaign. It was a standing-room-only affair, as more than one hundred of Bill's friends and neighbors crowded into Bogey's Restaurant in Middletown, which probably put us over the legal capacity of the room—but if the fire marshal came by to issue a summons, we would have found a way to recruit him to the cause, too.

I discovered early on that I loved events like this one—small enough to have a chance to meet everyone who'd taken the time to turn out, but large enough that you could really feel the energy and excitement about what we were trying to do. At events like this, I always made it a special point to stay to the very end, to be sure I had a chance to talk to every single voter, only on this night the last straggler wasn't even old enough to vote!

It was a fourteen-year-old boy named Anthony, and he'd been waiting until the room cleared out so he could talk to me one-on-one. He came over to introduce himself, and told me his father ran a chicken farm in New Castle County. "It's my dream to run that family farm someday," Anthony said, "but if the death tax is reinstated in January, and anything ever happens to my father, I won't be able to do that."

I was astonished to hear a young man talk so knowledgably, so passionately about an issue that was very much on the minds of Delaware voters. It saddened me that a kid like

Anthony—and let's face it, he was certainly a kid—had to worry about this sort of thing. I even said as much. I said, "You should be worrying about girls and grades, not about losing your family farm."

He said, "You're right, I should. But this is important to us."

It was important to me, too, and I explained to Anthony that I had always been opposed to this unfair tax and wanted to see it permanently eliminated. I assured him that I would move it from a plank in my platform to a top priority of the campaign agenda, and from that night on I looked for ways to keep this issue out in front of voters. Soon, I heard a story to rival Anthony's. Two young people came up to me at a rally and shared their grandfather's struggle. He'd spent his entire life sacrificing and working hard to build a family business that he could pass on as a legacy to his children and grand-children. The business was more than a job for family mem-bers—it represented decades of overcoming hardship; all those late nights and sacrificed vacations. Now the grandfa-ther was seriously ill, and was worried that if he died after January 1, 2011, there was no way his heirs could pay the in-heritance tax that was due to be reinstated on that date. They'd be forced to sell the business just to pay the tax.

These two grandchildren, clearly pained by what they were about to share, confessed that their grandfather was planning to kill himself before the end of the year to avoid the tax. This chilled me to the core. I wanted to cry, for what these good people were facing. It was unconscionable, really. I mean, this hardworking family man had already paid taxes on the money he earned each year; he paid taxes on the money that had been generated by saving that money; and now because he was successful in his business and doing well for himself, the estate tax (death tax) would be so great his family would have to sell the business in order to pay it.

It's *triple* taxation—and it's just plain wrong—and yet I don't share this story here because it packs such an emotional wallop. Yes, it's heart-wrenching, but I mention it here for two reasons. For one, it shows how our tax policies are crippling the American Dream that if you work hard and save responsibly, anyone from any background could create a better life for his or her family. Now, it's nearly impossible to both turn a profit and pay taxes.

The second reason is that this story illustrates one of the great lessons of direct campaigning. By talking with people as much as possible, and by listening to every last story and every last concern, you keep yourself open as a candidate to what *really* matters to your constituents. It's easy for politicians to forget that our policies and positions have a direct impact on the lives of real people—hardworking Americans who count on us to do the right thing by them and their families. These encounters are an important reminder of this, and here I was inspired to dig deeper into the changes that we could expect in our tax code and to do what I might be in a position to do about it as a U.S. Senator.

One of the telling things I learned about the death tax, by the way, came from a quote one of my staffers found on the IRS Web site, describing the perceived societal value of an inheritance tax: "The purpose of this tax is to raise revenue and redistribute wealth in order to prevent the concentration of wealth."

Sound familiar? It's almost a direct quote from the tenets of Marxism, which aim to abolish all rights to an inheritance.

As we looked ahead to the primary in September, we knew we were facing an uphill slog. We were gaining in the polls and on the issues, but Mike Castle had the name recognition. Unfortunately, party leaders were able to circumvent the local media in a great many areas of campaign coverage, creating the impression among voters that there wasn't even a contested race. Everywhere we turned, the talk of the campaign was all about Mike Castle and Chris Coons, the New Castle County executive who was now the Democratic Senate nominee.

These guys loomed as our name-brand competition, and their parties' "anointed" candidates, and it was generally assumed by pundits and analysts and armchair voters that Castle would clean the floor with us in the primary. Judging from some of the press accounts from the early part of the campaign, it might have appeared that Castle had the field all to himself. Still, we were gaining momentum all summer, heading into the all-important Fourth of July weekend. In Delaware, this meant wall-to-wall parades—starting with two or three on July 2, and stretching all the way to five or six parades by July 4.

In a state the size of Delaware, the events are all staggered in such a way that a candidate can make it to almost all of them, if he or she is so inclined.

Believe me, we were absolutely so inclined.

My friend Krystina Hamilton, who was now our volunteer coordinator was single-handedly coordinating our parade effort, putting together all the directions and information packets and making sure the volunteers all had their passes. The tradition at these parades in Delaware, as elsewhere, is for candidates to give out candy to kids (and sweet-toothed adults!) along the route. Well, we decided that for these Fourth of July parades we'd give out "the good candy." We didn't have a whole lot of money, but the incremental cost of stepping up a couple notches on the candy front was hardly significant, so we thought it'd be a nice touch. We thought if we could stand out to the kids, we'd stand a better shot of making a good impression with their parents.

"The bad candy," just so you know, typically takes the form of hard mints. It's not that the candy is actually "bad," mind you, but who the heck wants it? Those hard mints are something you'd find in your grandmother's purse. We wanted to give out something these kids would clamor for, so Krystina went out and bought a bunch of packets of Swedish Fish and Sour Patch Kids. We took the time beforehand to put our campaign stickers on the packaging. It was a real labor-intensive effort, but that's the sort of thing you do in a grassroots campaign. You roll up your sleeves and have at it.

Krystina bought more than a thousand packets of candy, which we thought would cover us for the first day of parades, at least. But we blew through our inventory on the very first parade. The candy was a big hit! We'd hear kids running up and down the route on their sugar rushes, shouting, "Look! I got Swedish Fish from Christine O'Donnell!"

They were so, so excited—and so were we, because this was turning out to be an effective (and *cost*-effective) attention-getter for us.

After that first parade, we went to the nearest BJ's wholesale market and snapped up another five hundred or so dollars' worth of the stuff, and then to a Staples, because we'd run out of stickers. The guy at Staples turned out to be a supporter, and he put a rush on our order. That night we were back at it, putting our stickers on five thousand packets of candy. We were up until well past midnight—including the candidate!—even though we had to be at our first parade lineup at six o'clock the following morning.

But here's where we realized we'd stumbled across a good thing with our "good candy" strategy. By the next morning the Castle campaign was handing out their own yellow packages of Swedish Fish, with their own stickers on them. And the thing of it is, his lineup assignment was ahead of ours, so it looked like *we* were copying *him*! We were trumped, but it didn't matter. For that first parade, anyway, we'd had better candy, we had more volunteers, we generated more excitement. And now they'd hopped on our candy bandwagon and made it seem like they'd been there along, but *we* knew the truth. *We* knew the real story—and we had to think, in some way, our supporters knew it too.

Unfortunately, not all of our giveaway ideas were so successful. It was a constant puzzle, to try to come up with clever souvenir-type handouts we could distribute at all these different events. Chicken barbecues, livestock festivals, 5K road races . . . you couldn't show up at one of these things empty-handed, so we were always trying something new. Once, we tried a little too hard. It was the heat of summer, and someone (namely, *me*!) had the good idea to rekindle something we'd successfully done in 2008—giving out small packets of sunblock. Clever, right? Especially when we had printed on them:

"Don't get burned by higher taxes! Vote O'Donnell for U.S. Senate."

Unfortunately, we were a little too clever on this one, because this time around the packets of sunblock looked like packets of condoms. At least, that's what we were told . . . by more than one person, *way* more than one person. We were a little red in the face over our miscalculation, I'll admit, as if we were the ones who had gotten sunburned.

As we gained momentum leading up to the primary, the "ruling class" of the Republican Establishment tried to kill it by pushing the argument that I was a two-time loser and that even if I did defeat Castle I couldn't win the general election. My supporters disagreed and countered that the argument was cynical and self-defeating. This is best expressed by Jeffery Lord, a former Reagan White House political director, who wrote at this point in the campaign:

> *It must be said here that the reason Ms. O'Donnell is a "two-time loser" is that she had the guts to take on up-hill Senate races in the first place. Where was Mike Castle when it was time to challenge Democrat incumbent Senator Tom Carper in 2006? Where was Castle when it was time to challenge Biden in 2008—when Biden was playing the Ruling Class game and had a ballot spot for both reelection to the Senate and on Obama's ticket as vice president? Answer? Not running. Why? Because the man who so much wants to be a United States Senator from Delaware didn't want to mar his reputation with a*

loss—thus enabling some Ruling Class writer to de-scribe Castle as a "two-time statewide loser." Such things are important in Ruling Class circles, and the fact that O'Donnell paid no heed and took on Delaware's political goliaths Carper and Biden any-way is a sign of Country Class guts.

So too is the treatment of mistakes or personal problems treated differently, a Ruling Class trait that dates at least since the so-called "Nixon's Fund" issue of 1952. The fact that Democratic nominee Adlai Ste-venson had a similar fund (in which contributors paid for political travel expenses and the like) was a big no-deal to the Ruling Class. It was Nixon who had the "scandal" and was forced to go on national television to save his candidacy. This trait has sur-faced repeatedly since. Ruling Class candidates can catch a pass for everything from Chappaquiddick (Ted Kennedy) to the Keating Five (John McCain and John Glenn) to plagiarism (Joe Biden) to question-able financing of real estate deals (Obama)—and hey, no problem. If you're Christine O'Donnell or any other Country Class candidate, this is used as an example of un-electability if not bad character or worse. The interesting fact that her tax problems with the IRS says bad things to the Ruling Class and is seen as yet one more sign of an average American's struggles with government is a decided telling point in the dif-ference in perception between Ruling Class and Country Class.

When people like Jeffrey Lord and Pat Buchanan fired back at the establishment, it was like they'd shot a bazooka at an advancing tank and caused others to take notice as this battle played out. This led to the anticipation over when, whether, or if we might receive an endorsement from Sarah Palin, who by that point, nearly two years removed from her own vice presidential run, was treated like a rock star on the Tea Party circuit. A thumbs-up from Sarah would have carried a whole lot of weight among primary voters in our state, so we had our fingers crossed—but it's not like we could twiddle our thumbs and just sit back and wait for the former governor to get around to it. We had a campaign to run.

Toward the end of August, it looked like we'd finally have a chance to meet. There was a big Glenn Beck rally being planned for Washington, D.C. They were expecting as many as a million people on the Mall, and there were all these tie-in events and meetings. Matt and I had spoken with Todd Palin, who was running interference for his wife at the time, and he was helping us schedule a meeting in D.C., connected in some way to the rally. However, we kept hitting one snag or another. We were also working with Pam Pryor, one of Sarah Palin's political advisors, trying to get something going.

And so, we had every reason to be hopeful, and we arranged for tickets to a VIP breakfast, where Sarah Palin was scheduled to speak. The tickets were set aside for us by Meredith Iler, one of the movers and shakers I'd met in Houston, and the plan was for her to meet us there and hand us our tickets and escort us inside.

Matt and I arrived at the breakfast about a half hour early, but there was no sign of Meredith. As the breakfast was about to start, there was still no sign of her. The volunteers at the registration table said to go ahead and wait inside the room until our tickets arrived.

After a couple minutes, a pleasant-seeming gentleman sidled up to me and said, "Um . . . excuse me?"

Right away, I jumped to conclusions and thought there was some new problem with our tickets. "We have tickets to this event," I started to explain. "It's just that we don't actually *have* them on us."

"That's not it," the gentleman said. "I just stopped you to say hello. You're Christine O'Donnell, aren't you?"

I nodded, not sure where he was going with this.

"I'm Mike Lee," he said, extending his hand.

"Mike Lee? From Utah?"

"Yes," he laughed. "Mike Lee, from Utah." Then he introduced his wife Sharon.

Mike Lee—now Senator Mike Lee—had just won his own Republican nomination over his own establishment opponent. Like me, he was the underdog everyone said couldn't win, only he'd gone and done just that, and here he was crossing the room to shake my hand.

He said, "I just want to encourage you in what you're doing. I've been following your race with my wife, and we're big fans. We're praying for you. You keep at it because you can win this. Just don't lose heart."

I said, "You too, Mike! Congratulations to you, too. I love what you're doing out there, what you're about."

We exchanged a few more pleasantries, but then it appeared that the breakfast would be starting soon, so we said our good-byes and he moved toward his table. Matt and I still had no idea where we were supposed to sit, so we stayed put by the back. Just then, Governor Palin walked in, and for a brief moment I didn't quite know what to do, so without really thinking about it I began walking toward where she was standing in the front of the room. I ended up walking right up to her, so I put out my hand in greeting and said, "Governor Palin, I'm Christine O'Donnell. I was on the phone with your husband the other night. He said you might be interested in endorsing me, once we had a chance to meet."

She flashed a warm smile of recognition and said, "Oh, Christine, yes!" Then she leaned toward me and in a hushed tone said, "They're really going after you, aren't they?"

Governor Palin couldn't have been more gracious, more encouraging, and as we parted, she said something like, "Let's get on it." Something encouraging.

By now, folks were starting to take their seats, and the presentation was about to begin, so Matt and I had to find Meredith. As I walked away I thought, *How about that? Governor Palin knows about our race. She of all people knows exactly what I'm going through.*

A couple days later, we were home in Delaware and still hadn't heard from the Palin camp on our "chance" meeting in Washington. But there was so much work to be done, so I instructed everyone to push forward. We'd all been hoping for Governor Palin's endorsement; it would put a giant exclamation point on our efforts, and help to put a charge in the movement in the final days leading up to the election. But in the meantime we had a campaign to run—and we meant to cover every darn inch of the state. There are only three counties in the state, and in just about two hours you could drive through them all. We were in each and every one of them, each and every week, sometimes each and every day. Between scheduled events, we'd pop into diners, churches, markets . . . wherever we might find a good group of decent, hardworking people.

There was this one place that became a kind of favorite stop for us—a mom-and-pop diner called Kirby & Holloway Family Restaurant in Dover. We went there first for the convenient location, because Dover is right in the middle of the state, but we kept going back for the terrific home cooking, the colorful local personalities, and the true flavor of Delaware.

On this one day, about a week after the Glenn Beck rally, we stopped at Kirby & Holloway to hand out some of our new literature. With the primary election just over a week away, we were beginning to get some traction. Our numbers were inching up in the polls and we were raising money. Of course, this last was relative. When you're running in a primary race in a small state like Delaware, raising $20,000 or $30,000 was huge, but we'd just crossed the $100,000 mark in donations, which was positively off the charts!

Whatever Mike Castle and his friends at the National Republican Senatorial Committee were doing with these attack ads and these smears about my finances, it seemed to be working against them. To answer some of these attacks, we started posting a "Christine Counters" section to our Web site, providing all the documentation to refute these baseless claims, and what we were hearing from voters was that the more the Delaware GOP grasped at straws, the more desperate they seemed.

(And yes, we had it on good authority—namely, Neil King Jr. of *The Wall Street Journal*—that the NRSC was briefing reporters (negatively) on me, in clear violation of party protocol, which calls for them to remain neutral in a contested primary race. Someone from the NRSC, in their infinite wisdom and witless defense, acknowledged that they were indeed circulating these materials against me, but because they weren't printed on NRSC stationery, beneath the committee's letterhead, the tarnishing couldn't be counted as "official" briefings from its communication office. I heard *that* lame explanation and thought, *Oh, good to know.*)

The message of our citizen-politician-versus-entrenched-establishment campaign was catching on, even among Democrats and independents. Right here at Kirby & Holloway, I was shaking hands with a good number of Democrats and independents who told me they were pulling for me in the primary because they wanted to vote for me in the general election. It was an exciting thing, to be shaking the hands of these good people, to join them for a cup of coffee or a bite of pie.

And it would get even more exciting still. As I sat at the table with one local couple, my cell phone vibrated with a text message. I found a point of pause in our conversation, and excused myself to steal a peek at the screen, and what I read nearly knocked me out. It said, *Gov. Palin just endorsed you on Sean Hannity's radio show!*

I was so pumped I didn't quite know what to do with myself, so I held my phone out across the table to show them the display. I said, "Look at that! Governor Palin just endorsed me."

I wasn't all that loud, I don't think. And the diner wasn't all that big. But somehow, every last person in that place had heard me. There must have been about forty or fifty people in the diner, right in the middle of the lunch rush, and everybody started clapping. Some folks stood up and started whistling, and shouting, "Woo-hoo!" or "Yee-ha!" or "You go, girl!"

It was just about a perfect moment—and it found me in exactly the right spot, at exactly the right time. And best of all, I was surrounded by the very people I was hoping to serve, at precisely the kind of mom-and-pop business that was getting squeezed by all these liberal tax policies and by the recession. The folks here were Republicans and Democrats and die-hard Independents, but they all found a way to share in our excitement, that on Sean Hannity's national radio show, with millions of people listening in, Governor Palin had heartily endorsed me in the U.S. Senate race in our home state.

For every "high" that found us in the 2010 campaign, there was a low moment to match. The day the Tea Party Express rolled into town, my candidacy had a little bit of both. We'd been building a nice head of steam as we rolled toward the primary. Our rallies were becoming more spirited, more hopeful; the voters we were able to directly reach were more enthusiastic, and more determined to help us bring about change. Mark Levin, Sean Hannity, and Rush Limbaugh were talking about us on their radio shows, calling positive attention to our effort. The more they spoke about how we were pushing principles over party, the more voters seemed to respond.

As a matter of fact, in a Fox News interview with Carl Cameron, Mike Castle *thought* he was dismissing my candidacy by saying, "She's got no money; she's never held office . . . all she has is her principles."

I heard that and thought, *Okay, if this is Mike Castle's idea of a slam, bring it on!* (And he did—and then some.)

As our campaign team knew full well, the more momentum we gained in the polls, the more likely it'd be that we'd capture the attention of these grassroots organizations that were spurring the middle-class movement around the country.

But I digress. . . . The Tea Party Express is an outgrowth of the Tea Party movement, founded by a group of California-based conservatives as a kind of national bus tour to call attention to Constitutionalist candidates seeking state and federal offices. I don't know if you've ever been to one of their traveling road show–type rallies, but they really do know how to work a crowd. They do a great job of whipping folks into a patriotic frenzy. We'd heard that they were coming to Wilmington for an event, which may or may not have included an endorsement of our campaign. Whatever their plans, we couldn't hear it directly from them. As a political action committee (PAC), they were restricted in their ability to coordinate with political candidates. They couldn't coordinate their efforts with ours, so we had to go to their Web site to follow what they were doing.

And so, of course, we played by the rules, which basically meant we crashed their press conference. It all happened organically—and yet Tom Ross and the Delaware GOP ended up filing a complaint against our campaign *and* against the Tea Party Express for illegal coordination, so that kind of put a damper on things. The complaint had been drawn up by Michael Toner, Senator Cornyn's legal counsel and Karl Rove's good buddy. It might have been funny to see the bigwigs scramble like that, if it weren't such a serious complaint. (And, by the way, the complaint was dismissed almost nine months after election day.)

I saw the party response as a kind of Hail Mary pass, as time was running out on Mike Castle's campaign. We'd done nothing wrong. The Tea Party Express had done nothing wrong. And yet these paper-pushing cowards didn't have it in them to fight us on the issues or the politics, so they looked to trip us up on a technicality.

And the thing of it is, there was no violation of FEC policies. I'd simply shown up at a rally that had been announced in the media and on the Internet. When the group's organizers were told that I—a local candidate who shared the values of many of the group's members—was in attendance, they invited me to the microphone to speak. After a few brief remarks, I handed the microphone back to the organizers and slipped back into the crowd.

That's all. No biggie—except, as it turned out, it was.

Understand, I was certainly allowed to speak at the rally. I just couldn't coordinate with the event's organizers, or discuss with them how long I would speak or what I would say. That wasn't why I'd given up the microphone so quickly. No, my real concern was that I didn't want to steal any Tea Party thunder. They had a lot of good, powerful speakers lined up; their program was jam-packed as it was, so I wanted to leave it to them to do their thing. This press conference, this breeze through town . . . it wasn't *just* about my campaign. Heck, it wasn't even *mostly* about my campaign. Rather, it was about the people who had turned out for this rally and for a whole bunch of similar rallies across our fine state. It was about the folks in Upstate New York, in Massachusetts, in Utah, in Kentucky, in South Dakota, in Alaska, in Nevada, and in districts all over this country, who were turning out in record numbers in support of Tea Party values and candidates and initiatives. This was about them. Their voices needed to be heard, and I didn't want to be the one to drown them out, so I slipped from the podium and tried to leave these good people to their rally.

I found Jennie somewhere in the crowd and she reminded me that we needed to get to our next event, so we tried to leave quietly through one of the back doors.

Yeah, I caught myself thinking, as a scrum of reporters and media-types pressed into our path, *good luck with that.*

What happened next was the most remarkable thing—not to mention that it was a little strange. It was like the whole press corps was joined at the hip, the way they all seemed to move as one, toward me. For the first time, I understood what people in the public eye mean when they talk about "the press," because these reporters were doing just that. I'd never been on the receiving end of so much media attention, and I didn't like it, not one bit.

We were at a meeting room in the DoubleTree Hotel in Wilmington, and as we moved toward the exit at the back of the room there was a pinch point. We couldn't move left or right, forward or back. The main exit was blocked. All I could see was a sea of reporters, microphones, cameras, lights. But I didn't have it in me to panic. I did, however, have the presence of mind to think how I might redirect all this attention back to the podium, where it properly belonged. I was grateful for the endorsement, but the purpose for my being here was to put the focus on the Tea Party Express, not the other way around, and I didn't like that I'd become a distraction, but by this point I'd come too far to double back. There was nothing to do but move forward.

The reporters were pushing at each other to get to me, and

at some point they started pushing Jennie and me. Jennie, being a good and protective big sister, put out her arm, to try to gain some separation between the reporters and me, and I tried to follow her as she blocked them. One of the reporters later claimed that Jennie had somehow assaulted him as we worked our way toward the exit, and when we heard that we couldn't think whether to file that in the *sublime* or *ridiculous* column of charges being leveled at our campaign. Jennie's got a great big heart, and a fiery personality, but she's a tiny little thing; there's no way she could have "assaulted" anyone. She'd just put her arms out in front of her, to cover her face and mine, to clear a path. Besides, this guy stood about six feet tall, so how he came away thinking my "little" big sister was out to assault him was beyond me.

Meanwhile, the Delaware GOP was surveying the scene, looking to bring all these charges of collusion against our campaign. They arranged for Senator Cornyn's legal counsel to draft the formal complaint claiming that I had somehow been in cahoots with the Tea Party Express, which set in motion another round of charges and allegations that I was some kind of criminal, playing fast and loose with our election laws. As our attorney and advisors helped to sort through the mess, I could only wonder how far we'd come from the days where "the voice of the people" was more euphemism than reality—and how far we still needed to go.

In his sheepish post-election defense, Tom Ross justified his actions in authorizing these charges by saying, "I just signed what they put in front of me." The "they" in this case referred to John Cornyn's legal counsel and Priscilla Rakestraw, our

Republican National Committeewoman—which one actually handed it to him, I could only imagine.

Have you ever been to a bull roast?

We went to one at the Elks' Lodge in Dover, about a week before the primary, and it was a revelation. First of all, it was a hoot—lots of good food, good people, good vibes, and all that. The revelation, though, came in a simple exchange with a Vietnam War veteran named George. I sat down with him and a group of his buddies at a picnic table, and started to introduce myself.

George interrupted me. He said, "I know who you are. I know what they're doing to you, what they're saying about you. But you can't listen to any of that. You can't let those people slow you down."

He then told me how when he'd returned home from overseas, he didn't get such a warm reception. People would spit on him, or scoff at him, or ignore him completely. They didn't understand what he'd been fighting for. But this was okay, he said, because *he* knew what he'd been fighting for. He knew what he was defending, and what it was worth.

He said, "It hurt, Miss O'Donnell. Don't let anybody ever tell you otherwise. But I knew the greater good. I knew these people were acting out of ignorance, and what I see today, going on down in Washington, it hurts even more. It's the same kind of disrespect, but it's bigger, because the very men and women who are supposed to be protecting our freedoms are instead taking them away . . . well," he paused to sigh, "they are just spitting on all the veterans, all the fallen soldiers, all of us who've given our lives, by taking away the freedoms we've fought so hard to protect."

When it came time to leave, he reached across the table and put his hand on top of mine. There was something so warm, so gentle about this man's demeanor. So caring. Something in his eyes reminded me of my grandfather, and as he spoke I thought back to all the stories I used to hear from my grandpop about the army buddies *he'd* lost.

George wouldn't let me go without pressing his point yet again. He said, "Do not give up, Christine O'Donnell. Let them spit in your face, but do not give up. What we fought for, what you're fighting for, it's worth it. We had to fight in a war, but your struggle is here."

It was a beautiful, uplifting moment—and just the tonic we needed to power past the nonsense, the venom, the vitriol being tossed our way by our opponents.

Beautiful moments like this one with George far outweighed the ugly, hateful moments; the one helped us shoulder the other. There's another one I want to share, for the sheer surprise value of it. This one found us as we were on our way to an event at a farm in Sussex County, in one of the more rural parts of our state. It was Monday, September 13, the day before the primary. By this point in the campaign, at the eleventh hour, the national media had picked up our scent. They could tell that we were on the brink of accomplishing something truly special in the First State, that Delaware voters were about to stand up and be counted and send a powerful message to party leaders that they were sick and tired of the entrenched establishment. Wherever we went, it seemed, we were followed by a big-time news organization. Kelly O'Donnell—(no relation!)—NBC's Capitol Hill correspondent, was meeting us at the farm for a *Today* show interview. Jessica Yellin, a CNN political reporter, was joining us later that afternoon. I was honored by the national attention, but I didn't want to take time from the campaign, so I told these reporters I'd be happy to talk to them if they met me on the campaign trail.

This type of setup worked out great for reasons other than time management: When we met with these reporters "out in the field," they had a chance to show their viewers some of the hardships facing our small business owners—specifically, how much the return of the death tax would *destroy* our family farms. This came into full focus for us as we pulled into a pizza parlor in Sussex County where we had arranged for a quick meet-and-greet on our way to a farm. There, by the side of the road, we could see a big beat-up pickup truck, with hand-painted signs saying, "Farmers for O'Donnell." There was another sign that said, "Honk if You Support O'Donnell."

And so, of course, we honked. Over and over. And as we stepped out of our car we were met by the farmer who'd been standing on the hood of his pick-up truck, waving to people as they passed.

"Oh my gosh!" he said, as we approached. "It's *you!*"

"Yeah," I said. "It's me." Then I pointed to his truck, and the signs, and said, "Thank you for this, that's so great of you."

"No," he said. "Thank *you.*" His name was Donald Goldsborough and he told me how important it had been to him and his fellow farmers to hear me in interviews talking about what the death tax would do to our small farms. He liked that we were putting it out there, forcing our leaders to face this all-important issue.

The awful thing about this was the way Donald was later ripped apart by my opponents. This guy had dipped into his own pocket to pay for gas money to drive up and down the state; he'd taken the time to paint his own signs and to miss an afternoon of work; he'd done these things to protest what he believed would be an unfair burden on his family, in the only way he knew. And what did he get for it? He got a whole bunch of attacking, antagonistic questions from liberal journalists; he got called a "nut job" and a "whacko," which I guess is what you can expect when you stand up and demand to be heard.

Later that day, just before the primary, Jennie and I stole a special, private moment at Rehoboth Beach. We had about a half hour to fill between events, and without either one of us talking about it, or asking the other what she wanted to do, we wound up in the beach parking lot. It was a cool, late summer day. Perfect and beautiful. Without a word, we got out of the car and kicked off our shoes and began walking toward the shoreline. It was like we were being pulled along, without a conscious thought.

It wasn't quite swimming weather, but it was warm enough to dip our toes in the water, so we walked along the shore for a while until it was time to turn back. As we did, Jennie turned to me and said, "Take this in, Chris. Enjoy this moment."

And so we did. For a few stolen moments, in the calm before the storm.

• • •

Primary day.

The plan was to go from polling place to polling place, shaking hands, thanking our volunteers for their support, making our final push. I cast my own vote first thing in the morning, at Wilmington's Cab Calloway School of the Arts, at about seven o'clock. Every time I step into a voting booth, I feel like I am part of something much bigger than myself, much bigger than the here and now. It's even more surreal when it's your name on the ballot. From there, we visited voters wherever we could find them—mindful of keeping a proper distance from the polling place doors. A lot of politicians don't even bother to campaign on Election Day, on the theory that if they haven't gotten their point across by then it's a little too late, but I prefer to keep at it. My thinking is if I can turn one voter around at the last minute it will have been worth it, so I spent the day looking for that one voter.

Jennie and Matt made a funny picture, trailing after me with lawn signs, which they pressed into the ground along the way, hoping to reinforce the point one last time as people made their way to the polls. If people looked like they wanted to talk, I stopped to chat; if they didn't, I left them alone, although when I could I thanked them for voting. I wanted to thank them for voting for *me*, but that would have been presumptuous, so instead I merely thanked them for taking part in the political process.

After all, this alone was something; this alone was *everything*.

There were reporters parked outside several polling places, so we stopped for interviews here and there as well, and as I spoke to members of the local and national media who'd decided to treat this primary election as a big story, I began to realize that we had tapped into something bigger than any of us could have imagined when we'd started out in this thing. I thought back to my modest, but surprisingly impactful write-in campaign back in 2006, and to my second try in 2008, as the party's nominee going up against a powerful incumbent. Those efforts were the foundation upon which this campaign had been built.

I'll mention here what I was wearing that morning, because it became a part of the story a bit later on: a red Jones New York blazer that I'd bought for six dollars on one of my trips to the St. Anne's thrift shop the previous year. It was, I thought, a fun, snappy look for what promised to be a fun, snappy sort of day, and the time fairly flew by as we dotted all the i's and crossed all the t's on the campaign. I wouldn't let myself think that this was the last day of our campaign, because we were hopeful that we'd win the primary and continue on to the general election in November, but I have to admit there was a certain amount of wistfulness to these final moments of this part of the election cycle. I wouldn't have wished the attacks on my character on anybody, the gutter-sniping, the hateful rhetoric, but a part of me was sorry to think the campaign might end. As tough as things had been at times, I would have signed on for it all over again, just for the chance to meet all the wonderful friends and supporters I'd gained along the way.

Late in the afternoon, I started hearing from Katy French, a dear friend who also worked in the political arena and was watching my race closely. She wanted to know if I had a speech ready. She said, "Win or lose, Christine, you're going to have to say something."

She was right. The eyes of the national media would be upon me, either way, so I supposed I should give some thought to what I might say, but I much preferred to speak from the heart. This frustrated my staff, all during the campaign, because I was always going off script, so I promised to huddle with Katy in one of the back rooms at the Elks' Lodge, where we were planning to wait out the results. That's where we were, in the early evening hours after the polls closed, when a CNN feed flashed on one of the monitors with a scroll at the bottom of the screen announcing that the network was calling the Delaware race for me. I wasn't expecting the race to be called so early, so a part of me thought I hadn't read it right. Through the CNN monitor I could see my sister, my parents, and the rest of my family standing behind Jessica Yellin as she reported the breaking news to the rest of the world. I wanted to be in the room with them, not watching it on TV. O'Donnell 53. Castle 47. It was a darn respectable margin and an historic, record breaking turnout. Not bad for a candidate who experts said had no chance and was outspent by millions.

I couldn't believe it, but my first thought was for my tireless campaign crew, because I knew full well they'd been running on fumes these past couple weeks; "tireless" is one thing over the course of a primary campaign, but to have to turn the page and work toward a general election without a chance to recharge their batteries . . . well, that was something else again.

The next moments are a bit of a muddle. There was such a crazy swirl of excitement. I have a clear memory of making my way to the podium. I had to run past a gauntlet of well-wishers and back-slappers. I wanted to stop and talk to everyone, to thank everyone for their hard work and endless support, but I would have never reached the front of the room! Katy kept pushing me along, but I didn't want to appear rude, so every time I made eye contact with someone in the crowd I mouthed, "I'm sorry, I need to keep going."

Somehow we made it to the podium in a reasonable amount of time. Once we got there I looked at the talking points Katy and I had prepared on paper, put them down, and simply spoke from the heart instead. Yet, I did reach back for a quote we'd planned on using, from Thomas Jefferson: "When the people fear the government, there is tyranny. When the government fears the people, there is liberty." Then I looked out from the podium at a roomful of smiling, cheering, hopeful revolutionaries—most of whom I'd gotten to know quite well over the past several months—and I looked out at the sea of faces in the packed room, most of them belonging to first-time campaigners. Cheers were deafening. Elation reached new levels. There was an electric sense of optimism and I said, "I wish you could see what I see." From the podium, I saw hope.

Later that night, there was a great celebration with friends and family, staffers and volunteers. There was a lot of excitement, as you can imagine, although one memory stands out. I was standing with my friend, a Delaware Democrat who herself challenged the Delaware Way. She couldn't have been happier for me—for what we'd all accomplished, together. She said, "Your winning tonight, it almost feels like I won."

"You did!" I said. "You did!"

After a beat or two, she said, "The way you feel right now,

remember this. Put it in your memory files. As good as this feels, you need to carry this with you, because the next part of the campaign won't be easy. It's important that you remember this. Hold on to this moment."

I didn't stay too terribly late at the party. We had to get up bright and early for a round of morning show interviews. We'd taken a block of rooms at the Fairfield Inn. Jennie and I were bunking together, as we usually did during the campaign, to cut down on expenses. Neither one of us could sleep, and we lay there in the dark for the longest time, like we used to do when we were kids, talking through the night.

"Jen?" I whispered at one point. "You awake?"

"Yeah," she whispered back.

"I can't sleep," I said. "There's too much racing through my head."

"Me, neither," she said.

"Yeah," I said. "But we should try. I have to be up in two hours."

As we drifted off to a sweet silence, I heard from Jen one last time that night.

"I love you," she said.

"I love you, too," I said.

Oh, and let me just finish up about what I was wearing on primary day, because it came into play in the general campaign. I got a text from a friend of mine that said, *Nice shot of you on the cover of Newsweek.* She'd just passed an airport newsstand and saw my smiling face and felt like she had to reach out. We were certainly glad that she did, because we had no idea *Newsweek* was planning a cover story. The idea for the piece was to play off of the "Mama Grizzly" phrase Sarah Palin had been using in some of her speeches to refer to the female candidates she'd been endorsing or working with around the country, and it was a real honor to even be considered in such company. The folks at *Newsweek* had the idea of putting a group of us on the cover, with the headline "The Bear Truth," each of us wearing the power red suits favored by Mama Grizzly–type politicians that season. And sure enough, when the magazine hit newsstands in late September, there was a head shot of me, in a *Hollywood Squares*–type collage, alongside Governor Palin, Minnesota congresswoman Michelle Bachmann, and South Carolina gubernatorial candidate Nikki Haley . . . each sporting our Republican red suit jacket.

I bet nobody could have imagined that I'd bought mine for six dollars at a local thrift store.

Jennie knew the story of the jacket. So of course, I had to have fun with this. I plucked a copy of the magazine off one of the desks in our office and held it out for her inspection. Then I started singing that *Sesame Street* song we used to hear all the time as kids: "One of these jackets is not like the other. One of these jackets doesn't belong. Can you guess which jacket is not like the other, before I finish this song?"

Then we both had a good laugh.

The kicker to this story was that *Time* magazine came calling a couple weeks later, for a cover story *they* were planning on challenger candidates in Tea Party–backed races around the country, hoping to tap in to the populist energy that was rapidly changing the American political landscape—for the good, we all fervently hoped. The journalist doing the piece, David Von Drehle, wanted to feature me, along with U.S. Senate candidate Marco Rubio of Florida, U.S. Senate candidate Rand Paul of Kentucky, and California gubernatorial candidate (and former CEO of eBay) Meg Whitman. The photo editor called specifically to ask if I could wear that beautiful red suit jacket I'd worn on the night of the primary.

I know admitting that was a secondhand suit jacket sets me up for ridicule, but it proves my point—that you don't need to be a millionaire to run for office. You just need to know where to shop.

CHAPTER TEN

Silver Linings All Around

Mike Castle wasn't the most gracious loser. All along, he and Karl Rove had given voice to working for the good of the party, suggesting that we all come together after the primary and join forces to ensure that this U.S. Senate seat wound up on the Republican side of the aisle after the special election in November—but it turned out this talk was just a bunch of hot air.

Those election night congratulatory phone calls are not only gracious, but also mark the official concession of the defeated candidate. Sure, they can be phony. But that doesn't mean they're not important. Especially in a primary race, they can lead to a conciliatory tone between two candidates who now must work together on a general campaign. At the very least, they're a last-ditch attempt at good sportsmanship and good manners to counter the bad temper that characterizes many contentious campaigns. Like them or not, obligatory or not, they've become an expected part of the Election Night routine, but on the night of my primary victory when Mike Castle hadn't called, I could only assume that his phone wasn't working properly. Apparently, it was only able to handle *incoming* calls, because in the wake of his defeat he heard personally from both President Obama *and* Vice President Biden. And, according to the *Delaware News Journal*, his concession e-mail to staffers and supporters didn't even mention my candidacy, so I guess we can only conclude that he didn't *lose* the election so much as throw up his hands in despair and walk away from it.

(All of this begged the obvious question: Why would President Obama take the time to place a call like that to a *Republican* U.S. Senate candidate like Mike Castle? I could only imagine the true nature of the call, but were we expected to simply forget the failed primary runs of Arlen Specter, and Charlie Crist—moderate Republicans who all bolted the party rather than accept conservative voters or policies?)

Funny thing is, *my* phone seemed to be working just fine, so it's not like the Castle camp could claim they weren't able to get through. Governor Mitt Romney managed to put in a call of congratulations. As did Rep. Michele Bachmann and a bunch of other folks. Another notable call was from Senator Jim DeMint, U.S. Senator from South Carolina, who's been a bulwark in Congress fighting to preserve our founding principles.

The next morning when I stumbled out of bed at four A.M. to meet the hair and makeup artist who would magically make me look presentable for my first interview of the day, it was all I could do to focus on the full slate of morning show appearances and international press interviews without worrying about any political scores that may or may not have needed settling. CNN, *Good Morning America*, the *Today* show, *Fox and Friends* . . . they were all lined up and waiting for me.

Reporters from all over the world were descending on our makeshift hotel command post to see what they could see about our surprising result, which overnight had become symbolic of a desire for change among American voters. The small public relations firm we'd hired to coordinate media requests for the primary campaign was immediately overwhelmed with interview requests—there were *hundreds upon hundreds* of calls, no exaggeration—so there's no way we could have even gotten back to all these news organizations in any kind of timely fashion.

For the time being, we could only handle what we could handle.

The hotel lobby was set up like a kind of control center, with a satellite truck in the parking lot out front, and the place was really buzzing, humming. A reporter for one of the British newspapers came over as I was getting fitted with a microphone, and I couldn't believe an overseas reporter was sent to the Fairfield Inn just to talk to me. He said, "Welcome to the second American Revolution. That's what they're calling it back home."

I liked this phrase so I started using it myself in interviews.

One of the questions I kept hearing all morning had to do with Karl Rove, and why he was slamming me on Sean Hannity's program the night before, after I'd been declared the primary winner. I had no ready answer, so I responded as honestly as I could. I said, "Perhaps his ego is bruised. He calls himself the Republican Architect, and he got this one wrong. He said there wasn't a shot in *whatever* that I could win, but I won."

The curtain had been pulled back, and the whole world could see Karl Rove for what he was—a bandwagon pundit who liked to take credit where it was hardly due and place blame where it was hardly deserved. To borrow a phrase, there wasn't a whole lot of *there* there when it came to Karl Rove, and the American people were finding that out. He had a book out at the time, called *Courage and Consequence*, and in one of my interviews I pointed out that he had a fistful of neither. I said, "The man doesn't have the courage to face the consequences when an outsider conservative beats his insider liberal."

The big bulletin of the morning, at least among our campaign staff, was the news out of Washington that the NRSC would not get behind us in the general election. The message from Karl Rove and the NRSC was that we were on our own, here on out. Senator DeMint even brought it up when he called to congratulate me. He said, "Don't worry about the talk that the party won't get behind you. You're not alone in this. We're gonna make sure you get the funding you need." I was grateful for his words.

With or without the NRSC, the money started pouring in that first morning. Overnight, we'd received over $380,000 through our Web site—more money than we'd raised over the entire primary campaign. By early evening, after talk radio hosts like Mark Levin, Rush Limbaugh, Bill Colley, and Sean Hannity had once again been talking about my campaign all day, railing at party leaders for not getting behind me now that I'd earned the nomination, we were fast approaching $1 million—even after our Web site crashed for a few hours as a result of our own virtual stampede.

Rush Limbaugh suggested to his listeners that if they each sent in a dollar to my campaign, we'd have enough money to do without any NRSC funding—and Rush's devoted listeners took him at his word, and within a day or so we were receiving bundles of mail, with one-dollar donations, in cash and checks. It was astounding—even more astounding was that after the second day we'd raised over $2 million, an incredible sum for our little campaign-that-could.

I thought back to how things were in Kentucky earlier that summer, when Rand Paul emerged from his outsider-challenger status to win his party's nomination. All during the primary, Rand Paul was trashed by the Republican establishment, right up until the day of the election, but the very next morning he stood with Senator Mitch McConnell, the Senate Minority Leader, who put his arm around Rand Paul and said, "All that's behind us. Rand is our guy now."

But there was none of that here in Delaware—not even close. And there wouldn't be any of that any time soon.

We did finally get a call from a Castle staffer on Friday, three days after the primary, but it was not the call we were expecting. Matt Moran answered the phone. "Oh," he said, somewhat ironically, once he realized who it was on the other end. "Is the Congressman calling to offer his congratulations?"

At this, the staffer was momentarily tongue-tied. He had no idea what Matt was talking about. He said, "Actually, I'm calling because one of your people showed up at our office."

What had happened was that over the summer, the Republican National Committee had set up a "victory" office in Delaware, in anticipation of the general campaign. This is standard practice in Senate races all over the country, especially when there's no incumbent in the race, in order to have a seamless transition that gives the candidate the best momentum leading up to the general election. But what was out of the ordinary this time was that the RNC team assumed that they'd be working with Castle's staff after the primary, because he had been the clear favorite to win the nomination. They'd installed desks, phones, Internet service . . . the whole package, all of it prepared with the Castle campaign in mind. It was a turn-key operation, ready to open for business immediately after the primary. But somehow, Mike Castle had swooped in and started thinking of the place as *his* office, and when our people turned up and tried to put the space to its intended use the Castle folks got their backs up.

To his great credit, Chairman Steele managed to reach us the morning after the primary election, to offer his congratulations and his assurances that the RNC would support our candidacy in the general election no matter what we were hearing from Karl Rove or others. This was welcome news, indeed. The chairman then told us what we needed to know about *our* victory office, and we were good to go—or so we thought.

We gave the address to some of our key people and sent them down to inspect our new digs. Their marching orders had come directly from the RNC Chairman, but when they stepped inside they found Castle's people, and they weren't exactly rolling out the welcome mat.

We'd yet to hear from our "trespassing" staff, but the call from the Castle office made the situation abundantly clear, and before Matt let this poor, unsuspecting staffer off the phone, he gave it to him pretty good. With mock surprise, he said, "Oh, so you're calling to *yell* at us! And here I'd thought you were calling to *congratulate* us." He then mentioned that for the past three days we'd been taking calls from reporters, wondering if we'd heard from the congressman. He said, "Now we can tell them, yes, the congressman has finally called, but only to tell us to get the hell out of his office."

Ten minutes later—which was now about three days and ten minutes too late—Castle finally called. He said all the usual things, and I politely thanked him. Then I said all the usual things, and he politely thanked me. But before I'd let him off the hook, I put it to him straight. I said, "By the way, your endorsement would really go a very long way."

After that, there was a *really, really* awkward silence. And then, after *that*, Castle quietly said, "Okay, thank you very much." Then he hung up.

As I hung up on my end, I thought that had to be the most painfully halfhearted congratulatory political phone call in the history of painfully halfhearted congratulatory political phone calls.

Meanwhile, Karl Rove and the Delaware GOP operatives continued to make the rounds of the political talk shows, reiterating their disinterest in our campaign. This was a darned shame. We now had some money coming in, directly from Delaware voters and supporters around the country, so it wasn't *just* about the money. No, we needed our party leaders to campaign against our Democratic opponent, Chris Coons, in ways that we couldn't. We needed the strength that comes from a divided party locking arms and moving forward as one.

Also running interference and undermining our campaign was the chairman of our own state party, Tom Ross, who dismissed my candidacy: "She's not a viable candidate for any office in the state of Delaware. She could not be elected dog catcher."

This was from a guy, we later learned, who abused GOP

funds and his own authority to telephone every Republican voter in the state on primary day, with a "robo-call" urging them to vote for Mike Castle over Christine O'Donnell. Keep in mind, this was the Republican Party placing these calls, not my opponent; as if that wasn't bad enough, the calls contained some of the most unprofessional and unseemly language I'd ever heard from Republicans attacking another Republican. And it's not like I was some fringe candidate—in which case his behavior would have still been inexcusable. I'd been the official GOP nominee for this same seat in 2008, so the disrespect and gutter language were especially galling, and all the more surprising.

Further, Tom Ross used Delaware GOP funds to dispatch "trackers" (including his own staff member) to trail my campaign with video cameras, hoping to capture damaging footage of some kind, which he might then use to smear me. Such dirty tactics are not uncommon between opponents, but I'd never heard of a party official deploying these methods within his or her own party, in a race that would determine that party's eventual nominee. When I called Tom Ross out on this, he said I was "delusional," despite the reporting by local reporters and bloggers, who offered a detailed account of Ross's crusade against me, in the heat of our primary campaign. In addition to the straightforward news accounts, there was also corroborating video, which we made sure to post online, showing the Delaware GOP staffer crowding my campaign team, baiting our guys to respond in a negative, unprofessional way.

Here again, the use of "trackers"—or "stalkers"—to trail an opponent in a political campaign is fairly common. In fact, we got to know the guy hired by the Coons campaign to follow me around to try to catch me doing or saying something foolish. His name was Ken, and I came to like him. We'd offer him snacks or drinks whenever we saw him tailing us on the campaign trail. (He never took us up on our offer, but we always made the gesture!) Still, in our experience it was fairly unprecedented for a state party official to authorize the use of trackers in a primary campaign *before* the party had designated a nominee.

And—get this!—once we'd won the nomination, the NRSC and Delaware GOP trackers who'd been assigned to me were let go; they didn't use them against Chris Coons, and I certainly could have used the help. Coons was always contradicting himself and getting caught in one lie or another, although for some reason the media always gave him a free pass; it would have been great to have footage of some of these foot-in-mouth moments, to counter whatever his campaign was digging up on me! But it's astonishing to me that the Delaware GOP used their trackers only in this internecine way, against one of their own. Against *me*.

To be sure, the politics of personal destruction severely harmed my efforts to reach out to independent voters. Once again, I don't mean to get ahead of the story, but I want to make this point here while I'm on it. Besides, I don't think I'm blowing the ending for anyone when I mention I ended up *losing* the general election to Chris Coons, despite the momentum rush that seemed to have been working in our favor just after the primary. Understand, in a small state like Delaware, winning the support of independents is essential for a Republican victory. Why? Well, in 2010, there were 293,817 registered Democrats, and 183,623 registered Republicans, with 146,925 independents and third-party voters. There's no two ways about it. The Delaware Dems had totally out-hustled the Delaware GOP for an incredible enrollment advantage of over 110,000 from what had essentially been par a decade ago. Until recently, Delaware was *not* always a blue state.

The toxic environment and polarizing attacks against me by Republican insiders damaged opportunities for my campaign to reach across party lines to attract independent and third-party voters. According to exit polls, the independent vote in the general election was fairly split between my Democratic opponent and me. But to overcome the gap in registered voters, Republicans must do a substantially better job of getting out the vote than their Democratic counterparts, or win the independent vote outright if they hope to prevail on Election Day.

We lost a good chunk of time in the confusion over our victory office—time we could have used to hit the ground running in the general campaign. Consider: In the space of a few days, we went from a staff of about eight, with two or three volunteers in the office and hundreds around the state, fielding over one hundred calls a day, to the same staff of about eight, with the same group of volunteers, now fielding up to a thousand calls a day. In spite of the negative press, there was a good deal of positive attention coming our way as well, and we had to scramble to keep up with it.

With the million things we had to do in the days immediately following the primary, we didn't spend a whole lot of time on new office space, because we'd thought it was all taken care of with the victory office Chairman Steele told me about. But here in Delaware, the "victory" office had become the "not-your-victory" office, which didn't exactly leave us where we needed to be. This meant we'd have to start from scratch, and lose another few days, but I refused to see it as a willful act of sabotage, or even as a stunningly childish temper tantrum. It was better to look at it as a chance to make a fresh new start, to find our own new digs and give them a personal stamp.

No matter how I looked at it, we were still up against it, because soon after we moved into our new headquarters, we were told to expect an important visitor. Former Delaware Governor Pete du Pont had long been a great champion of the conservative movement; he was well respected across the state *and* across the country. He'd supported Mike Castle in the primary, for reasons having nothing to do with me (I don't think), but now that I'd won the Republican primary he wanted to meet and see about throwing his support our way.

The only problem with this was that our office wasn't *quite* ready to receive such an important visitor. Our phone lines were not yet installed, so our volunteers were making their get-out-the-vote calls from home. We were not fully staffed, and only partially furnished. Volunteers had to work around the clock to hang pictures and signs on the wall to give the place a "lived-in" feel. One group pulled an all-nighter, just ahead of the Governor's visit, to make sure the place was looking right by morning.

It was still very much a bare-bones operation, and we worried that if Governor du Pont came in and saw our offices looking like that he'd come away thinking we couldn't run an effective campaign. It would give him something to think about, some reason to doubt us. So we called in every volunteer who'd been making calls from their homes, and quickly established a call center in our new office; we only had a day to get up and running on this, but we went at it double-quick, and by the time the governor took a tour of the place he was impressed. He told me so himself. He said, "There's a great buzz here, Christine."

I had to agree. Although that buzz just might have been the sound of exhausted volunteers snoring at their desks.

The biggest debate leading up to the general election took place at the University of Delaware and it offered one of the most surreal moments of the campaign. It was covered by CNN. Wolf Blitzer was sent in to moderate, and 1.7 million people tuned in to watch. Wolf Blitzer! 1.7 million! It was an unfathomable number, but the real kick came in the debate prep, where I huddled with Jennie, two members of our press team, and the former McCain/Palin political debate prep team. And yet underneath this major league scenario was our own minor league way of doing things in the O'Donnell camp, as my aunt Barb, who did double duty as our campaign scheduler, flitted in and out of the room, bringing us coffee and sodas and all kinds of good things to eat as we worked; she even roasted a whole turkey for our group, with a heaping bowl of her special mashed potatoes.

My entire family turned out for the debate itself, which was a great big deal. They came back to the dressing room that had been set up in Mitchell Hall: my parents; my sister Jennie and my brother Dan and sister-in-law Kristina; my sister Eileen; my nieces and nephew. When I took the stage, I could see them all out front, sitting in the first few rows, and it helped me to relax. It's one thing to prepare around the clock with a presidential debate prep team, but the only way to *really* prepare for a moment like this is to surround yourself with friends and family and trust in yourself to make them proud.

Another controversy of the 2010 campaign had its roots in some remarks I'd made in previous years, in my role as an activist and strategist. This story needs a bit of a setup, so here goes: I'd been speaking out on the ethics of a controversial development in the field of medical research and scientific experimentation. Like most Americans, I was opposed to the practice of human cloning, and what I considered the Frankenstein-like mixing of the DNA of different species. All along, this had been the stuff of science fiction, but it was becoming more and more of a reality. In fact, our own congressman, the remotely Republican Mike Castle, had sponsored a piece of legislation with Colorado Democrat Diana DeGette, the so-called Castle-DeGette bill—or, the Stem Cell Research Enhancement Act—which would have allowed federal funding of embryonic stem cell research.

I had a few one-issue, one-shot clients at the time, who'd pay me a couple hundred dollars to help them draft a press release or to speak out on this or that issue. I never really made money on these assignments, but I took them on if I believed in the cause, and here I'd been fighting a state version of the Castle-DeGette bill that would have essentially legalized human cloning in Delaware through a kind of loophole.

I researched this issue on behalf of this one client, and discovered a 2005 *National Geographic* article that reported on a group of California scientists who'd grown laboratory mice with functioning human brain cells. "Critics of this research would have you believe that to grow our cells in other creatures is repugnant and inhumane," the article reported. "Mice already grow human ears and are used in many experiments to grow colonies of other human cells." This mad science was also reported by the Associated Press and on MSNBC.

Personally, I didn't find this reporter's explanation the least bit reassuring. This type of science degrades the dignity of human life, and yet advocates for such experimentation introduced Delaware Senate Bill SB5 which would have opened up our state to all kinds of scientific immorality. You see, SB5 was presented as a ban on human cloning, but in reality it was just the opposite; it was a legislative trick. It was sold as a ban, but exempt from the ban was the process known as "somatic cell nuclear transfer," which just happened to be the only known and proven method of human cloning. This was a classic example of The Delaware Way—a slick piece of political maneuvering to deceive the voters, although I'm afraid the backroom sleight-of-hand is not exclusive to our state.

And here's another thing: approximately two-thirds of the world's *Fortune* 500 companies are incorporated in Delaware, so the pressure on our little state to cozy up to these giant corporations can be enormous. On an issue like this, where researchers who found a way to perfect somatic cell nuclear transfer techniques stood to earn a fortune, this was especially so. As I saw it, SB5 was introduced to benefit one specific,

Delaware-based pharmaceutical company, by giving them a kind of free zone within the First State and allowing them to possibly obtain a worldwide patent on this type of research.

Together with Jordan Warfel, now a dedicated member of the Delaware Family Policy Council, I testified before our state legislature in Dover and spoke out against these practices— and against the creation of chimera hybrids among species. The sponsor of the bill countered my testimony by claiming that I was misinterpreting the special provision I found so objectionable.

"If that's the case," I challenged the state senator, "why don't you simply cut the language about the somatic cell nuclear transfer that seems to have everyone so confused?"

I even took the challenge one step further, coming up with language that would have made the bill a clear ban on human cloning in our state, but this was unacceptable to the sponsor. He appeared to grow visibly upset as I pressed the issue, until he finally exclaimed, "That's not what [the company] wants!" He did, in fact, name the pharmaceutical company that had been quietly promoting the bill, but I don't see the need to reference it here. My point is to show the Delaware Way of political maneuvering in full flower, and not to indict the company working the system behind the scenes. Clearly, the sponsoring senator had no authority to change the language of the bill because he wasn't really the author of the legislation.

It was, I thought at the time, a stunning admission, but before I could call good and proper attention to it, Lieutenant Governor John Carney Jr., now our Democratic Congressman, ordered that I be removed from the chamber—for no reason but to contain the public relations damage that would surely attach to his admission if we didn't let it drop. Fortunately, Delaware's pro-life bloggers reported the incident and exposed the bill for the sham that it was—and, in the end, SB5 was defeated, thanks in large part to the efforts of a group called Rose and a Prayer that successfully rallied Catholic Democrats and evangelical Republicans against it.

In November 2007, I was asked to discuss this issue on *The O'Reilly Factor* on Fox News. I was to appear on a panel to debate the ethics of human cloning, but before any real debate could get underway Bill O'Reilly launched into a strange discussion about cloning research coming from Oregon. He said, "It's monkey business in the state of Oregon, and we mean that literally. Scientists there say they have cloned the world's first monkey embryos, deriving stem cells for medical research but potentially paving the way for cloning human embryos as well. The question is, is cloning monkeys morally wrong?"

At this point, the show's producers cut to some stock video footage of a monkey walking on its hands, and a group of monkeys playing in the trees. As the footage aired, O'Reilly turned to me and challenged me to respond, so I did. I tried to bring the conversation back to the salient, alarming point of all this, that the researchers boasted this would bring them one step closer to human cloning. Bill denounced my slippery slope argument, so I said, "American scientific companies are cross-breeding humans and animals and coming up with mice with fully functioning human brains. So they are already into this experimentation."

Of course, I'd meant to say human brain *cells*, referring back to the *National Geographic* story and other press accounts—including one on MSNBC, one of the news outlets that ripped into me for my remarks—but I left out that all-important word. It was a regrettable slip, but it was just that—a slip. Nevertheless, even with this slight gaffe, my meaning was clear to everyone else on O'Reilly's panel. One of them, Dr. William Morrone, from the American Board of Osteopathic Family Physicians, referenced the same piece of research and didn't think it was necessary to correct me on this. My meaning, his meaning . . . *our* meaning was clear.

Such are the perils of live television. Even President Obama let loose a few whoppers in his time ("fifty-seven states with one left to go!") And there may even be a room reserved at the The Library of Congress for the volumes of Vice President Biden's gaffes. That said, it's not like I was randomly out there making these claims. It was another nonissue, and yet someone on Chris Coons's campaign dug up this old footage and retrofitted it for one of his commercials, and all of a sudden I was marginalized as some sort of fringe candidate, instead of a concerned activist calling reasonable attention to some very real and very disturbing developments in the scientific arena.

Looking back, many have said there was a strong chance I could have won in the general election against Chris Coons if GOP insiders had not launched their vicious attacks against me and the campaign had not turned rancorous and divisive. On July 12, a Rasmussen poll showed me not only gaining in the polls, but leading! I was beating Coons by 41 percent to 39 percent, with as large an edge as ever among the coveted independent voters. And let us not forget, this was a year marked by a growing discontent for our Democratic leaders, like Harry

Reid, Nancy Pelosi, and Barack Obama. Had the Delaware elites followed Ronald Reagan's "Eleventh Commandment," and kept the primary contest respectful and focused on the issues, we would have been well positioned to win the election in November and the everyday citizens of our great First State of Delaware would have been heard.

It was not to be. After oceans of publicity, not all of it fair, I lost the general election as the underdog Republican candidate for U.S. Senate in a predominantly blue state. And yet I refused to be defeated. I told a reporter that a loss is not a defeat, so long as you can truthfully say that you fought as hard as you could, for as long as you could, with whatever resources you could muster. In the case of our campaign, we faced not only a significant pushback from the White House, but also the persistent antagonism of the liberal leadership of the Delaware state GOP.

I emerged from the experience profoundly grateful to be an American, and for having the opportunity to speak up for my beliefs.

All of which left me to ponder the future of the conservative movement and the Tea Party revolution, and I had an opportunity to do just that with Bill O'Reilly when he invited me on *The O'Reilly Factor* just after the general election to talk about the campaign and my own political future.

I'll share some of that conversation here, for the way it crystallizes the mood of the campaign, and my frame of mind in its immediate aftermath:

O'REILLY: . . . the way they went after you. It was all personal . . . "you're this, you're that," you know . . . and I'm going to myself, "Why are they going after her? Why do they want to denigrate her personally? Why?"

O'DONNELL: You know the most frustrating part of all of that was if you asked the people, "Did you watch the speeches? Did you watch the debate?"

O'REILLY: They don't care. They just want to demean you.

O'DONNELL: They just wanted to attack me rather than look at where I stand on the issues. . . . It could be [that I was] a strong woman who had the audacity to challenge the system, and I busted up the backroom deal. I think there were a lot of bruised egos. A lot of, you know, "You're taking the power out of our hands." I think at least for the party in Delaware, the Republican leadership in Delaware, they would rather control the way they lose than lose control of their party.

It was a good line, I thought at the time (and still do!)— *they would rather control the way they lose than lose control of their party.*

PART TWO

My Thoughts

Government is not reason; it is not eloquent; it is force. Like fire it is a dangerous servant and a fearful master.

—George Washington

CHAPTER ELEVEN

Rise Above It

In the aftermath of the 2010 Senatorial election, I found myself reflecting on aspects of the campaign that might have gone differently, while at the same time looking ahead to whatever might come next for the movement, and for me. Clearly, we'd tapped into something, as we spoke to Delawareans eager to take back their government, to stand up and be counted, as well as to people wanting their government to accurately represent them, as it was intended by our forefathers.

On a personal level, though, there was still much to sort out. And there still is. It's been character-building to say the least. Throughout my years in advocacy work, a dear friend would remind me that God has to build and strengthen your character before He can release you into your calling. Otherwise, fulfilling your purpose could be the very thing that crushes you.

Certainly, I'd been beaten down for so long by my opponents (and even by members of my own party!) that out of necessity it seemed I'd become almost immune to the criticisms and attacks that came my way. I came to expect it, but at the same time it was a giant, looming frustration to know that in trying to represent the needs of the people of Delaware, I'd have to deflect all the slings, arrows, twisted stories, and misrepresentations that came our way. It was relentless, to the point where I'd sometimes wonder if it was all in vain, if I should have thrown in the towel and saved my reputation. After all, I was warned that if I continued, they'd make me toxic.

But that's not me, I know full well. I've never been the shy and retiring sort, and I wasn't about to begin now, so I tried to set these negative thoughts aside and continue whatever it was that we'd had a hand in starting.

It was in this mind-set that I came upon what I began to think of as a crisis of persona. It had to do with the kind of person I wanted to be, going forward. It found me one afternoon, a couple months after the general election; I overheard an anonymous young man slamming me to his friends and, well, something got to me. "She doesn't even know the First Amendment," he said, as if the more he mocked, the more he impressed his friends.

The encounter requires a bit of a setup, so here it goes: In the weeks leading up to Election Day, I participated in a noteworthy debate at Widener University Law School with my opponent, Chris Coons, who had been a corporate lawyer before entering politics. At some point in our back-and-forth, Coons brought up the issue of whether or not local schools could teach intelligent design. I've always maintained the position that communities determine their own curriculum, whether to teach intelligent design or to exclude it. Either way, teachers and local school officials certainly have the right to decide for themselves. Disagreeing, my opponent stated that the federal government should mandate that no public school should ever be able to teach intelligent design because it violates "separation of church and state."

To this I responded, "Where in the Constitution is the phrase 'separation of church and state'?" Of course it was a rhetorical question. As I've stated numerous times on shows like *Hardball* and *Politically Incorrect*, that phrase simply does not exist in the Constitution. Coons replied that separation of church and state is in the First Amendment.

"Really?!" I stated in what I thought was an obviously sarcastic tone. Apparently it was not . . . but I'll get to that.

I held firm, and at one point took it a step further, asking if Coons could name the five freedoms that are protected in the First Amendment. He could not, and appealed to the moderator to move on.

As my team and I left the debate, we were literally high-fiving each other because we had just exposed that Chris Coons, a lawyer, did not know the Constitution. What happened next was a whirlwind of bias, ignorance, or a bit of both, but it certainly was revealing.

Before we even made it back to the office, the Associated Press had erroneously reported that I didn't know the First Amendment and had to ask for help. They reported that in the middle of the debate I asked my opponent where is separation of church and state, and my opponent had to point out that it is in the First Amendment.

Whiskey, Tango, Foxtrot!! Are you kidding me? The AP didn't even know the First Amendment well enough to recognize the error in their reporting. It was a rather chilling revelation that so many leaders and influencers do not know the Constitution, the document by which our nation is *supposed* to be governed. And it explains why our country has moved so far away from its roots. If you don't know what *is* constitutional, how can you recognize a violation?

The story actually dominated the news for a large part of the campaign, and sparked a debate about what the Constitution actually does say. That's a good thing.

Yet, the dominant news coverage coming out of that debate seemed to mock those of us who take a literal approach to what our founding document says about a separation of church and state, while also suggesting that I was woefully unaware of these issues. I'd listen to the coverage and try to take it in stride, knowing how the left seems to always resort to personal attacks and smears, instead of engaging in an honest discussion of the issues. What was especially galling was that on the morning of the debate Coons himself hadn't been able to name the five freedoms protected by the First Amendment, and actually had to call for help from the moderator to evade the question. But here it was, almost two months later, and I was still being attacked for stating a simple, verifiable fact.

Now, the dust was settling on the campaign and I was sorting through the blur that had been the fall. I was enjoying a half-priced-burger break with Matt Moran and Krystina Hamilton at Cromwell's, a popular Wilmington pub. We were unwinding, relaxing, revisiting some of the pivotal moments of the campaign, and going over what our futures might hold, when my ears tuned in to the conversation going on in one of the booths near to ours. A young man, who I took to be a student, was going on and on about me, and to hear him speak, you'd think I'd just stolen his lollipop and shoved him into the sandbox. I heard him say, "She didn't even know that separation of church and state is right there in the First Amendment." He then went on to regale his friends with how little I knew about this and that. As I listened, I could hear that he was essentially parroting a diatribe he'd heard from every liberal commentator or critic during the campaign.

Well, usually this kind of thing doesn't bother me. You have to put it in its proper perspective. Yet, this particular day, I was beyond frustrated, because, of course, the First Amendment discusses no such thing. Matt and Krystina could tell I'd drifted away from our own conversation, and when they tried to pull me back I shushed them.

"Listen," I said quietly, thumbing toward the booth where the know-it-all student was sitting. "He's talking about the First Amendment debate, and me." I found this guy's chatter infuriating. It's funny, or perhaps telling, that it hadn't seemed to bother me when Mike Castle or Chris Coons got the facts wrong or went after me. I knew they were purposely twisting facts to portray me in a bad light. I'm not saying I was okay with it; but I knew that there was a good chance they knew the truth, and they were purposely misrepresenting facts as campaign tactics . . . but this kid? I thought he should know better, or at least he should know what's in our Constitution, or *not* in our Constitution—it wasn't that he was going after me, but that he was arguing so self-righteously, and incorrectly, for what he felt was in the First Amendment. And, right or wrong, it got under my skin.

"Where's my Constitution?" I said. "I'm going over there."

I was in the habit, when I was in campaign mode, of carrying copies of the Declaration of Independence and the United

States Constitution for ready reference, and here I wanted to slap that copy down on the table in front of this arrogant kid and say, "You show me. You show me where in here is the phrase 'separation of church and state.'" But cooler heads prevailed, thank goodness—meaning, Matt's and Krystina's.

Matt said, "I don't think that's such a good idea, Christine." Krystina was in the outside seat in our booth, and she wouldn't move to let me pass. "It's for your own good," she said with a smile. It's actually funny to think, after everything that had gone on, that small scene is what finally got under my skin.

In case you're interested (and if you've read this far in the book I can hope/assume that you are), the idea behind the separation of church and state comes from a letter of response Thomas Jefferson wrote to the Danbury Baptist Association in answer to mounting concerns they had over the establishment of a national religion. To the Danbury Baptists, Jefferson sent his assurances that in America there will always be a wall of separation between the church and the state, and that's where the phrase comes from. What was compelling about that letter was that Jefferson went on to write about how the church needs to have a vibrant role in the future of our country, because our newly formed government could not exist without it. It was all about how our Republic was being built on faith and character, and on people of faith and character—but unlike in England at that time, the United States would never have an established church of the land. Citizens would be free to worship as they chose.

It wasn't until a judge misused Jefferson's letter more than a century later to help define the original intent of the Constitution—even though Jefferson himself did not take part in drafting the Constitution (he wasn't even in the country at the time!)—that the phrase came into play. And yet a judge somehow took it on himself to define original intent, based on a *letter* written by someone who had virtually no role in the drafting of the Constitution, and in so doing managed to supersede all of American history. In our Widener debate, Coons was intent on talking about the judicial activism of the courts over the years, which had entirely obscured the Constitution, while I kept coming back to the actual text of the original document.

Just to be clear, the phrase "separation of church and state" appears nowhere in the U.S. Constitution. (And I do wish I had said that exact sentence, as clearly as that, in the debate.) Look it up if you'd like; you won't find it. And it doesn't appear conceptually, either. In our actual Constitution, the First Amendment establishes a balance between two distinct ideas: 1) no establishment of an official or "national" church and 2) free exercise of religion. (By the way, I've included a copy of the Bill of Rights, as well as the Declaration of Independence, as an appendix to this book, because it never hurts to keep these documents close at hand.)

Some liberals seize on the first part of the First Amendment while ignoring the second, but both requirements are constitutionally mandated. Many Tea Party folks take this to heart and are aggrieved by these types of things because they believe we should look to the Constitution as the precedent, our foundation. And we must; we surely must. That document is the lifeblood of liberty. To have it diluted by scholars and so-called experts and quick-fix politicians out to rewrite history sets up a dangerous equation. It gets to where we have all these new laws, based on precedent upon precedent upon precedent, and at some point there's a thick crust of legal precedent that no longer resembles the original document, let alone its original intent.

That's one reason these tossed-off remarks from this fellow at the pub bothered me. It wasn't because he'd judged *me* unfairly. It's partly because the wrong message had hit home with him.

Another reason it bothered me was because this young man is our future, and I wanted to shake some sense into him about the First Amendment. This scene as it played out seemed to indicate that "they" won. Yes, they won the election. But I'd like to think that by bringing important issues into the spotlight, we won in all accounts except in the detail of who is representing the people of Delaware in Washington. Yet hearing this young man parrot all the slams and hollow sound bites was just too much.

For a moment, it appeared that my anger at being misrepresented, lied about, having my family dragged into it, and all the rotten parts of the whole campaign would culminate at this moment, because this young man misunderstood the Widener debate and the Constitution. Just a couple months removed from the election, and I was obviously still bothered, not only at the way this debate moment had been played and replayed in the press, but also by all of the attacks and jabs hurled at me during the campaign, and I was prepared to let out my frustration over half-priced burgers.

I share this story not only because it helps to pull back the curtain on one of the more colorful controversies from the campaign, but more important, I see it as a tale of forgiveness for me. It brought me to question, with all of this going on, "Why is this getting to me? Why is it making me so resentful?"

Indeed, the very next day, I found myself watching a news story about an African-American pastor reaching out to a leader of the Ku Klux Klan. "Nothing you can say or do to me will make me hate you," the pastor said, "because I will not become a hateful person."

Although the TV was muddled in the background and I was going about my day, it was as if everything else suddenly went silent and that sentence shot out directly to me and made me look into my own heart. It became abundantly clear—that moment at the restaurant was the precipice, the reminder, that I really did have to exercise the muscle of forgiveness. As we moved further from the election and smears went unchecked, and it seemed there would be no consequences for the "politics of personal destruction," it became more of a struggle. Yet only I was to blame for that. Only I could take responsibility for how I chose to respond. Did I want to become a bitter person? Did I want to let my accusers win by robbing me of my integrity? If so, only I am to blame.

I would not, could not become a bitter, unforgiving person as a result of all of this. I had to find it in my heart to forgive this young man, just as I had to find it in my heart to forgive every careless reporter who filed dubious stories about me, my family, or my campaign without credible sources. I had made up my mind that I would allow these experiences to make me more open, more loving, more compassionate. Why? Because it's the right thing—the best thing—to do. Holding on to resentments inhibits a person's ability to grow and develop more fully. Freedom is found in forgiveness. How many times had I seen this lived out in my own home. My mother forgiving my father. My father forgiving himself. Without taking that critical step, perhaps my father would not have been able to continually get back up and try again to be the best he could be.

As I listened to this brave pastor on television, I recognized that forgiveness, above all else, is what will keep us from our precipitous slide toward socialism. There's an awful lot at stake; the pushback is greater now than it has been at any time in our history. For the middle-class movement to succeed and forge ahead, we need to forgive those who are doing the pushback. We must refuse to allow anyone else to turn us into someone or something we don't want to be.

"Nothing you can say or do to me will make me hate you, because I don't want to become a hateful person."

I heard those words and thought that if this pastor could forgive a man who'd been burning crosses on his lawn and making death threats, I could certainly find a way to forgive some college kid who was slamming me to impress his pals, reporters who don't do their research or knowingly report falsehoods, and politicians who purposely sling mud and put their own self-interests in front of those of their constituents. I had to forgive or I'd be of no useful purpose to anyone, including and especially myself.

And so I did . . . and in so doing I found another way to develop my character more deeply, so God might release me into my calling.

CHAPTER TWELVE

The Power of the Soundbite

In January 2010, I was invited to speak on media bias and socialism at an international conference at the School of Social and Media Culture in Toruń, Poland. It was quite an honor to be asked to appear on such a significant stage, to discuss an issue of such vital importance to our movement back home—and an issue that was especially relevant in that part of the world as well.

Not too long ago Poland suffered under Communist rule and the transition into a free market economy is marked with bumps and bruises. The conference organizers asked me to talk about mass media bias because even in Poland some see their media is an obstacle to their full transition to freedom.

My first thought was to list specific examples of how American newspapers and television news organizations were biased against those of us who unashamedly champion free market, limited government principles. But then I had another idea. Instead of laying out a whole bunch of evidence of the liberal media bias, I decided to address the root of the problem and examine how the media derives its power to influence the individual—or, at least, how I thought the media went about setting our national agenda. My main point was delivered as a kind of thesis statement at the very top of my presentation: Mass media lends itself to a nation's slide into socialism because it reduces all policy into sound bites.

As I gave my remarks from the podium, I looked into the large audience and could see grown men, tough looking men, with tears in their eyes. Then afterwards, as I greeted the crowd, a frail older gentleman moved toward me. He sort of shuffled as if every step was painful and when he approached, he handed me a note. His hands were thick with calluses. His face looked weary. Apparently he couldn't speak English, so he had someone translate onto a piece of scrap paper what he wanted to tell me. "Thank you. Thank you for speaking up for us." And as I read the note, he clasped my hands in his and nodded his head and shoulders as if to say with body language what he couldn't say in English. I looked into his eyes and could see such depth of both suffering and joy. I could only imagine the evils he witnessed in his lifetime having lived under a communist regime.

And so, I share these same remarks here—gently edited, because what works on the stage doesn't always translate to the page.

In my remarks I talked about capitalism. I'm not referring to the post-communist crony capitalism practiced in parts of Eastern Europe today. I am referring simply to its core principles as economic theory. America's economic system is based on free markets and free enterprise that serve the person rather than the other way around. A benevolent country's economic system should honor and uphold the dignity of every human. This is why we shouldn't legalize prostitution or sex trafficking and why we abolished the slave trade. One could argue there certainly is a free market demand for such things, yet they violate the sanctity and dignity of human life so they have no place in our economy. Capitalism, conservatism, and Judeo-Christian thought—all are based upon millennia of philosophical, economic, and theological history and scholarship. Each is made up of a set of core principles that have been time-tested, and verified.

For instance, our Western notion of capitalism as economic theory is based on the idea that the individual will be more productive when he or she can enjoy or direct the fruits of his labor, rather than the collective of which that person is only a part. And, it's based on another notion that markets constituted by millions of freely consenting actors transacting with each other are infinitely more efficient at setting prices than a central planning committee. These ideas are cold, scientific, historically demonstrable realities that may not play well with the American nanny-state crowd.

Among the basic tenets of Christian thought are the twelve articles of faith contained in the Apostles' Creed, but on top of these are centuries of theological development and clarity regarding the initial deposit of the faith that has become a touchstone of Magisterial teaching, including documents such as *Humanae Vitae*, the groundbreaking encyclical by Pope Paul VI on human dignity and personhood, the principles that should direct all aspects of governing and servant leadership.

It's compelling to note that every time the principles of *Humanae Vitae* are countered by totalitarian governments or the theories of secular humanism that drive most economies in Europe, demographic and economic disaster occurs. These are cold, scientific, historically demonstrable facts that simply don't play well with the sound bites of the "my body, my choice" crowd.

Among commonsense conservatives, there are core principles at play as well, such as the desire to protect individual liberty to make individual choices, which actually leads to a more moral and safer society. Another core principle of conservatism is that, in government, less is more. Here again, we have seen the demographic and economic disasters that have occurred when these principles are violated. These, too, are cold, scientific, historically demonstrable facts, but these soundbites don't play well with the nanny-state crowd.

In each of these cases, American mass media have successfully manipulated most of the general public and social justice advocates who play into the emotional sound bites of "take care of the little guy, demonize the successful." But the problem is that there is a complex set of ideologies behind the soundbites. The more you punish the successful, the productive, the prosperous . . . the harder it is for the little guy to join them. As a result, policies based on sentimental sound bites—as opposed to, say, centuries of quantifiable economic data—have brought about the gradual decline of partially socialized economies in Western Europe, Canada, and, increasingly, in the United States.

With regard to the fundamental dignity of the human person outlined in *Humanae Vitae,* the soundbiters can make a compelling thirty-second case for why abortion and assisted suicide are all "compassionate" uses of individual liberty. And, they can convince legions of college students looking for a cause of much the same thing; they can even persuade well-meaning politicians to enact such policies at taxpayer expense. But the sound bites ignore the history of societies which have lived under regimes that threaten the basic principle of human dignity. These societies have *contracepted* and *euthanized* their way out of existence. And we can never forget that once you decide that a person's right to life is based on the convenience or cost, eugenics follow, as we graphically saw with the genocide against not only the Jews, but also other ethnic minorities, the disabled, the old, and the sick in Nazi Germany. Historical facts dispute the sound bites and prove the time-tested wisdom of *Humanae Vitae* and its roots in Judeo-Christian principles.

I could go through a similar case study with conservatism, focusing on the consequences of expanding governments by using sentimental soundbites about taking care of the weak and the poor and vulnerable. I can show you how governments that propose themselves as nannies end up with the poorest and weakest populations. We need look no further than the collapse of Eastern European communism for the ultimate evidence of how incapable a statist approach can be at providing for its people.

So, can we point to France as a seemingly successful model of socialism? They require citizens to pay a majority of their income in taxes and social charges (euphemism for taxes) but they get something in return. So if that's the case, why not model our socialism after theirs the way we model French fashion, especially when the media portrays France as the epicenter of all things cool and hip? Well, there are two reasons why we can't ever use any socialist economy as a role model. The first is that the French model cements the chasm between the social classes. When you pay 60 to 70 percent of your income to the government in taxes, you simply can't earn enough money to invest in your business and cover your daily expenses associated with modern life. You're forever playing catch-up. If you are dependent on government programs, you and your family will most likely stay dependent for generations.

Second, socialism reduces the individual to a cog in the wheel. It's socialism's fundamental flaw. Under socialism, the individual exists to empower the state. It should be the other way around—the state should exist to empower the individual—and yet in a socialist economy the value of the individual is reduced to that which is cost effective. It is the sanctity of life versus the quality of life. History warns us of the evils that emerge when societies treat human beings as commodities. We learned from the evils of slavery and the horrors of communism that a society can never and should never put a price tag on a human being.

So why are the soundbite policies winning elections in the United States, even as their fecklessness is on such graphic display throughout Europe and South America? I mean, it was one thing to be a communist in 1953, when a reasonable person might think, *Hey, that sounds altruistic and right. Let's give that a try.* It's an entirely different thing to support communist programs in 2011, after watching the rationing and economic collapse of just about every industry that has been socialized in Europe; after seeing the gulags in Siberia and the solidarity strikes in Poland; after seeing the decline of Venezuela from a prosperous, resource-rich up-and-comer to the basket case it is today; or after seeing an agricultural and mineral-rich country like Zimbabwe turned into a place where its citizens can't even find a loaf of bread.

Okay, so we can see the evidence. We can all agree, there's no longer any reasonable excuse for supporting a socialistic program—either writ large, as in Venezuela, or by the slow bleed we find in places like the United States. The soundbites are merely the breathlessly emotional jingoism that mask these failed policies. We *get* it.

So why are we the only ones? Why don't all voters get it? Why is the United States sliding more and more into a socialism that has a 100 percent failure rate? In other words, why do the soundbites work?

The reason is that if there is historical evidence that demonstrates a principle clearly, then one must have knowledge of that history in order to observe the principle and internalize it. You can't possibly know that socialism destroyed Eastern Europe and is gradually doing the same to Western Europe if you can't even find London on a map. And how can you know that if you can't describe the horrors of Auschwitz or Lubyanka, the underground KGB prison they used to torture people in Moscow during the height of communism? How can you truly appreciate the principle of supply and demand and the necessity of market-based pricing rather than central planning if you've never seen the photos of the brutal winter bread lines in the Soviet Union? How can you know the liberating impact of free market principles if you've never studied their impact on society?

For a soundbite to be effective, good or bad, it must latch on to a value that already exists within the hearer. The hearer responds by ascribing more to that sound bite. They can respond in a visceral, purely emotional way. They can respond emotionally, based on facts. Or, they can respond emotionally, based on facts and faith. Let me give you an example of these three different responses.

At a recent World Economic Forum, many world leaders called for a new breed of capitalism. They said this new breed of capitalism would be more compassionate and that it would demonstrate a more equal distribution of wealth. They said that true equality would arise when everyone had exactly the same of everything.

The purely emotional response would have been, *I want to be compassionate. I want equality in the world. This must be a good thing.*

The emotional response based on facts would have been, *I want to be a compassionate person. I want equality. Yet, this sounds an awful lot like communism. I remember the death and suffering brought on by communism. This can't be right.*

Is that response right? Not quite. Something is still missing.

The logical conclusion, calling *only* on facts and emotion, might be that the principles of communism or socialism might just work with kind and compassionate leaders. *The world is different now,* we might tell ourselves. *Maybe the problem is not with the principles themselves but with the practitioners of the principles.*

However, watch how we tilt the argument when we respond not only with our emotions and a knowledge of history, but also with the principles of our faith. Now our thinking is, *this new breed of capitalism sounds compassionate. And yet equal distribution of wealth sounds an awful lot like communism. I have seen the death and suffering brought about by communism. Not only that, but the Church teaches that every human being has an unalienable, precious dignity. A man's worth and dignity should never be used for totalitarian purposes. It is not right.*

Let's be clear: The American education system has been hijacked by the nanny-staters who want to make sure children feel good about themselves rather than know history, economics, logic, or accounting. They want kids to find themselves rather than find God through the accumulated wisdom of the Magisterium of the past two thousand years. If the soundbite is about freedom for its own sake rather than freedom for good, freedom for righteousness, freedom for self-sacrifice, freedom for hard work, freedom for prosperity . . . well, then freedom simply becomes license. And a society filled with self-actualizers who value license above all else will self-destruct in a few decades.

Our education system is failing. But that is what happens when families are no longer the primary educators. Parents can only step aside for the public schools if they've already stepped aside for the televisions inside their homes, so we have a larger cultural decline. That is, we have some parents who have bought into the soundbites and are now letting the soundbites nourish their children's minds and drive their behavior, which then leads young people to become manipulated even more by soundbites as they become voters, who then lead our whole country into gradual socialist decline.

Ultimately, we have a chicken-and-egg problem—which came first, the chicken or the egg? In other words, is it the sound bite indoctrination of a society that leads it toward socialism, or is it socialism itself that fosters such sound bite indoctrination? I would argue that society declined first— families and education declined first. You don't elect someone who promises wealth through raising taxes if you understand the first thing about basic economics. And you don't elect someone who puts a Chairman Mao Christmas tree ornament on the White House Christmas tree, if you've ever studied revolutionary China. (And yet in 2009 President Obama did just that.)

So we have in America a crisis of education, which ultimately is a crisis of the family, which ultimately is a crisis of faith—the *true* faith, not feckless, amorphous faith in hope, rainbows, or good cheer. That's what we're facing in America today, a *true* crisis of *true* faith—faith in a living and active God; faith in the power of redemption and the need for salvation from real and pervasive sin; faith that evil is real but that truth can overcome it in love; faith that nurtures strong character, in which we learn to model Christ in His merciful grace and self-sacrifice in love.

The family doesn't break down where there is strong faith surrounded by neighbors with strong faith. And even though *individual* families might break down as they always do in a fallen world, the *institution* of family is not doomed when faith is still the reason people get out of bed every day, still the reason we go to work, still the reason we sacrifice. And yet the same so-called Enlightenment and postmodern secular *inhumanism* that destroyed the faith in Europe over a few centuries is now having its say in America as well.

Before I get all gloom and doom about the state of play in

the United States, let me get very politically incorrect and bring up the concept of American exceptionalism—usually a taboo topic at an international conference. There's a reason why socialism has been slower to "take" in America than elsewhere. Other countries sometimes poke fun of America for being so "new," but we have the oldest consistent representative democracy in the world. Our Constitution grants us freedom of the press; that freedom can be used for good. Right now, I have mostly focused on the negative impact of our soundbite-driven media. Yet if we make it our focus, we can use the power of our mass media for good. We may have to work harder at this. It will take more vigilance. But it *can* be done.

Freedom.

It's what's so great about the United States. America is exceptional because it wasn't founded on tribalism—that is, on the chance location of a certain ethnic group when the Romans found and conquered them, as in most of Europe. Our founders weren't a religious-cultural group held together by lifestyle and religion, like in much of the Mideast. They weren't a tribe of indigenous people occupying a certain forest or a plain until European colonists assimilated them, as in much of the Americas and Africa. No, what made the United States great were ideas.

The United States was a hodgepodge of misfits and pioneers; small groups of investors and land-grabbers; fringe religious groups driven from elsewhere; indentured servants trying to get free; dreamers, one and all. There wasn't any one thing that characterized American colonists in any cultural, ethnic, or religious sense. However, the one thing that ultimately united them was a document. That one thing that made them *one*—"*E Pluribus Unum*," from many, one—was the Declaration of Independence. But that Declaration didn't come down from the sky to Thomas Jefferson's pen out of nowhere. The Declaration insists that government serves something far above itself. Government is the handmaid and guardian of something that it didn't create and cannot destroy. The Declaration says: "We hold these truths to be self-evident; that all men are created equal and are endowed by their Creator with certain inalienable rights; that among these rights are life, liberty, and the pursuit of happiness."

In these words lie the core beliefs of capitalism, conservativism, and Judeo-Christian thought, all in one. These words, or rather the ideas the words express, are a natural immunization against socialism. As long as America is truly a country based on these ideas; as long as Americans, whatever their many, many differences, are united around these ideas . . . then America will stay America, and the infection of a socialist creep will be no more.

Even if the schools don't teach this anymore—and they don't!—American families continue to live and breathe these ideas. That's why, when a political candidate effectively presents these ideas in a persuasive way, he or she gets elected. *Message received*. And what does that say about us? It says we still believe this stuff. Not because we're special, but because these ideas are simply true. They're engraved on the human heart. In our need to be valued, in our desire to be appreciated, in our longing to be loved simply for who we are, freedom is inscribed on the heart of every human being. That's why the Declaration insists that the government can't take away these freedoms. People know this. All people. Yet it is one of those things that they don't know until they hear it. And when they hear it, they recognize it to be true.

Is the United States under siege from the socialist forces plaguing Europe and the rest of the world? Absolutely. Should we be worried? Definitely. Is it inevitable? No way! Because people know the truth. That's why a generation raised knowing nothing but Polish communism, who had never known a day of freedom, could be utterly transformed when a Polish Pope came to them and told them these things—because the human heart knows they're true. That's why the world cheered when that lone student stood down the Chinese tank in Tiananmen Square—because the heart takes one look at that picture and knows the difference between good and evil, between freedom and tyranny. That's why Berliners were dancing in the streets, and the whole world with them, when a cement wall crumbled. That's why President Ronald Reagan could sum up his whole foreign policy in four words: "We win; they lose." Because the human heart knows the difference between good and evil when it sees it. We know the truth when we hear it. The problem is that our side isn't as good at putting truth into sound bites, so we can't compete with the soundbiters.

The great hope we can stand on is that if we find the right words and use the media effectively, *we* have the distinct advantage of being right. People *already* agree with us, they just haven't heard us. The truth we advocate is already in their hearts. The forces of socialism have to rely on deception in order to win elections. We just have to get better at telling the truth—faster, with fewer words . . . with *better*, more powerful words.

In closing, I offer this: most young churchgoing kids don't grow up wanting to be public relations hacks. Typically, they don't grow up wanting to be in politics at all. They're out there being productive, raising families, serving mankind, serving the Church. Yet we need to send our best and brightest to journalism schools, marketing programs, and into academia. We need to teach our team how to compete in a soundbite universe. We're at an advantage because we're actually telling people the truth they already know. If Coca-Cola can do it, so can this middle-class movement and all of you.

I want to encourage you, all of you, to tell your stories far and wide. Actually, *encourage* is too soft a command, so let me rephrase that. I am *imploring* you to tell your stories far and wide. Most Americans have a sanitized version, a sanitized understanding of what took place under communist regimes. We need you to share your experiences. Warn us with your personal stories. Post YouTube videos, write books and blogs, give interviews and exchange ideas on social network forums like Facebook and Twitter. Start human rights groups in high schools, and book clubs in churches. Bring films that are true and powerful to local theaters. Raise funds for TV ad campaigns. And if you have money to spend, spend it on advertising time during the World Cup or *American Idol.* Get your message out there, in a big-time way, and at the same time don't be afraid to take it to the streets. Build from the ground up. Don't just speak to academic conferences. Share your stories over a cup of coffee at your local diner, and encourage others to pass them along. You are living witnesses to the truth, and the human heart loves the truth.

"Fellow citizens, we cannot escape history," Abraham

Lincoln said in an address to Congress about the ravages of the Civil War. He was speaking about slavery, of course, although if we transpose his words to those of us who are slaves to tyranny and injustice and the destructive powers of our soundbite-driven media, they are just as relevant today. Consider: "We of this Congress and this administration will be remembered in spite of ourselves. No personal significance, or insignificance, can spare one or another of us. The fiery trial through which we pass, will light us down, in honor or dishonor, to the last generation."

My friends, America is the last best hope on Earth—not because of some sort of cultural imperialism, but because of the ideas on which she was founded. These ideas are not our own. They never were. They belong to the whole world. They belong to every human. We are bound for greatness simply because of these ideas, which can make the world great, too. America must hold true to them, even if the rest of the world forsakes them, so let us pray for each other. Let us pray that these self-evident truths, these inalienable rights to life, liberty, and the pursuit of happiness, endowed by the Creator upon all men, will be an everlasting inheritance for us all.

CHAPTER THIRTEEN

The Freedom Food Chain

We hold these truths to be self-evident, that all men are created equal, that they are endowed by their Creator with certain unalienable rights, that among these are life, liberty, and the pursuit of happiness. That to secure these rights, governments are instituted among men, deriving their just powers from the consent of the governed. . . .

With these brief clauses stitched together by Thomas Jefferson, approved by his editing committee of Benjamin Franklin and John Adams, and signed by fifty-three other courageous revolutionaries, the nascent United States asserted to the watching world the only proper and legitimate role of the government: To secure the God-given rights of man. Others had made such an assertion, as a review of the libraries of our Founders confirms, but none had ever successfully insisted on it by force, or even tried.

America, you see, is a miracle. If you had asked Genghis Khan the proper role of the government, you might have heard something about protecting and expanding the territory belonging to the Mongolian people. Alexander the Great might respond, *To protect and expand the Greek territory.* Or Julius Caesar: *To promote the greatest possible prosperity for the Roman people . . . and to protect and expand their territory.* Henry VIII: *To enforce peace, order, and true religion on the English people . . . And to protect and expand their territory.*

Notice a pattern? The greatest and most powerful of all rulers, and their governments, never imagined that their sole legitimate purpose was to protect rights given to their people by someone other than themselves. Although dissidents and philosophers may have proposed such radical ideas, never had such impractical nonsense been asserted by an actual government, revolutionary or otherwise. And to be fair, the signers of the Declaration hadn't exactly formed a "government" just yet. But the events that followed would by necessity quickly convert many in that Second Continental Congress into a governing body that supervised and funded a military effort that would bring the greatest empire of the day to its knees.

So you see, it was kind of an unprecedented big deal, this American Founding. And it was nothing more than the forceful insistence on an idea.

But the twentieth century brought about a hundred-year assault on that idea. By slow and subtle means, in fits and starts, with measures coated in syrupy intentions and high-minded assurances, that idea has been undermined as the governing force in America in a way no armed redcoats were ever able to achieve.

The trouble for our modern-day ruling class of elites and nanny-staters, is that no matter how slowly the heat rises in the pot, eventually the proverbial frog does realize his mortal peril. For him, it is always too late. For America, it's never too late. As long as America still embraces that Founding idea, she can always throw off tyranny and insist on that idea as her ruling principle once again.

In order to do so, America must once again examine this idea in order to better embrace it and fight for it.

The idea is simply this: The proper role of the government is to secure the unalienable rights of man. All other ideas that have shaped governments are simply not the American idea. They may have merits. They may even be corollaries of the American idea or derivatives of it in some way, but they're not the same thing. To secure the welfare, the order, the peace, the happiness, the prosperity, the opportunities, or the protection of a people . . . these are all good things. Some of them may even be justly derived necessities of the original idea of securing unalienable rights.

But too often, these other ideas begin to take on a life of their own and smother the original purpose of the government. Even with the noblest of intentions and the purest of hearts, ruling elites can forget the Holy Grail that they are duty-bound to preserve—the unalienable rights of man—in favor of a sweet-sounding benevolence that can easily devolve into a comfortable tyranny, the likes of which we now see deadening the souls, and bankrupting the treasuries of Europe and many other places across the Earth.

The questions we face here in America are simple: Will we follow the same path? Do we have a means to escape that destiny? Or, are we simply a decade or so behind the economic collapse we've seen overseas? If so, what mechanism can we cling to if we wish to prevent this fate?

I would argue that a rigid, ideological reawakening is in order. It is our only hope. We must cling to our Founding idea; that the role of the government is to secure the unalienable rights of man. If we don't, if we choose some other priority for our government, be it security, a minimum standard of living for all, or some reasonable but infinitely less vital standard by which to judge our rulers, we will follow Europe over the spiritual, economic, and political cliff.

Take another look at the passage quoted above. From this very simple collection of assertions made by our Founders, we can derive some key points. First, that there are unalienable rights, and some of them are listed, but the list is not exhaustive. Fortunately, we have the Constitution, which lays out a longer (but still not exhaustive) list of rights in its Bill of Rights and subsequent amendments. Some of these aren't necessarily unalienable, however. For instance, under certain conditions (i.e., at time of war or national emergency) some of these rights could be temporarily suspended by the executive—as has happened!

Even without a clear indication from our Founders delineating that exhaustive list of rights, we do have a vital starting point: life, liberty, and the pursuit of happiness. Until those three unalienable rights are properly restored in the fullness imagined by the Founders, there's no point in arguing over anything else. Let's just start with the low-hanging fruit we know the government *must* protect rather than wasting time on everything else.

Preserving the freedom of all men means that one man is not perfectly free. For instance, if all men have the right to life, then I am not free to stab you to death. So, paradoxically, the notion of freedom for all necessarily implies a certain abridgment of freedom at the same time. This means that the government is in fact justified in abridging some freedom in order to secure a greater freedom.

(And by the way, here's another shout-out to my critics. I am using the word *men* as a gender-neutral term. I am not implying only *men* have rights.)

I have freedom of speech, but I can't publicly lie or slander you to the point where it causes you damage—at least that's how it's supposed to work! I am free to choose whatever religion I want, but no governing body can ever demand that I practice one particular faith or deny me the right to exercise my religion wherever I choose—again, at least that's the idea.

But here's where the trouble really starts. Reasonable people can disagree about that balance. Every day we are faced with infinite examples of this. Some people argue that the liberty to drive the car I own is dependent on the competence and safety of all drivers on every road. In order to protect my life and liberty to drive safely, the government is thus justified in depriving all would-be drivers of the liberty to drive if they try to do so without a license and insurance, or with reckless disregard of the rules of the road.

But there are some libertarians among us who would argue that the world is a dangerous place and it's not the government's job to rob us of liberty in order to protect us from the risks of exercising liberty. What's more, the level of safety required of drivers might depend on where they drive. The kind of competence it takes to drive a car on long, flat highways in the rural plains states might be totally different from the competence needed to drive a taxi cab in New York City.

So maybe the controversy as to the right balance will split along geographical lines, with New Yorkers thinking one type of balance is right and Kansans having a totally different view. Who wins? The Constitution doesn't resolve these controversies for us. After all, the Constitution says we all have to be treated the same under the law, no matter where we plan to drive, right?

(Stick with me here. I'm making a case for local control as opposed to federal control.)

Think of it as a kind of freedom food chain: Not all rights are created equal; invariably, the lesser are sacrificed for the greater. Your right to life is infinitely more valuable than your neighbor's right to drive on the wrong side of the road. But who defines the lesser and the greater?

The practical implication of the freedom food chain on the proper role of the government is this: If the government's only legitimate purpose is to secure the unalienable rights of man, then the government may only deprive man of rights and freedoms in order to protect rights and freedoms. Usually this means restricting lesser freedoms (such as the freedom to drive on either side of any road) in order to protect greater freedom (to protect the lives of others on the road).

Implied in this *legitimate* trade-off is the notion of what would be an *illegitimate* trade-off: You don't deprive anyone of a right or freedom in order to preserve *lesser* rights and freedoms. That's why we don't usually make robbing a bank a capital crime, because the right to our property, no matter how grievously violated, is never greater than the right to life. In that vein, we generally only take life in order to preserve life, rather than to preserve property, or some other lesser liberty. We generally wage a shooting war only on those who would kill our citizens, not those who merely annoy them.

The problem with the freedom food chain is that it is all about balance, and people disagree on such a subjective notion. When two groups have different ideas about where in the freedom food chain a particular right falls, who wins?

The Declaration of Independence uses the word "governments" as the institution tasked with securing the rights of man. The implication is that there is no *one* "government." Government in and of itself contains many expressions and levels. Fortunately for us, our constitutional framers created the concept we call Federalism. At the time, they did not call it that. To them, Federalism simply meant "Constitutionalism." Federalists were those who supported the ratification of the Constitution by the states and argued their position against the anti-Federalists who opposed the Constitution. The anti-Federalists thought the Constitution infringed upon state sovereignty too much. However, our modern concept of Federalism appears to be just the opposite. Today it means the system created by the Constitution, of taking most of the power away from the federal government and reserving it solely for the states and the people themselves.

The last item in the Bill of Rights is the brilliant locus of Federalism known as the Tenth Amendment:

The powers not delegated to the United States by the Constitution, nor prohibited by it to the States, are reserved to the States respectively, or to the people. . . .

In other words, if a power is not explicitly given to the federal government in the text of the Constitution, we cannot expect that power to reside in the federal government. Instead, it is reserved only for the states or the people themselves. Note that the Constitution gives no guidance as to how to divvy up the power reserved for the states and the people. That's for state constitutions to sort out. It merely says, "If it ain't written in plain ink here on this page, the feds can't do it. We don't care who does it, but it ain't gonna be the feds."

End of argument.

James Madison, one of the famous authors of the Federalist Papers, defending the Constitution against accusations of federal power-grabbing, expounded more on this amendment:

The powers delegated by the proposed Constitution to the Federal Government, are few and defined. Those which are to remain in the State Governments are numerous and indefinite. The former will be exercised principally on external objects, as war, peace, negotiation, and foreign commerce; with which last the power of taxation will for the most part be connected. The powers reserved to the several States will extend to all the objects, which, in the ordinary course of affairs, concern the lives, liberties and properties of the people; and the internal order, improvement, and prosperity of the State. . . . (Federalist No. 45, 313–4)

In essence, this is Federalism. Only a few powers are reserved for the federal government. The rest belong to the state or the people themselves if they aren't delegated to the state in state constitutions. So why does Federalism help us so much with figuring out the proper role of the government? After all, doesn't this Tenth Amendment just say that there are an indefinite number of powers and they are reserved either for the federal government or the state government—either of which are still governments?

The reason why Federalism helps us is found in understanding the reason why a federalist system was enshrined in the Tenth Amendment. Why would the Founders have wanted to limit the federal government to so short a list of powers? They must have done it for a reason. And that reason is related to the freedom food chain.

The more power we give to others, the less freedom we have. It is the same with our rights and freedoms—so much more precious than a diamond. The farther away from us, from our homes, our communities, our cities that those entrusted with our liberties are, the fewer our options are when we seek recourse. It goes back to the concept of "the consent of the governed." Basically, this can be interpreted to mean that as you get farther from a delegation of power, the use of that power is less subject to your consent.

That's why we want the freedoms that sit the highest on the freedom food chain to be protected by those closest to us. The Founders envisioned that only a tiny portion of taxation would come out of Congress. They expected states and cities to have the highest taxes. They expected that the vast majority of executions would be by states and localities, and only in the most rare cases of high treason or military crimes during time of war would the federal government ever have the power to deprive anyone of life.

Not only would the power over our highest rights be delegated to those most subject to our consent, but also it was expected that the more common, everyday deprivations of liberty would also be preserved to those authorities closest to us. In other words, it was expected that if we were to be controlled in ways that deprive us of liberty, no matter how small, it was almost always going to be at the local level. Put another way, if an infringement of liberty was *grave*, it better be local, or if it was *frequent*, it better be local. Because it is the grave and the frequent encroaching policies which need to be most accountable to those governed by them.

Never in a thousand years would the Founders have imagined the federal government depriving us of liberties from the time we get up to the time we go to bed. And yet today the federal government controls the voltage powers of the alarm clocks that wake us up in the morning, the type of toilets we use when we roll out of bed, the water that flows in our showers, the ingredients and permitted labeling of our toothpaste and cereal, the standards under which we raise the cows that produce the milk we pour on that cereal, and on and on . . . until we lay our heads down on our government-approved synthetic pillows.

If you do not consent to the legion of federal rules, what is your recourse? In practical terms, very little. You can vote for your representatives in Congress, but no matter how good your guy is, he can be outvoted by the rest of the members. And as we all know, it's really hard to vote out an incumbent.

Without time and money to organize beyond your sphere of existing contacts, you are literally powerless to retaliate against those who abuse the power you delegated.

What's more, as we discussed above, the specifics of the proper balance between infringing on rights in order to preserve rights is something people can vigorously disagree about. That's why it's best if the vast, vast majority of those debates are local. I might be willing to give up a little more of my income to provide a safety net for down-and-out neighbors if I can see them every day and know the people taking care of them. But I'm much less likely to give up the right to my income for strangers living across the country, who might spend my money in ways that would offend and insult me. I might understand the need for a speed limit on my busy Main Street, but why should I have any say over the speed limit on a highway five states over?

The fact is, by keeping these decisions local, *Federalism, when properly observed, provides the greatest accountability for the greatest source of would-be freedom-raiders.* If those who restrict my freedoms are my neighbors, they are going to be a heck of a lot more careful to exercise that power reasonably than an elected official in Washington who never has to answer to me.

Secretary of Health and Human Services Kathleen Sebelius once said in reference to ObamaCare, "The essence of good government is trust." In other words, don't question us. Just trust us. I heard that and thought, *Oh, give me a break!* Secretary Sebelius had it exactly 180 degrees wrong. The essence of good government, and the essence of the American system of government, is distrust. It is all about installing the maximum amount of accountability over those with the maximum power. That's why Federalism matters. And that's why we must insist on a federal government that limits itself to the powers enumerated in the Constitution, and leaves everything else to the states or to the people themselves.

CHAPTER FOURTEEN

Reimagining the American Dream

God who gave us life gave us liberty. And can the liberties of a nation be thought secure when we have removed their only firm basis, a conviction in the minds of the people that these liberties are a gift from God? That they are not to be violated but with His wrath? Indeed I tremble for my country when I reflect that God is just, and that His justice cannot sleep forever.

Thomas Jefferson

Let us accept that the only proper role of the government is to secure the God-given rights of man. In doing so, we acknowledge that the government must by necessity deprive all of us of lesser liberties in order to preserve for all of us the greatest liberties. This is the case in requiring licenses to exercise certain rights (to drive, to own a gun, to build a house, etc. . . .). There are even times when the government must deprive us of a few of our greatest liberties in order to preserve those great liberties for others. This is the case in capital punishment, general incarceration, or quarantine.

Notice that in each of these *legitimate* deprivations of liberty, the objective is the preservation of greater liberty. Notice, too, that these legitimate deprivations are most often and most appropriately carried out by local or state governments—that is, levels of government that are more accountable to the people than the federal government is. For example, we receive our driving, building, and gun licenses from the state or the city; similarly, foster care systems are run by local municipalities or states, and so forth.

In other words, two principles emerge: the freedom food chain and Federalism. Freedoms can only be "eaten" by freedoms higher on the food chain. You can only suppress freedom in the service of a greater freedom. A government cannot legitimately suppress freedom in service of some other cause, no matter how nice the cause is.

The more you respect someone, the more you trust his judgment . . . and the less likely you are to try to tell him what to do. It would be as absurd as telling Mother Teresa to "behave herself" on her way out the door, or urging General Patton to "win one for the Gipper."

So it is with the role of the government. The more respect we as a society have for the individual, the more likely we are to get out of that person's way, to let him arrive at his own conclusions, chart his own course. If we think that all humans are mediocre, then we might think the government should provide for their basic needs, and that should be well and good.

But if we look at humans as God's priceless masterpieces created for earthly greatness and imitation of God, and destined for eternal glory . . . well, then we're going to be sure that nothing gets in their way, aren't we? Who'd want to micro-manage *that*?

Conversely, the less respect we have for someone, the more likely we are to intervene. Control is merely a sign of distrust. The less we trust someone's competence, greatness, or potential, the more we will try to control him—for his own good, we'll say, but also for the good of everyone he might affect. This is to be expected; it's why we control our children. They may have great potential, but their competence and judgment are still taking shape, so we control much in their lives until they grow in these areas and we can lighten up.

In this way, independence becomes the product of competence.

Because of this basic truth, we can draw certain conclusions about a government that is highly interventionist or controlling. We can understand its root assumptions about its trust of its citizens by looking at how it treats them. We can assess just how glorious and great a society views the individual human soul by how hands-off or hands-on that society is with its government authority.

It comes down to this: The more a society values the freedom and greatness of the individual soul, the more willing people will be to die for it. People will die for what they prize the most. And so the reverse must also be true. When a government honors people, people honor the government. Remember, even baboons and elephants innately protect their family circle. What separates us from the beasts is the ability to value something outside our own interests. If we don't have that innate ability to love something greater than ourselves, then it is easy to lose freedom in order to preserve ourselves—a survival of the fittest argument, if you will.

There is a societal choice when it comes to freedom. We are seeing this in the uprisings in the Middle East. Dictators, despite the seeming paradox, can only rule with the consent of their people. If their people refuse to play along and instead seek to shut down the country, usually by bravely risking life and limb and liberty, then the dictator has little recourse.

Bravery isn't just fearlessness or reckless risk-taking; it's an expression of our deepest values. What we call bravery is usually an expression of valuing something more than our own life. Our most heroic risk-taking demonstrates our greatest values, because we're willing to risk more for what we value more. A mother will risk her own life to defend her child against an attacker. A Christian in a Muslim country will risk his life in order to protect his relationship with God. A political dissident will risk his freedom to defend his God-given right to free speech or assembly or . . . whatever it is that ultimately gets him jailed.

Our American revolutionaries demonstrated that they valued freedom and independence more than life. People who value something more than their own lives almost always win. We saw a similar type of risk-taking in the civil rights movement. People decided they wanted freedom and equality under the law more than they wanted their own safety. They were willing to risk being hosed down, spit on, beaten, jailed, or worse. And, ultimately, they won.

One beautiful side effect that occurs when people value something more than life and safety and liberty is that it is a mental and spiritual challenge to those watching. This challenge is often why motivated minorities can overcome powerful majorities. Because of the challenge their risk throws out to a watching world, sometimes the risk is all it takes to win. And since they value it, they must protect it for others. This process can sometimes overthrow tyranny without a single bullet being fired, or at least without the mass violence that might otherwise be required.

In the United States today, we've lost touch with these ideals. We've grown fat in our freedom and have willingly exchanged our freedom for government-provided comfort.

Ask yourself, "What is the American Dream?" When I asked that question to folks I met on the campaign trail, so many answered that it meant to own a house or a car, or to be able to do whatever they wanted. Sadly, that is not the answer. That is not what the American Dream meant for generations before mine. The American Dream meant the chance to work hard, to save and sacrifice, to *earn* the house or the car or the freedom to do as they please. Everyone had a shot at the American Dream, if you were willing to pay the price. Today, the American Dream is government-subsidized. By its very nature, it can't exist that way.

In previous generations, character was developed through hard work, sacrifice, planning for the future, and being challenged regularly to put the needs of others before your own. The reward was in the pride and love that were deepened by meeting these challenges—and this, in turn, created a better, stronger America.

Also, for most Americans of all races and ethnicities and

religions, the basic family structure was still the norm. Children were born to married couples who usually stayed married. Judeo-Christian values strengthened the family. The family was the central provider, not the government.

So did the overgrowth of government create the collapse of the family, or did the family collapse because of government overgrowth? One could argue it was both, sort of like when a drowning victim takes the lifeguard down with him.

Today, the size of government has grown far, far beyond anything imagined at the Founding. With that overgrowth comes the countless losses of liberty, the infinite amount of control over the souls of citizens. As a society, we have accepted this. We have seen occasional backlashes at the ballot box, such as in a "post-LBJ" Nixon victory or a "post-Carter" Reagan landslide. But nothing has completely stopped the downward spiral. We enjoy fewer and fewer freedoms, while the government exhibits more and more control.

The Depression/New Deal era legitimized government as God. The sexual liberation and authority-challenging of the sixties and seventies legitimized the rejection of Judeo-Christian traditions. Today, the decades of intellectual justification for rejecting faith in the mind, which had already been rejected in practice, is about to be the last nail in the coffin for our Judeo-Christian culture.

Why is this important? Well, as we've moved away from our fundamental Judeo-Christian worldview on which this nation was founded, there has been a slow surrender of liberty to our new government saviors and our willingness to surrender to the "collective good" because of a devaluation of unique human dignity. Every person, by virtue of being created in the image and likeness of God, has an unrepeatable precious human dignity.

By unrepeatable I mean just that. It can't be repeated. Think of someone you love. Now, even if there was a way to clone humans, and someone was able to duplicate a whole new person with the exact DNA, exact look, exact voice, it still wouldn't be your loved one. It's that unrepeatable quality that makes a person uniquely who they are, that makes you uniquely who you are.

This unique worth is in everyone, regardless of race, physical ability, or circumstance. Every single human being has an unrepeatable preciousness that is worth protecting. That, and that alone, is why government was created.

Let us not forget—God gave us our rights, not man.

As the Founders said, a government's "just powers are derived from the consent of the governed." Infinite worth and power resides with the people. Under the American system, we bestow on others the freedom and power to hurt us only when we trust them enough to know that they won't! If I am free to be different or try different things than my neighbor, without interference from my neighbor or any governing authority, then I am truly free indeed.

Our Founders understood this link between faith and the proliferation of human freedom. The ample evidence of their own faith is widely available, as are their assertions that the government they designed was based on a transcendent respect for the sanctity of mankind. The Declaration of Independence justifies its own necessity with an assertion about the rights and dignity of man. In light of that foundation, all the other assertions in the document flow as logical necessities. If man is indeed *this* free, if his life is *this* precious, then any government that offends his dignity and suppresses his freedom is, by necessity, illegitimate and must be thrown off for the sake of God and man, His masterpiece.

These beliefs have consequences. And the gradual dilution and diminishment of these beliefs will of course also have consequences. A government founded on such truths will only remain faithful to them as long as those who govern and those who sustain them also hold those truths with unwavering fervor. Even in the zeal of our Founding, the risks of dwindling conviction about this reverence for humanity were known and warnings duly given. In 1781, Thomas Jefferson, the author of that Declaration, said this about the Divine origin of human liberty:

> *God who gave us life gave us liberty. And can the liberties of a nation be thought secure when we have removed their only firm basis, a conviction in the minds of the people that these liberties are a gift from God? That they are not to be violated but with His wrath? Indeed I tremble for my country when I reflect that God is just, and that His justice cannot sleep forever.*

As we abandon our Founding notion that liberties are given by God and ignore Jefferson's warning that their violation cannot escape His wrath; as we not only willingly and casually surrender our own liberties like sheep to the slaughter, but also sit tacitly by and allow even more grave and frequent liberties of others to be taken by force of law, it is inevitable that the consequence of this devaluation of human dignity will not only offend a just and holy God, but will make us less and less human, more and more like savage and un-thinking and mute animals, who act only on our passions and not on our reason, a little more with each passing year.

CHAPTER FIFTEEN

Our Follower in Chief

If you set out to be liked, you would be prepared to compromise on anything at any time, and you would achieve nothing.

—Margaret Thatcher

Barack Obama's penchant for popularity could be the downfall of our country. I'll admit, that's a pretty bold statement, right here in the opening of this chapter, but I offer it in all seriousness, recognizing full well what it means to question the ability of our president to lead, to make good decisions, and to protect our most cherished Constitutional rights. And I do so with the utmost respect for the office of the presidency.

When a little boy gets his first red plastic fireman's hat, we all *ooh!* and *ah!*, take pictures, and tell him encouraging things about helping people and being a hero. But nobody actually expects Junior to put on heavy equipment and carry a fire hose up twenty flights of stairs to put out a fire. That's how I see our forty-fourth president. As if he were a child playing cops and robbers, words have no meaning for President Obama. He shouts, "Bang, bang, you're dead!" but he doesn't really mean it. He puts handcuffs on his playmates (like Wall Street moguls and other Democrat donors), but he doesn't really take them to jail. As long as he gets the rush of saying the right things and going through the motions, it seems to count in his mind as *actually doing stuff.*

Like our aspiring little firefighter, President Obama wants to dress up as president and enjoy the fawning press and fancy perks of the office. Did he think no one would expect him to lead? He campaigned on leadership vision, intellectual seriousness, and management know-how. America *ooh'd* and *aah'd*, encouraged him to be a hero, and put him in the White House. Problem is, we expected him to actually govern—especially when leadership and seriousness would be most put to the test, as in the Gulf oil spill, the economic meltdown , the crisis in the Middle East, and many more grave situations facing our nation in his first (and, let's hope, *only!*) four-year term.

The disaster in the Gulf was a great example of the glaring chasm between what the country expects to motivate a president and what motivates *this* president. Driven by public perception rather than public good, the *appearance* of competence was, as it always is for Mr. Obama, just as important to him as *actual* competence. As long as his critics weren't blaming him for the problem—or, better yet, were blaming someone else!—the president could convince himself that he had all but solved the problem.

Any actions being taken to *actually* contain the spill—as opposed to containing the PR damage—were taken on the part of BP and heroic state officials like Republican Louisiana Governor Bobby Jindal, rather than the feds. President Obama didn't make one move until the media were clamoring for him to. Like an annoyed teenager asked to do his chores before he goes out for the night, the president dragged his feet, waiting on the media to suggest a to-do list.

It took the president over a week to even declare an emergency or visit the Gulf region. And the roster of the snap-delegation the White House sent in the initial weeks after the explosion? Department of Justice lawyers, EPA "SWAT teams" (whatever *they* are), and a climate-change czar. Only *after* being goaded into it by public pressure did the president approve requests from local officials, meet with victims' families, and meet with BP execs. And who can forget the butt-kicking vulgarity he dutifully "emoted" after being chastised by Hollywood director Spike Lee for not "going off"?

Obama lacked the maturity to recognize that he could have provided comfort and solidarity for our Gulf neighbors with the small sacrifice of purging from his schedule events too frivolous for the leader of a nation in crisis. Such a purge might have started with the three high-roller fundraisers, six rounds of golf, two family vacations, and two parties with rock stars and other celebrities.

And then there was that Oval Office address . . . fifty days too late, with starry-eyed zeal about how the crisis somehow justifies bullying America into an unaffordable, job-killing, economy-choking national energy tax.

Based on his actions, rather than rhetoric, we were left to conclude that continued leakage in the Gulf and the subsequent destruction of the coastline, coastal industries, and wildlife were all just fine with President Obama, as long as nobody thought less of *him* for it.

Then we have the economy. To be fair, the deficit spending

and skyrocketing debt was already in place when Obama took office. The TARP bailouts and unprecedented spending and associated annual deficits started under President Bush (though the spending spree reached unprecedented reckless-ness when the Democrats took over Congress in 2006), with then-Senator Obama voting in favor. The housing bubble that generated this economic meltdown started under Democratic policies to force banks to lend to uncreditworthy borrowers. In the Clinton and Bush years, nobody did a thing about this, though there were some who were trying to warn us. To their credit, some Republican lawmakers earnestly tried to seek Fannie and Freddie reform, but were powerless in the minor-ity to influence the corrupt favor factory that was the House Financial Services and Senate Banking Committee leader-ship.

Those shady loans and all their subsequent risk were then quickly offloaded by the banks that made them turn to Fannie and Freddie in the first place, who bundled them up into packages bought by the big investment banks and there morphed into complex securities with risk portfolios that no one could really appreciate or even understand. As the under-lying mortgages were defaulted on at higher-than-expected rates, those securities tanked, bringing the banks most lev-eraged on those securities down with them. The housing mar-ket collapsed, the banks had to be bailed out with TARP, and the broader economy spiraled.

I agree, it's not fair to lay all of this at the president's feet, although *Senator* Obama was certainly part of the dysfunc-tional Congress that fiddled while Rome burned. Nonetheless, he was a junior senator who did next to nothing in the Senate except run for president, and the crisis was well on when he won that most coveted prize.

As president, Obama's economic policies have doomed an entire decade of what should have been reasonable economic growth out of a short recession. He has spouted endless amounts of words on the subject, consulted with so-called experts, and promised laser-like focus, special commissions, and whatnot. As long as he has appeared to care and to be doing something, he has successfully avoided blame (at least by the media and professional Democrats). And it seems that this is sufficient for him—avoiding blame, that is. Because certainly the lack of actual economic improvement has not caused him to change course. This leads us to ask a fundamental question: Does he not know how to create economic recovery, or does he not want to?

The reason that question has only two possible answers, neither of which is fitting of an American president, is that pro-growth policies are not hidden in some secret lockbox.

Regardless of origin, whether man-made or part of the natural cycles of a normal economy, recessions, once under way, respond predictably to government policy. What I mean by *predictable* is this: They get worse under certain policies, and they are minimized under other policies. This is historically demonstrable and irrefutable over a century of well-documented American recessions and varying federal responses to them.

Indeed, when pro-growth policies are put in place, recessions are short and minimally damaging. It doesn't matter if these pro-growth policies are put in place by a Democrat as with President Kennedy or violated by a Republican, as with President Nixon.

(Such pro-growth policies include lowering tax rates, eliminating particularly perverse tax disincentives to growth and investment, cutting government spending to keep more capital in the private economy, and eliminating bureaucratic red tape and regulation that slows down economic activity or punishes growth or suppresses competition.) When the federal response is instead to increase the size, scope, and heavy hand of government over the economy, recessions drag out and turn into national nightmares that rob a generation of Americans of the income, return on investments and savings, and career opportunities they otherwise would have had. This can reverberate through generations, especially for those at the bottom of the economy. That's why you need a president who actually understands the seriousness of his impact on the lives of hundreds of millions of Americans and their children, and who views that responsibility with the grave humility and caution it requires.

It seems that Obama is either perfectly okay with an economy in permanent meltdown, or doesn't know enough basic economics to fix it. He seems content to simply *look like* he both cares and knows what he's doing . . . *instead of actually fixing it*! Take the so-called "stimulus," for example. It seems Obama was just interested in having a stack of paper to *call* a stimulus bill and didn't actually care whether or not the policies contained therein would really stimulate economic growth. I say this only because if he had cared, then the content of the stimulus bill could not have been what it was. We were told the stimulus bill would go to "shovel-ready" construction and infrastructure projects. The argument was that the projects themselves would require workers, and once completed, the infrastructure built by them would help economic activity by facilitating transportation, better power grids, and so forth. We can argue about the dubiousness of these claims, but let's give him the benefit of the doubt on this one. The problem, however, was that there were no shovel-ready projects, as the President himself later, rather stunningly, admitted. Instead, the money was slated for pork projects and bailouts of state governments that had spent themselves into bankruptcy. Those uses of funds may have had merit had they been fully disclosed and debated in another context, but no one can seriously claim that they stimulate new jobs or lasting economic growth. And no one can seriously defend the NIH plan to spend $2.5 million of that stimulus money to teach prostitutes in China how to drink responsibly.

Did President Obama not realize that his stimulus would fail? Or did he know it wouldn't work, and hoped he could put a nice enough ribbon on it that we wouldn't notice? Does it even matter?

That kind of image-driven psychosis is what is wrong with Obama's presidency, if you ask me. As long as he's not being blamed for our problems—by the media, or by the voters around election time—he really seems unconcerned about whether his policies make those problems worse or better. It's almost as if he's interested in the presidency because it's cool to be President, this is a one-man illustration of an obsession with self-esteem for its own sake rather than as a result of accomplishment.

You see, it appears words simply have no meaning for President Obama. He says he's going to have a "laserlike focus" on jobs. But instead, he focuses like a laser on forcing through

a broken health-care bill. And that "temporary" oil drilling mor-
atorium that shut down an entire industry and its jobs, in violation of a federal court order? Nearly a year later, that was still
in place. How's that for laserlike? The President says projects
are "shovel-ready," but then admits that this is not the case. He
claims to have "saved or created" millions of jobs, but the unemployment rate keeps going up. He says he "will not rest" until
the BP oil spill is contained, but he goes on serial golf outings,
family vacations, and political fundraisers while the oil gushes
onto Gulf shores. He says he will not tolerate a nuclear Iran,
but Iran is steadily going nuclear under his watch. He says he
is committed to a secure southern border, but then he sues
Arizona in federal court for trying to help ICE enforce the
border.

His 2011 State of the Union address included this nugget:
"Because you deserve to know exactly how and where your
tax dollars are being spent, you'll be able to go to a Web site
and get that information for the very first time in history."

Actually, the very first time that happened in history was
in 2006, when the Coburn-*Obama* Federal Funding Accountability and Transparency Act was signed by President Bush
and implemented shortly thereafter in the form of the groundbreaking new Web site: www.usaspending.gov. That's right, it
was a Coburn-Obama Bill. Senator Obama was there at the
White House signing ceremony. Did he forget that this Web
site already existed? Was he planning on starting a new, re-
dundant Web site in addition to the one he *personally* created
four years ago? And if so, wouldn't that really be the "second"
time in history rather than the "first time in history"? It's a
small point, but given how much effort and hand-wringing

goes into deciding what's in and what's out of a State of the Union address, this bizarre episode speaks volumes about Obama's total disregard for the plain meaning of words.

It's not like this waffling is unknown in politics, but usually wafflers . . . well, they *waffle*. They're more vague than this president. They speak in vague generalities and platitudes. They try to avoid specific positions like the plague. In Obama's case, he actually takes positions. He's articulate. His speeches, if you pretend that what he's saying might actually be true, can be quite moving. It's just that he never seems to mean what he says or do as he says. So, if a position later turns out to be unpopular or unwise once the facts are known, he just changes position, and then he tells us about it with an articulate flourish.

He's at his worst—or *best*, depending on your point of view—when he's out campaigning. He simply takes the opposing view, whether or not he really believes it. You get the feeling these are just lines in speeches to him, words on a teleprompter, not actual policies that he has arrived at through study and conviction and that he intends to fight for. When he gets elected, he has no tendency whatsoever in favor of policies he has previously endorsed. If he discovers that there are reasons why his opponent may have taken a different view and that those reasons still exist, he just switches his position and does what his advisors tell him he must. A few examples come to mind. First, to distinguish himself from Hillary Clinton, his 2008 primary opponent, he claimed to oppose the Iraq war, especially the surge that ultimately led to victory. He promised to withdraw troops almost immediately upon taking office. His opponent, with great cost and agonizing, took difficult votes to support Iraq funding, including the surge, and stood by her position because she thought it was right even if it wasn't perfect. Once in office, of course, Obama looked at the facts, apparently for the very first time, and arrived at the same judgment as his primary opponent and predecessor—namely, that the surge must be continued and that timetables for withdrawal were foolish. He just switched positions, escaping all the consequences of taking that painful position that his more serious opponents took during the campaign.

The same thing happened with the terrorist detention facility at Guantánamo Bay, Cuba. The flippancy of his opposition to Gitmo for purely campaign purposes was exposed when he simply switched positions as soon as he was shown the information that his opponent already knew—namely, that these were dangerous guys who would be difficult to prosecute legally, but who would nonetheless do us harm if we let them go. National security isn't always black and white—sometimes difficult decisions have to be made. But criticizing those who take the tough positions, only to take the same position himself once elected, just further proves that Obama is disinterested in policy. He uses words about policy to win elections, but those words have no bearing on actual policy once elected.

Then, of course, we have the individual mandate to buy health-care insurance as part of his health-care reform package that will wreak havoc on our economy. Then-senator Clinton included the mandate in her reform proposal during the primary campaign. She didn't dance around or deny her support for this (horrible) mandate as Obama did. Obama saw an opportunity to gain support by opposing an unpopular, but what he later claimed was a necessary, element of the Democrat health-care policy. He criticized Clinton for the mandate. Then, when he passed his own reform once in office, he included the mandate. When the mandate was challenged in various courts, his lawyers argued vigorously that the mandate was an absolutely essential lynchpin on which the entire reform package depended.

So do we have a President who's just learning as he goes? Or is it that, once again, his opposition to the mandate during the campaign was just words. When he was elected and actually had to craft policy, he did what his advisors told him he must and supported the policy he had savaged his opponent for endorsing.

There are so many nonsensical and flippant examples of words that Obama doesn't mean, I'm losing track of them all. He promised during his campaign to convert the entire White House auto fleet to plug-in cars within a year of becoming president, an idea so blatantly absurd that no one even reported it back then. He promised to double the Peace Corps, and double funding for after-school programs. He has done no such thing. He promised to support a human mission to the moon through NASA by 2020. Instead, his budgets have gutted NASA funding and have actually dismissed human lunar landings in favor of robotics and other priorities.

Serious politicians know better than to make such specific claims in a campaign unless they are absolutely sure they can accomplish them or are at least willing to fight for them, even if they end up losing.

As incredible as all these examples are, this bad habit of making promises you won't keep and claiming results you don't and couldn't obtain reaches new heights of disingenuousness with the health-care reform process of 2009–10.

First, the process. He promised to put the meetings and debate on C-SPAN. He didn't. He promised to include Republican ideas. He didn't. He promised to allow five days of public comment before signing bills. He rammed the bill through Congress using outrageous and arguably illegal procedural gimmicks and signed the bill almost immediately afterward.

Next, the policy. He promised that you could keep your insurance plan if you liked it. But the bill allows employers (through whom most Americans have insurance coverage) to dump all their employees into the government insurance market. In order to prevent hundreds of unions and employee groups from dropping all the coverage they offer members, Obama has had to provide more than two thousand exemptions from the law. He promised that the bill would lower the deficit. Even his own actuaries have openly mocked and denied this claim. He promised that insurance premiums would go down. They have gone up, dramatically. He promised (in writing, in an executive order!) that abortions would not be funded by taxpayers under the law. The leading abortion experts in the country have exposed in painstaking legal detail exactly how taxpayer-funded abortions will be dramatically expanded and even mandated under the law. He promised that no one making less than $250,000 in annual income would see any kind of tax increase under his presidency. Yet, when the law's penalty for not purchasing health insurance was challenged in court, his lawyers argued that it was constitutional, precisely because it was a tax increase, allowed under Congress's authority to levy taxes, rather than a penalty.

In the area of foreign policy, perhaps more than anywhere else, Obama has shown that he is a follower and not a leader. He simply doesn't want to have a policy on any foreign policy issue. He just wants to use words. Policies require choices of one path over another path, with the sad but necessary sacrifice of all the good that might have come with the sacrificed path, in favor of the supposed greater good of the chosen path. He seems either unwilling or unable to make such choices. Unfortunately for him, in foreign policy matters making no choice is in fact a choice in itself—a choice that carries real and tangible consequences. By letting chips fall where they may, Obama has tacitly endorsed and enabled the status quo.

Now, please don't get me wrong. We are all grateful that Osama bin Laden was killed under his watch. But based on Obama's pattern of indecision in foreign policy, one can hardly claim that the death of bin Laden was a direct result of his leadership because up until that point, there had been no decisive leadership coming from the White House. Best example: the democratic uprising in Iran. By saying nothing for days, until the regime had effectively mobilized to crack down and suppress the uprising, Obama missed a huge (and, potentially, our *only*) opportunity to bring about democratic regime change in the nation posing the greatest threat to American security.

In Asia, where South Korea is a treaty ally of ours, North Korea sank a South Korean ship, killing dozens of sailors. Emboldened, North Korea bombed a South Korean island a few months later, killing civilians. It was only massive South Korean preparations for retaliation, which North Korea took as a credible threat, that stopped the aggression in its tracks.

Regarding the Gaza blockade–running by a Turkish ship, which had to be boarded by Israeli soldiers subjected to violence, Obama said absolutely nothing in defense of Israel's blockade and its legitimate right to enforce it. As a result, the very next minute, there was another ship on its way to run through the blockade and force a confrontation. Fortunately, Israel was not cowed by universal international condemnation and threatened to use force again, and the ship was eventually steered to a legal port.

As I write this, we are still trying to understand the outcome of the Egyptian crisis, although I suspect our president will be unable to grasp it for some time. Here again, Obama said absolutely nothing until events were already determined. He did not seek in any way to influence those events, despite the very real possibility that the uprising could empower a Muslim Brotherhood takeover of a critical U.S. ally and threaten war with Israel. The Muslim Brotherhood is the group known for incubating terrorist organizations such as Hamas and al-Qaeda. Now, Obama didn't have to stand by Egyptian president Mubarak in order to still demand the rights and freedoms of the Egyptian people for a *secular* democratic government. (*Secular* . . . this would have been a key code word against the Brotherhood.) Instead he has done nothing and the world holds its breath to see if the largest and most important Arab nation falls to radical Islamists.

A leader would make sure that doesn't happen. A follower holds his breath.

To sum up, President Obama has been disastrous for our

nation because he is satisfied to merely avoid blame for problems rather than solve problems, because words have no meaning for him, and because he is a follower rather than a leader. This lethal combination of character flaws means that no substantive policies are put forward by him; rather, they are allowed to be put forward by others either *through* him, or through others with his approval. This approach places America at the whim of events or the leadership of others, either members of his staff, those from the radical wing of his own party (Pelosi/Reid), or worst of all, the most dangerous of rogue nations in the world.

His problem is basic: The man seems just not interested in *doing* anything. As if he became president because he wanted to *be* something, wanted respect and admiration and awe. But he didn't want to have to actually *do* anything to make the world a better place, or to make America stronger.

His presidency is one long, sad illustration of this preference for being remarkable over doing remarkable things.

As I wrote at the top of this chapter, I don't mean to be harsh. Barack Obama is our President. He holds an office that commands our respect. But that doesn't prevent us from recognizing our own mistake: putting him in that office in the first place. American voters are catching on to the unbelievable fraud they've been sold in Barack Obama. The 2010 midterms were a complete rebuke to those in Congress who have enabled Obama's adolescent policy rampage. That's a great first step, but it'll take another year before the grown-ups can wrest the executive branch away from left-wing protesters and economic illiterates currently surrounding and influencing our Community Activist in Chief.

It grieves me to admit it, but when then-senator Hillary Clinton tried to warn us that then-senator Obama wasn't ready for the grave phone call at three A.M., she was right. When then-senator Joe Biden told us that Obama wasn't ready for prime time and would require "on-the-job training," he was right. And when then-senator Obama himself protested in 2006 that he wasn't going to run for president because that job required more experience than he had, he was right.

Fortunately, it's not too late to shut down Woodstock and send the kids home. A Republican sweep in 2012 is desperately needed to rescue our nation from the brink of more disasters than we care to count . . . brought about by Obama's failures.

Winning an election might have made him president, but it didn't make him presidential. Americans know the difference.

PART THREE

My Hope

A genuine leader is not a searcher for consensus, but a molder of consensus.

—Dr. Martin Luther King Jr.

CHAPTER SIXTEEN

Apathy to Activism in Seven Steps

In my campaign speeches I repeated over and over that my goal, my whole candidacy, was about putting the political process back into the hands of the people. But the problem is that way too many good people are standing on the sidelines saying, "I don't want it!" Because unless you've been cordially invited by the Lords of the Backroom, when you step up, you risk being torn apart, chewed up, beaten down, and all sorts of viciousness. And then you're worse off for it.

I've also said in my campaign speeches that a victory on Election Day meant a victory over the politics of personal destruction. It would mean that more good men and women, but especially women, could stand up and run for office without worrying about devastating consequences and risking unnecessary hardships on their families.

But we didn't win on November's Election Day. So does that mean the toxic way of doing things still rules our political system? Does that mean the politics of personal destruction had a victory over us? Well yes and no.

No major advancement in history ever took root because *one* person won his or her battle. Every significant milestone in humanity was the culmination of the tireless work of previous dissidents; ending slavery, the woman's right to vote, the civil rights movement, these didn't just happen overnight. Countless heroic individuals battled for decades before the dam finally broke.

Such is the case here. Each time we fight, each time we step up to challenge the corrupt status quo, we are increasing the pressure on the proverbial dam. It's about to break.

Freedom is a light for which many men have died in darkness.

This challenge calls to us from the Tomb of the Unknown Soldier of the American Revolution, and I believe it calls to us more forcefully now than ever in my generation. We cannot experience a Second American Revolution without first having the character, qualities, and determination of the first American revolutionaries. We have to be willing to sacrifice everything, if necessary, even if we won't see the reward in our own lifetimes; even if it might not benefit us personally. America was never intended to be a nation of spectators.

Over the past few months, the Tea Party Movement has gone from grassroots to groundswell, as disenfranchised voters around the country are standing up in greater numbers than ever before, raising their voices in protest to ObamaCare, rising taxes and a spiraling economy. A few— too few—have been elected to Congress, but that is only the beginning. There are hundreds of thousands of elected officials in America. We need more citizen politicians serving in every level of government—from school board presidents all the way to the President of the United States.

That's easier said than done, right? Of course it is. But it can be done if we put our minds to it and if we're as fierce in our determination to win as they are in their determination to crush us.

So let me share with you what I think can be the seven steps to turning the tide in America.

Hopefully by this point in the book you're saying *Okay, count me in!* Or, perhaps you're still a little hesitant because you don't know where to start. You're not alone.

One time on the campaign trail Jennie ran into a convenience store for a quick pit stop and when the woman behind the counter saw her *O'Donnell for U.S. Senate* sticker, she said, "Oh, please tell Christine we're all rooting for her! I really hope she wins." Jennie thanked her for her much needed encouragement then reminded her she could do more than hope, "Don't forget to vote on November 2!" Then the woman responded, somewhat timidly, "Oh, I don't vote . . . I mean . . . I'm not the type . . . I mean . . . I guess . . . . I just don't know how. I don't know anything about politics."

When Jennie told me about her convenience store encounter, I could relate to how that woman was feeling. I'll let you in on another little secret, although I registered to vote when I was eighteen I didn't actually cast my first vote until I was *already* working with the Bush-Quayle team. Up until my own political revelation that I mentioned in earlier chapters, voting seemed like something *other people* did—the rich people, the brainiacs, the people who sat on student council and got straight A's. Not people like me.

Unfortunately, too many good Americans, everyday

citizens still feel this way. Voting can be an intimidating process, but it doesn't have to be.

So let's start with the first step:

STEP ONE: VOTE.

If you're not registered to vote, go register. Don't be embarrassed, regardless of how old you are. More people than you realize are not registered. And usually it's simply because they don't know where to begin.

Registering to vote is pretty easy. Just look online, or open your phone book to the government section, to get the phone number for the Department of Elections. When you call, if you get an automated message, you can keep pushing pound or zero until you get a live person. Tell that person you're not registered to vote but that you want to be. Usually, he or she will gladly walk you through every step of the process.

Once you've done that, go get your friends and family members registered to vote as well.

Find out where your polling place is. This information should be on your voter ID card. But if you can't find it, it is available on most Department of Elections Web sites, or by calling them. All you need is your address. Make sure you bring your photo ID with you on Election Day.

When you get to the polling place, it's okay to let them know it's your first time voting and you want a little direction. Don't worry, it won't be like you're the millionth customer at a grocery store. Balloons won't fall from the ceiling and they're not going to announce it over the loudspeakers. They will probably say congratulations and then help you on your way.

STEP TWO: VOTE OFTEN.

That saying *Vote Early, Vote Often* is intended to mock voter fraud. But there is a legal way to answer that call to action, and it is important!

Vote in party primaries, general elections, and midyear school board and city council elections. Sometimes, because of the low turnout, your vote can literally make the difference in these off-cycle races. A few have been won by just a handful of votes, and sometimes even *one* vote.

It's important to know which elections are coming up and who your candidates are. Most states mail out sample ballots directly from the Department of Elections. However don't count on it. We don't do that here in Delaware, or if we do, I've never received one. But they are made available at the Department of Elections. So get a sample ballot. Get a list of all the election dates and research the candidates. Information technology has made this easier these days.

My advice is to go directly to the candidate's Web site and not just rely on the news clippings, for obvious reasons. (Now if you put emoticons in books this is probably where I'd put a wink.)

Get involved with campaigns early, before things heat up, when you'll probably have a chance to talk personally with the candidates and get the best sense where they stand on the issues that are important to you. And who knows—you just might be persuasive enough in articulating your own position to influence a candidate's approach on an issue going forward.

STEP THREE: SEEK OUT MENTORS.

Go to those in your community who seem to be making a difference and ask them for a leg up, or a bit of insight, or a gentle push toward an area of need. Tag along and help them out for a while; you'll learn a lot, but you'll also give others a chance to learn about you. You never know what projects or initiatives might fit perfectly alongside your personality and abilities.

STEP FOUR: DEFEAT THE SOUNDBITE, OR BETTER YET, USE SOME OF YOUR OWN.

Unhappy with the news media? Work around them. Remember in an earlier chapter we talked about how the power of the soundbite is rendered harmless by the power of knowledge? It's like Superman and kryptonite, only Superman is a good guy, so the metaphor doesn't completely fit here. But you get the picture.

Armed with your own talking points, you can become your own informal communications network. Just as our Founders had Committees of Correspondence leading up to the American Revolution, we should do the same in this Second American Revolution. It sounds like a lot of work, but don't be overwhelmed. Keep in mind the big impact of *many* participants each taking a *small* part. "Many hands make light work," the proverb goes, and this is especially true at the grassroots level when trying to get out a message. Thanks to the Internet, building an arsenal of facts, figures, and your own soundbites is right at your fingertips. One of the goals of my new Political Action Committee, ChristinePAC (www.christinepac.com), is to do just that, to provide this crucial information to up-and-coming virtual town criers.

Information technology is changing. It's in the hands of the people now. Our Primary victory is due in large part to the online activists who fed the momentum leading up to Election

Day. These folks tweeted, retweeted, Facebooked, and blogged. At one point before the slams got overwhelming, whenever a nasty article was written, a virtual volunteer was quick to set the record straight in the comments section.

If you're not sure how to get started with online activism, do a quick search. Dozens of online articles will pop up with great ideas on taking that first step. Here's another little secret . . . a lot of those articles will be written by liberals. But they're helpful, so dig in and take their suggestions. Just ignore the barbs and jabs aimed at good candidates and become your own informed electorate.

As we're spending so much time online, we have to be careful not to ignore the time-honored traditional media sources outside of the Internet: newspapers, radio, and TV.

Write letters to the editor, especially when you see a biased or hostile article. Some have said the Letters to the Editor page remains one of the most read sections of a newspaper, so there is a great forum begging to be used. Keep in mind, shorter letters have a better chance of being published, but check the letters column in your local newspaper to get a sense of the average word length.

Talk with activists who are good writers and listen to their guidance. You'll find that most people who write frequently to newspapers will send in many more ideas than they get published. They will be delighted to work with you to develop timely, important, and strategically valuable letters of your own.

Make the most of local call-in radio shows. *Come on in, the water's fine!* To my knowledge, no one has ever been injured by calling in to a radio talk show. Pay close attention to the subject preferences of each host. Tip: Sometimes if you wait to place your call until there are fewer than twenty minutes remaining in the hour, you probably won't get on before the topic changes at the top of the hour. But you can tell when a host is streeeeeeetching for time and desperate for an interesting caller to help make it to the next commercial break.

And when it comes to TV broadcasts, don't forget you can have a say there, too. Don't just yell at the screen when a TV journalist is utterly biased (although this can be cathartic). Grab a pen or your laptop and write the station manager a letter. And why stop with the station manager? Write to the GM, the news desk, the editor, the reporter. Sometimes all their contact information is right on their Web site so it's simply another click on your e-mail.

**STEP FIVE: BECOME A PART OF THE SOLUTION,
TAKE A LEADERSHIP POSITION.**

You might be disenchanted with your local party leaders, whether Democrat or Republican. So don't just beat 'em, join 'em. You'd be surprised how many leadership positions might be open in these organizations—like, say, precinct captain— simply because there aren't enough volunteers to go around. At the local level, parties often run on only a few volunteers who end up doing all of the work—a thankless job, for sure. If you've been unhappy with what you've seen from the outside, you may be surprised how quickly you can become a part of the solution.

Do keep in mind, however, that no matter how you feel right now it makes no sense to approach the local party with a chip on your shoulder. Just hope for the best and try to win over those who might be suspicious of our populist movement.

STEP SIX: RECRUIT AND ENLIST.

Remember how one conversation with my dear friend, Eileen Rooney, set my whole life on an entirely new trajectory? You can have that same impact. Sometimes a conversation around the proverbial water cooler, or between innings at a little league game can be more powerful in swaying a voter than a campaign commercial. So take those talking points you've gathered in step four and interject them into your daily conversations. I know there's that old warning about not talking about religion and politics, but that rumor was started by the same nanny-staters who wished we *had* curled up in the fetal position over the past few years.

Then, invite folks to join you. They may say, "But I know nothing about politics." That's okay, at the grassroots level it is okay to learn as you go along. You don't have to be a perfect policy analyst to stuff envelopes or put up yard signs.

Be a Paul Revere. Or, better yet, a Caesar Rodney.

"The first to present his case seems right, until another comes along and questions him." Something to keep in mind from Proverbs 18:17.

STEP SEVEN: HOLD OUR LEADERS AND ELECTED OFFICIALS ACCOUNTABLE.

Now I'm not saying nitpick or hold them up to an impossible standard, but you should certainly follow their voting record.

Sit in on local budget meetings. Speak up at town halls. Don't be afraid to ask questions. That's not only our right, but our obligation. Learn to track the voting activity of your elected officials. Start small and work your way up. Research the tools available to monitor votes, speeches, and events. Today's tools are easier to use and more informative than you might expect. Don't hesitate to ask officials, no matter how well entrenched with the establishment, to defend their votes and activities. Make sure that the rest of us know what you're learning. (But be truthful in what you're spreading. Don't play by their rules to win by any means necessary, including spreading lies.)

And just for good measure, here's an eighth step, but this one's extra credit. Put *your* name on the ballot! Win or lose, simply by having more citizen politicians run for office the entrenched political process will be changed, and you'll be changed in the process.

Rick Green, a former Texas state representative, is one such inspirational Constitutional defender. He's a dynamic speaker, who's done a lot of work on building grassroots organizations, and he doesn't mind at all if I share a few of his ideas to keep our movement *moving*:

A: Read the Constitution and the Declaration of Independence.

This is the foundation, the formula for America's success. If we do not know our rights, we will not know when they have been violated, nor will we know if a candidate supports the basic principles that made our nation great in the first place. I've included the texts for the Bill of Rights and the Declaration of Independence at the back of the book, so you can see for yourself what the Founding Fathers intended.

B. Attend citizen trainings.

Just as the Founding Fathers prepared for the coming battle, we must get trained and equipped with the weapons of our warfare: ballots, not bullets. Go to trainings and seminars held by the Torch of Freedom Foundation, Heritage Alliance, and other organizations educating Americans about our foundations and how to work the process.

C. Get plugged in to a modern committee of correspondence.

We have an amazing advantage over the Founding era through our communications tools. Can you imagine waiting weeks for a response to a letter you may have sent to John Adams to warn him about certain actions or movements of the British? By using social media tools like Facebook, Twitter, YouTube, blogs, and plain ol' fashioned e-mail, we can immediately communicate with an unlimited number of fellow patriots around the nation.

D. Know your stuff.

If a stranger knocked on your front door, would you give him the keys to your home and car? Share your social security number and date of birth? Allow him to babysit your children or choose their textbooks or teach them morals? Too often, we do worse by voting for total strangers to make, execute, enforce, and interpret our laws . . . and then totally forget about them until it's too late.

As I write this, I see the middle-class movement having a huge impact on the budget process in Washington.

I see President Obama pulling back from the most leftist elements of his legislative and governing agenda.

And I am hopeful. . . . There are more of us than there are of them. . . . And we're being heard.

Epilogue

"Freedom Is a Light for Which Many Men Have Died in Darkness."

> —from the Tomb of the Unknown
> Revolutionary War Soldier, Philadelphia

Have you ever heard the quote "The only thing necessary for evil to triumph is for good men (or women) to do nothing."? But what happens when the good men and women are tired, or broke, or just flat out exhausted by life's other problems? We all feel like that at times.

Inherent in our Constitution is a system of checks and balances. Yet, that system only works when America has an actively engaged citizenry. We've grown apathetic and allowed the Lords of the Backroom to stomp all over the Constitution. And now that system of checks and balances is . . . well, out of balance.

But so many of us are war weary, too tired to fight. How do we find the inspiration and strength to soldier on? When I felt that way on the campaign trail, inspiration came when I'd be reminded that we're fighting for people, not merely political philosophy.

Generations before us had that same understanding. It kept them fighting when it seemed impossible to win. Nathanael Greene's leadership of the Southern Continental troops in the Revolutionary War is a powerful reminder that the resolve of the human spirit is stronger than any well-outfitted army.

Greene was not even permitted to join the military at first because of a limp. Yet his will and wisdom overcame his physical limitation. He rose all the way up to the rank of general. As he led the Southern troops against British General Cornwallis, he knew he was outresourced. Cornwallis's troops were well-trained, well-fed, and well-dressed in their lavish military uniforms. Greene's guys wore tattered clothes, had holes in their shoes, were hungry and inexperienced. But they had passion. Greene kept them inspired with a vision of a free America; an America in which their children could build a better life for themselves. Many of his soldiers were poor and could not afford land to pass onto future generations. This free America, a land of opportunity, would be their legacy. America would be the inheritance they'd leave their "children and their children's children."

General Greene's troops lost just about every battle. After each one, they were depleted, but not defeated. They forged ahead and ultimately they won! They simply had more passion than the other side. What Cornwallis's troops lacked, Greene's had: a vision worth dying for. A fierce determination and the hope of a new America is what kept them charging the battlefield.

We, too, must cling to our vision of a free *and solvent* America. We must ask what sort of America we want to leave for our children. One in which they depend on the federal government for everything from Band-Aids to bread? And have to surrender some of their freedoms for their needs?

Or do we want to leave an America where life may be hard, but our hard work makes life better? An America where citizens are free to disagree with those in power, an America in which leaders are accountable to the people they serve?

If so, run to the battlefield, barefoot if you must! But don't give up. What we've heard these past few years is the mere rumblings of a revolution that's on its way. In 2010, we sent shockwaves of fear into the core Establishment and they're lashing out like never before.

They will use everything in their arsenal to bully us out of the fight. Unscrupulous reporters will write stories using any source eager to trash us. It doesn't matter if that source happens to have a history of drug addiction or domestic abuse. As long as they are willing to "go negative," to trash-talk, they're deemed "credible." And political attack groups aren't any better, seeking out disgruntled former staffers to smear us, not seeming to care about the truth of the allegations they're promoting or even checking the credentials of their sources.

Expect it. Then rise above it.

It's tempting to defend every little stupid thing they'll throw at you: Trust me, I know! But don't get distracted. Forgive them, let it go, and move on.

Seems like a contradiction, doesn't it? I tell you to charge the battlefield and then I say forgive them. So how do we know when to forgive and when to fight like heck?

Let's look at Jesus's own example. He tells us to turn the other cheek in forgiveness. But he himself started flipping over tables, tossing a whip around, driving out animals when the Holy Temple was used as a marketplace. When do we forgive, and when is it time to turn over some tables?

I'm not a theologian, but I am someone who has grappled with this question. And I've come to see there is a clear delineation between when to rise above it and when to fight back, not to mention *how* to fight back.

The first distinction is that when the offense was against him, Jesus turned the other cheek. The very same people who praised him later falsely accused him and spit on him. Did Jesus respond, "Traitor! I once trusted you!"? No; instead, he prayed for them: "Father, forgive them. They know not what they do."

So why didn't he simply say "Father, forgive them" when these same imperfect humans misused the Temple? In my understanding, it seems that when *others* were attacked, when God was blasphemed or when the system was abused, that's when Jesus fought back.

That's the line in the sand. When the offense is a smear against you, try your best to rise above it. But when the system is abused, when justice is trampled on and ignored, start flipping some tables. (Figuratively, not literally. As cathartic as it may be, don't go into the next candidate's forum and flip over your opponent's sign-up table.)

Now it's time to fight back! It's one thing for a disgruntled employee to record a malicious robocall to ingratiate herself with the elites. It's something else entirely to file a false affidavit in a politically motivated complaint to the U.S. Attorney's office.

The day after I won the 2010 Republican primary, the left

wing, George Soros–funded group Citizens for Responsible Ethics in Washington (CREW) went on the attack. Two days later they filed a politically motivated complaint against me with the Federal Election Commission (FEC). Their complaint relies on the false affidavit of one man, David Keegan, and a manipulated, almost incomprehensible reading of the legitimate campaign expenses I had filed with the FEC. According to CREW's own fund-raising e-mails, the purpose of their actions was to stop me from getting elected.

Not content with pursuing the trumped-up charge in the political arena, CREW also requested that the U.S. Attorney's office begin a criminal "embezzlement" investigation. They abused the justice system in the process. The justice system is in place to protect people, not to be used as a political weapon.

David Keegan was a volunteer with my 2008 campaign. We cut ties with him less than two months after he joined the campaign. He's been disgruntled ever since. Before working with CREW, he worked with my Republican opponent to file a similar politically motivated complaint with the FEC (which was dismissed). CREW just took it to the next level after our primary win.

Because CREW needed a Delaware citizen to officially file the FEC complaint, their executive director, Melanie Sloan (a former Biden staffer) turned to her father, who just so happens to have been a major donor to both Joe Biden and Tom Carper's U.S. Senate campaigns.

George Soros is up front about his agenda to change America into a socialist nation. And CREW is the same group that went after Governor Palin and dozens of other Constitutional Republicans and conservative groups. Every once in a while they file a token complaint against a Democrat, but nothing comes of it. They don't grandstand in the media about it and they don't use it to fund raise. Not coincidentally, it's mostly Republicans who get that fanfare treatment.

The justice system should not be used as a political weapon. It hurts those the system is designed to protect and taints the political process. Imagine if every time CREW didn't like a candidate, they got an ex-employee to file a phony sexual assault charge against him?

Crying "embezzlement" is no different. The tactic is to file complaints just before Election Day so that in the court of public opinion, the damage is already done. Whether it's Sarah Palin, Charles Taylor, or me, it doesn't matter if the candidate they go after is cleared after Election Day, CREW's purpose was served.

They toss out multiple complaints with the FEC, the IRS, or the U.S. Attorney's office and hope that one of them sticks. By the mere action of lodging a complaint, the U.S. Attorney's office is then obligated to investigate.

CREW does this because it works—send a complaint letter to the U.S. Attorney's office and then issue a salacious press release. Headlines will read "U.S. Attorney's office investigates Candidate X for fraud."

Adding insult to injury, CREW is also politically selective in who it goes after. It's gone after Republicans for (alleged) influence peddling, but never raised any questions about Vice President Biden, whose son raked in huge consulting fees while his father peddled legislation that directly benefited his son's lobbying clients. (For more on this, read Chapter 3 of Michelle Malkin's *Culture of Corruption*.)

There are laws that are supposed to prevent the filing of false claims. There is reason to believe that Melanie Sloan and CREW were well aware that their complaint was supported by a false affidavit. Keegan even suggested as much to a reporter in 2011. But many candidates and their families are so emotionally and financially tapped out after defending themselves from a CREW attack that there is little left to fight back.

The more CREW gets away with their tricks, the more viscous their attacks become. Their blatant disregard for truth is emboldened.

Enough is enough! I've assembled a legal team and am fighting back. It's time to stop CREW from browbeating good candidates—to stop the corrupt practice of abusing and misusing the justice system for political gain.

Whether liberal, conservative, Republican, or Democrat, good people should be able to run for office without concern for getting trashed in the public eye or having phony claims thrown at them. Thug politics have to stop.

There is an epidemic of good people withdrawing from public office. According to the *Los Angeles Times*, fewer women are running for office because of the nasty process. Who wants it?

If we don't fight back, the attacks against good people will continue. The justice system will continue to be used as a political weapon.

CREW abused the system. Now we are using the system for its intended purpose, to vindicate an injustice. We've assembled a legal team and as part of my defense, we're filing countercomplaints of our own. While I'm on it, please allow me to set the record straight on CREW's complaint.

CREW is claiming I used $20,000 from the 2010 campaign to pay my rent, meals, gas, and the like. They got David Keegan to sign an affidavit claiming $1,500 of that was for supposed 2009 rent payments. Well, first, David Keegan hadn't been around the campaign since August 2008, so how could he know what was happening in 2009 or leading up to the 2010 campaign? Moreover, despite being termed a "financial consultant," Keegan was merely a two-month volunteer who held a fund-raiser and had zero access to my financial accounting—something that became perfectly clear when he admitted that he didn't actually know what he had attested to.

At the time of writing this epilogue, we are planning to file our own misconduct countercomplaint. Part of this is to request that the proper authorities investigate Keegan for perjury.

Second, the $20,000 was the annual rent for the townhouse the campaign rented to use as an office. And gas, fast food, and a bowling event with volunteers? Those are valid campaign expenditures that amount to a few hundred dollars total. Joe Biden spent tens of thousands of dollars from his 2008 U.S. Senate campaign on restaurants, travel, and lodging after he became vice president. The FEC questioned him, he was fined, and that was it. No criminal charges, no investigation.

Behind the beige siding and red shutters, our campaign townhouse was transformed into a nonstop bustling office. Desks and filing cabinets occupied every bit of the living room, dining room, and even basement and kitchen. At its peak, five staffers lived upstairs where bunk beds and cots were crammed in the bedrooms.

CNN reported this, panning their camera around the room to show that the house had very much been morphed into an office with no resemblance to a townhome. (You can see excerpts from their story at www.troublemakerbook.com.)

The real story is that I paid rent to the campaign (not the other way around) in order to use that address as my legal residence. In 2008, our campaign office and my home were broken into complete with nasty threats graffitied on the walls. For security reasons, when I moved, I wanted to keep my new home address private. There is nothing illegal about that. Unorthodox perhaps, but not illegal. The typical U.S. Senate candidate is a millionaire or an incumbent who lives in a gated mansion and security isn't as much of a factor. But for a single woman it is. For the sake of safety, I don't want my address made public. And I think even Melanie Sloan would have to agree.

I'm fighting back not for myself but for every candidate or group that CREW wrongly attacks. What's the worst they can do? Lob on more charges? Well, I won't be the first political dissident to be wrongly accused, and I won't be the last.

APPENDICES

The Declaration of Independence

THE UNANIMOUS DECLARATION OF THE THIRTEEN UNITED STATES OF AMERICA,

When in the Course of human events, it becomes necessary for one people to dissolve the political bands which have connected them with another, and to assume among the powers of the earth, the separate and equal station to which the Laws of Nature and of Nature's God entitle them, a decent respect to the opinions of mankind requires that they should declare the causes which impel them to the separation.

We hold these truths to be self-evident, that all men are created equal, that they are endowed by their Creator with certain unalienable Rights, that among these are Life, Liberty and the pursuit of Happiness.—That to secure these rights, Governments are instituted among Men, deriving their just powers from the consent of the governed,—That whenever any Form of Government becomes destructive of these ends, it is the Right of the People to alter or to abolish it, and to institute new Government, laying its foundation on such principles and organizing its powers in such form, as to them shall seem most likely to effect their Safety and Happiness. Prudence, indeed, will dictate that Governments long established should not be changed for light and transient causes; and accordingly all experience hath shewn, that mankind are more disposed to suffer, while evils are sufferable, than to right themselves by abolishing the forms to which they are accustomed. But when a long train of abuses and usurpations, pursuing invariably the same Object evinces a design to reduce them under absolute Despotism, it is their right, it is their duty, to throw off such Government, and to provide new Guards for their future security.—Such has been the patient sufferance of these Colonies; and such is now the necessity which constrains them to alter their former Systems of Government. The history of the present King of Great Britain is a history of repeated injuries and usurpations, all having in direct object the establishment of an absolute Tyranny over these States. To prove this, let Facts be submitted to a candid world.

He has refused his Assent to Laws, the most wholesome and necessary for the public good.

He has forbidden his Governors to pass Laws of immediate and pressing importance, unless suspended in their operation till his Assent should be obtained; and when so suspended, he has utterly neglected to attend to them.

He has refused to pass other Laws for the accommodation of large districts of people, unless those people would relinquish the right of Representation in the Legislature, a right inestimable to them and formidable to tyrants only.

He has called together legislative bodies at places unusual, uncomfortable, and distant from the depository of their public Records, for the sole purpose of fatiguing them into compliance with his measures.

He has dissolved Representative Houses repeatedly, for opposing with manly firmness his invasions on the rights of the people.

He has refused for a long time, after such dissolutions, to cause others to be elected; whereby the Legislative powers, incapable of Annihilation, have returned to the People at large for their exercise; the State remaining in the mean time exposed to all the dangers of invasion from without, and convulsions within.

He has endeavoured to prevent the population of these States; for that purpose obstructing the Laws for Naturalization of Foreigners; refusing to pass others to encourage their migrations hither, and raising the conditions of new Appropriations of Lands.

He has obstructed the Administration of Justice, by refusing his Assent to Laws for establishing Judiciary powers.

He has made Judges dependent on his Will alone, for the tenure of their offices, and the amount and payment of their salaries.

He has erected a multitude of New Offices, and sent hither swarms of Officers to harrass our people, and eat out their substance.

He has kept among us, in times of peace, Standing Armies without the Consent of our legislatures.

He has affected to render the Military independent of and superior to the Civil power.

He has combined with others to subject us to a jurisdiction foreign to our constitution, and unacknowledged by our laws; giving his Assent to their Acts of pretended Legislation:

For Quartering large bodies of armed troops among us:

For protecting them, by a mock Trial, from punishment for any Murders which they should commit on the Inhabitants of these States:

For cutting off our Trade with all parts of the world:

For imposing Taxes on us without our Consent:

For depriving us in many cases, of the benefits of Trial by Jury:

For transporting us beyond Seas to be tried for pretended offences:

For abolishing the free System of English Laws in a neighbouring Province, establishing therein an Arbitrary government, and enlarging its Boundaries so as to render it at once an example and fit instrument for introducing the same absolute rule into these Colonies:

For taking away our Charters, abolishing our most valuable Laws, and altering fundamentally the Forms of our Governments:

For suspending our own Legislatures, and declaring themselves invested with power to legislate for us in all cases whatsoever.

He has abdicated Government here, by declaring us out of his Protection and waging War against us.

He has plundered our seas, ravaged our Coasts, burnt our towns, and destroyed the lives of our people.

He is at this time transporting large Armies of foreign Mercenaries to compleat the works of death, desolation and tyranny, already begun with circumstances of Cruelty & perfidy scarcely paralleled in the most barbarous ages, and totally unworthy the Head of a civilized nation.

He has constrained our fellow Citizens taken Captive on the high Seas to bear Arms against their Country, to become the executioners of their friends and Brethren, or to fall themselves by their Hands.

He has excited domestic insurrections amongst us, and has endeavoured to bring on the inhabitants of our frontiers, the merciless Indian Savages, whose known rule of warfare, is an undistinguished destruction of all ages, sexes and conditions.

In every stage of these Oppressions We have Petitioned for Redress in the most humble terms: Our repeated Petitions have been answered only by repeated injury. A Prince whose character is thus marked by every act which may define a Tyrant, is unfit to be the ruler of a free people.

Nor have We been wanting in attentions to our Brittish brethren. We have warned them from time to time of attempts by their legislature to extend an unwarrantable jurisdiction over us. We have reminded them of the circumstances of our emigration and settlement here. We have appealed to their native justice and magnanimity, and we have conjured them by the ties of our common kindred to disavow these usurpations, which, would inevitably interrupt our connections and correspondence. They too have been deaf to the voice of justice and of consanguinity. We must, therefore, acquiesce in the necessity, which denounces our Separation, and hold them, as we hold the rest of mankind, Enemies in War, in Peace Friends.

We, therefore, the Representatives of the united States of America, in General Congress, Assembled, appealing to the Supreme Judge of the world for the rectitude of our intentions, do, in the Name, and by Authority of the good People of these Colonies, solemnly publish and declare, That these United Colonies are, and of Right ought to be Free and Independent States; that they are Absolved from all Allegiance to the British Crown, and that all political connection between them and the State of Great Britain, is and ought to be totally dissolved; and that as Free and Independent States, they have full Power to levy War, conclude Peace, contract Alliances, establish Commerce, and to do all other Acts and Things which Independent States may of right do. And for the support of this Declaration, with a firm reliance on the protection of divine Providence, we mutually pledge to each other our Lives, our Fortunes and our sacred Honor.

The Bill of Rights

Amendment I

Congress shall make no law respecting an establishment of religion, or prohibiting the free exercise thereof; or abridging the freedom of speech, or of the press; or the right of the people peaceably to assemble, and to petition the Government for a redress of grievances.

Amendment II

A well regulated Militia, being necessary to the security of a free State, the right of the people to keep and bear Arms, shall not be infringed.

Amendment III

No Soldier shall, in time of peace be quartered in any house, without the consent of the Owner, nor in time of war, but in a manner to be prescribed by law.

Amendment IV

The right of the people to be secure in their persons, houses, papers, and effects, against unreasonable searches and seizures, shall not be violated, and no Warrants shall issue, but upon probable cause, supported by Oath or affirmation, and particularly describing the place to be searched, and the persons or things to be seized.

Amendment V

No person shall be held to answer for a capital, or otherwise infamous crime, unless on a presentment or indictment of a Grand Jury, except in cases arising in the land or naval forces, or in the Militia, when in actual service in time of War or public danger; nor shall any person be subject for the same offence to be twice put in jeopardy of life or limb; nor shall be compelled in any criminal case to be a witness against himself, nor be deprived of life, liberty, or property, without due process of law; nor shall private property be taken for public use, without just compensation.

Amendment VI

In all criminal prosecutions, the accused shall enjoy the right to a speedy and public trial, by an impartial jury of the State and district wherein the crime shall have been committed, which district shall have been previously ascertained by law, and to be informed of the nature and cause of the accusation; to be confronted with the witnesses against him; to have compulsory process for obtaining witnesses in his favor, and to have the Assistance of Counsel for his defence.

Amendment VII

In Suits at common law, where the value in controversy shall exceed twenty dollars, the right of trial by jury shall be preserved, and no fact tried by a jury, shall be otherwise re-examined in any Court of the United States, than according to the rules of the common law.

Amendment VIII

Excessive bail shall not be required, nor excessive fines imposed, nor cruel and unusual punishments inflicted.

Amendment IX

The enumeration in the Constitution, of certain rights, shall not be construed to deny or disparage others retained by the people.

Amendment X

The powers not delegated to the United States by the Constitution, nor prohibited by it to the States, are reserved to the States respectively, or to the people.

Litany of Humility

O Jesus! meek and humble of heart, *Hear me.*
From the desire of being esteemed, *Deliver me, Lord.*
From the desire of being loved . . .
From the desire of being acclaimed . . .
From the desire of being honored . . .
From the desire of being praised . . .
From the desire of being preferred to others . . .
From the desire of being consulted . . .
From the desire of being approved . . .
From the fear of being humiliated . . .
From the fear of being despised . . .
From the fear of being dismissed . . .
From the fear of being calumniated . . .
From the fear of being forgotten . . .
From the fear of being ridiculed . . .
From the fear of being wronged . . .
From the fear of being suspected . . .

That others may be loved more than I, *Lord, make this my prayer.*
That others may be esteemed more than I . . .
That, in the opinion of the world, others may increase while I dimish . . .
That others may be chosen while I am set aside . . .
That others may be praised while I am overlooked . . .
That others may be preferred to me in everything . . .